The Curious Traveler Series

ROME
THE SECOND TIME

15 ITINERARIES
THAT DON'T GO TO THE COLISEUM

DIANNE BENNETT AND WILLIAM GRAEBNER

CURIOUS TRAVELER PRESS

Rome the Second Time
Published by Curious Traveler Press
info@curioustravelerpress.com
716.353.3288

ISBN-10 0-61527-998-8
ISBN-13 978-0-61527-998-5

Cover design by James Duncan Creative, Nashville, Tennessee

Printed in the United States of America

1 2 3 4 5 6 7 8 9 10—12 11 10 09

"You gotta know your way around Rome
to have any real fun."

—Riccardo, in Federico Fellini's *I Vitelloni* (1953)

CONTENTS

LIST OF SIDEBARS

FOREWORD

THERE ARE different ways to know and love a city, and at times tourists feel at home precisely where they have no house.

Those streets are not their streets, but they seem familiar. They have never been in that piazza, and yet they have already walked its stones. They discover that walls they have never seen before are somehow part of them. A courtyard, an alleyway, a fountain appear for the first time yet seem pieces of their lives.

Rome can create this magic, can make citizens of those who don't live in the city. But to experience this enchantment requires some help. A good guidebook can be a compass. But not just any guidebook. An appropriate guidebook is one that defies the genre. It tells a story rather than catalogs monuments and museums. It values the discovery of details, because Rome is most enchanting if one appreciates small treasures as well as great ones. It suggests not the shortest street but the most beautiful, because the marvel is in becoming aware of what we have around us and have yet to see. A guidebook must also have a practical sense, because Rome is full of cultural and gastronomic opportunities, of connections waiting to be made.

It's not important to speak Italian, to have an Italian passport, or to live in Rome. The *caput mundi*—the capital of the world—is open to intelligent visitors, visitors who are eager for knowledge and always ready to be surprised.

Wherever we go, wherever we visit, the best spirit that travelers can bring to their journey is perhaps described in the words of a great American poet on his arrival in Italy: "My ignorance is immense, and so, too, is my happiness." And so we are, curious travelers of the world.

—WALTER VELTRONI, Mayor of Rome (2001–8)
on *Rome the Second Time*

INTRODUCTION

Imagine Rome

THIS BOOK isn't for you—if you're going to Rome for the first time. Not for you if you want to see the Coliseum, the Roman Forum, the baths of Caracalla, the Trevi Fountain, the Pantheon and Piazza Navona, the Spanish Steps, Trajan's Column, and St. Peter's and the Vatican Museum. This book is not for you if you're thinking about evenings in Trastevere with a bottle of beer in hand or perhaps a midnight frolic with the rowdies in Campo dei Fiori. This book is NOT *Rome for Dummies*.

If you want another Rome and another way of being in Rome, keep reading. We offer a Rome we discovered after we had seen (more than several times) the great monuments and piazzas, after we had stood in awe in St. Peter's and wandered, finally bleary-eyed, through the dozens of rooms in the Vatican Museum, after we had baked in the noonday sun, trying to make sense of the Forum, after we had recognized the Trevi Fountain and the Spanish Steps from photographs. (We never did the Trastevere thing, but we have our own version.)

The Rome we offer is a Rome we'll bet you haven't experienced before. It isn't Bernini's Rome, or Nero's Rome, or the Rome of the popes, though now and then you'll run delighted (not numbed) across those Romes and others, as you walk with us through the city streets and parks, along the banks of Rome's rivers, and in the hills beyond.

NAZIS IN ROME: One of our Romes is the Rome of the late 1930s and especially of World War II, when the Nazis occupied the city and committed one of the worst atrocities of the twentieth century. You'll see where Hitler met Mussolini in 1938, the headquarters of the German high command on the famous via Veneto, the prison where the German SS tortured political prisoners, the street where members of the resistance exploded a bomb as a German column moved through, and the caves where more than three hundred victims of Nazi retaliation were killed and buried.

ROME AND WATER: Three of our itineraries frame and bring to life Rome's fascinating experience with water, a history that includes the aqueducts, the beneficent and destructive Tiber River (Tevere), drainage systems that predate the empire, the city's glorious large fountains, and even the ubiquitous street-corner fountains, those *nasoni* at which Romans drink—as well as wash their cars. The first of these itineraries takes you into the outskirts of Rome, where several great aqueducts emerge from ground in grace and splendor. The second follows the story of the Renaissance aqueduct Acqua Paola as it climbs the Gianicolo Hill and "shows" in one of Rome's most spectacular fountains. A third takes you to the banks of the Tevere, where you'll learn why the river today is so far removed from the busy streets above it, and so distant, emotionally, from the lives of Rome's citizens.

MODERNIST ROME: Another set of itineraries takes you to Piazza Bologna, a new "suburban" neighborhood in the 1920s and 1930s, populated then by Fascist bureaucrats and those removed by Mussolini's inner-city "urban renewal" projects, now home to Rome's prosperous middle class and to an unusual number of modernist structures, many of architectural merit. On these walks, you'll see a charming 1920s public housing development (now pricey condominiums), a post office designed by one of Fascism's best architects, the villa that was Mussolini's home, and the house occupied by the renowned twentieth-century playwright Luigi Pirandello.

TREKS INSIDE AND OUTSIDE ROME: Our Rome is a rich, complex space that begs for a certain physicality, and to that end we offer a variety of walks and treks inside and outside the city, many on paths, trails, neighborhood streets, and back roads where few tourists (and at times, few Romans) set foot. You'll walk along the via Sacra (Holy Road) to one of the highest points in the Alban Hills twenty miles from Rome, take a delightful little-known path to a café at the summit of Rome's Monte (Mount) Mario, explore the mysteries of two of the city's less-traveled parks, get a bird's-eye view of Tivoli in less than thirty minutes, or walk the banks of Rome's second river—the Aniene—where Romans cultivate private gardens on public space, away from the eyes of the authorities.

PLAYING WITH GUSTO: Skilled in the fine art of relaxing in Rome, we offer suggestions for having a good time "after 6:00" (exploring the city's small art galleries, social centers, bookstores, jazz clubs, and houses of culture) and "after 8:00" (dining inexpensively in neighborhoods unknown to tourists, enjoying a glass of wine at one of Rome's elegant rooftop wine bars).

HELP FOR THE CURIOUS

In all of this exploration you'll have plenty of help. We offer our advice on when to go; which subway, tram, or bus to take; which paths to walk (or avoid); what to take with you; and whether a particular itinerary is suitable for small children. When there's a choice of routes, we explain the options and let you decide. Even if you don't read Italian and don't want to learn, we help you "read" the entertainment section of the daily newspaper *La Repubblica* and decode what you'll need from the weekly guide *Roma C'è*. We suggest the locales where the best foreign cinema, contemporary art, and interesting music are most likely to be. We list addresses and, where English is available, telephone numbers and helpful Web sites. (A note on telephone numbers: 06 is the Rome city code. The numbers that follow can be of different lenths and spacing; there is no normalized way of writing Italian phone numbers.) We translate salient parts of the Italian and Latin on plaques, arches, fountains, building facades, and prison walls. Here and there, we offer background: why the Tevere is flanked by fifty-six-foot walls; why Hitler came to Rome; how aqueducts work; the styles and forms of Fascist architecture; Italian imperial ambitions in the 1930s; why Tivoli's Villa d'Este is profoundly different from Villa Gregoriana only a half mile away; why so many Italians drive scooters. When we have different opinions about what you should see or what it means, we make that clear too, with parenthetical references—(Bill says) and (Dianne says).

The pleasure of touring is often found in details and subtleties, in understanding in some depth what one observes on the streets; in fact, in being inside Roman culture rather than outside it. We try to help with that process, including in our itineraries information about illegal immigrants inhabiting public parks, tips on distinguishing a "modernist" building from a "monumentalist" one, or background on how a new set of sidewalks can change a neighborhood. In some cases we go further, using sidebars to explain, for example, the layered meanings of the arch for Romans and Fascists, the Italian experience with malaria, how you (or your kids) can figure out which pope commissioned the fountain you're looking at or what year the Fascists built the neighborhood school, or how to tell a via from a viale or a villa from, well, a villa.

WE DON'T GIVE AWAY THE PLOT

Rome is a curious place for tourists. On the one hand, the city is magical and wondrous. On the other, it is exhausting and potentially—we hesitate to say it—mind-numbing to the point of uninteresting. Numbness usually comes with a guidebook in hand or from the sense that one has seen it all before: seen the Coliseum on a travel office poster, seen the Trevi Fountain in countless films, seen St. Peter's and most of the other well-known tourist sites in any one of a hundred television documentaries or docudramas. So *Rome the Second Time* is not just for second-time visitors but for those who could use a respite from the "known" Rome, from the Rome that all of us think we have seen before, from the "requirements" of Rome tourism, one might say. It's for those who want to use their own (rather than someone else's) imagination. We take you there (that much is necessary), but we promise you a fresh experience. To ensure that freshness, we deliberately keep most of the photos small. They help you find your way while preserving your sense of discovery. We try not to overdescribe what you can see for yourself. We love using our own imaginations; we hope you do too. It is often better to read about something after you've seen it, rather than before. Most of us prefer not to know the plot of a film before we see it and rue reviews that tell us too much; yet most guidebooks that lead us to an encounter with great architecture or to a museum exhibition fail to exercise proper restraint.

LIVING WITH ROME'S FRUSTRATIONS

Jimmy Cliff unwittingly captured a salient quality of Rome tourism in his 1970 hit "You Can Get It If You Really Want." "Rome was not built in a day," he sang, "Opposition will come your way." He was right. Even with the aid of itineraries and directions, Rome can be a frustrating, irritating place for tourists. Romans are famous for unannounced and irregular hours and unannounced and canceled events, for everything from museums to music to food. As good as we are at this game, we are hardly immune to the slings and arrows of outrageous fortune that Rome tourists regularly suffer. We were excited about visiting Forte Mario (on Monte Mario), only to find that it exists solely as a modern military installation that is completely blocked from view (hence, it's not on our itinerary; we spare you that). We paid a special, additional fee to enter the Coliseum to see a video installation by a contemporary artist, only to discover that the brightness of the day made the video unviewable. A free bookstore basement performance by jazz pianist Stefano Bollani was canceled at the last minute, as he stood at the piano, when it was discovered that his record company had not granted the required permission (but on another trek to the same basement bookstore we were treated to one of the best and most spontaneous jazz performances we've ever encountered). We enjoyed a recent exhibition at the MACRO Future art gallery in an ex-*mattatoio* (slaughterhouse), but on three previous visits we found the gallery was closed when it was supposed to be open. And in spring 2005, we arrived at St. Peter's Square an hour *after* the new pope made his first public appearance. And so on. You'll soon have your own list.

If you experience every event of this sort as a defeat, a failure, you're sure to be miserable at least half the time. Our experience is that we have to adopt the Italian way of going with the flow and let some of our American-bred attention to detail slide (not all that easy to do). Here are some other ways we've found to think about what's happening around you.

ENJOY THE PROCESS

Enjoy getting there and getting back. A long bus ride can be an irritation (we recently took a bus the wrong way for an hour), or it can be an opportunity to piece together the city in your mind, to understand how one part connects to another, or just to observe how Italians manage and behave in public. If you've found yourself in a new neighborhood with "nothing" to do (because a museum wasn't open or a performance was canceled), take a slow walk around the neighborhood or find a café and check out the ambience, the patrons, the *tuttofare* (the one person in the café doing all the work; *tuttofare* means "do everything"). Follow the advice of travel philosopher Alain de Botton in *The Art of Travel*: "Once I began to consider everything as being of potential interest, objects released latent layers of value." Examine brickwork, sidewalks, metal gates, pedestrian behavior, double-parking, landscaping standards in a park, garbage removal, lines of laundry, police giving tickets, or pretty girls and handsome guys riding motor scooters. Take some "art" photos; write in a diary. If you're looking for "authentic" Rome, try the local housewares (*casalinghi*) store. Buy your friends back home a set of three short, fluted drinking glasses—the cheapest gift possible and absolutely "authentic." Look around and see how much of the merchandise is made in China. Think about what it means to describe something as "authentic."

GOOD DAYS AND BAD DAYS

There are two main reasons you'll have good days and bad days. One of them has little to do with Rome or with this book but everything to do with your presence in the city. "It seems," writes the astute de Botton, "we may best be able to inhabit a place when we are not faced with the additional challenge of having to be there." What he means is that when we travel, we bring with us our moods, our complex bodies, personalities, idiosyncrasies, tendencies, desires—in other words, ourselves—which on any given afternoon or evening, even in Rome, can contribute to our unhappiness. It's bound to happen, and it will. You can avoid having this kind of bad day by staying in your hotel (or leaving your bad-mood travel partner at home) curled up with a good book.

The other reason is more straightforward. If you spend enough time in Rome, sooner or later—like the casino gambler or the three-point shooter—the odds will get you, and you will be visited by a string of failures. It happened to us in May 2005. Bill took Dianne on a scooter to the Crypta Balbi Museum (near Largo di Torre Argentina in the Center), which was offering special tours (she had been longing to go there, but he's not into that). She waits for an hour to be fourth on the waiting list (turned out there were reservations), and they take three. Arguments with the museum clerks get her nowhere; she feels wronged (a later visit makes her conclude she should have gone off with Bill on the scooter). We go to Monti, supposedly one of Rome's best neighborhoods for action. The streets are closed for a heavily promoted street fair, but absolutely nothing is happening—no music, no art, no fair. We head to a nearby church to see Michelangelo's *Moses*, only to be blasted physically and emotionally by a loud guide droning in English to a tired and intimidated flock that blocks all views of the statue. Back to the street fair—what street fair? Still no action. Off to a favorite wine bar on the street. Closed. Dianne's sunglasses break, so we pop into an eyeglass store. Nice guy, but he can't fix them. We give up and go to dinner at a local *osteria;* it's okay, but worn out by the day, we scrap over the meaning of a full moon. Dianne's diary concludes: "A nothing-works day. Finally home & bed."

But there's also the potential for an unexpectedly good day. After the usual coffee, we shop at the local market and find the first Ravenna cherries of the year, chat with the bread people, vegetable folks, and the tamely lecherous (they all are, say Romans) butcher. We do a little shopping for friends by scootering around the fashionable Parioli neighborhood. Then we're off to a bookstore to line up to get illustrious American author Richard Ford's signature on a book. Finding ourselves the only ones in "line," we chat with Ford and his publisher, Carlo Feltrinelli, of the gigantic Feltrinelli publishing house. Discovering that the Wine Institute is having a free tasting, we walk up and down the Spanish Steps trying to figure out where to get a (free) ticket. Inside are twenty sommeliers and dozens of wines and, it turns out, a view to die for along the length and top of the steps. We talk others hesitating outside into going in. What's to debate? Head out on scooter to another lovely hilltop, the Celio, and the summer jazz series featuring we know not who. For €5 we enter this lovely park made into a jazz setting (Villa Celimontana) and find a free buffet, wine, and tables, courtesy of the Slovakian Embassy. We listen to Eastern European jazz, which turns out to be terrific, including an older male singing in English and great (universal language) scat. Dianne's diary concludes "fantastic evening."

SOMETIMES YOU GET WHAT YOU WANT
SOMETIMES YOU GET WHAT YOU NEED

Inevitably, we are now and then disappointed by an event—a concert, an exhibition, a film—that just isn't as compelling as we thought it would be. Yet there are frequent compensations, especially in Rome, where events provide entree to fascinating buildings and spaces. We were disappointed, for example, by an exhibition of works by the painter Giorgio Morandi in Palazzo Colonna, just off via del Corso. But the exhibition provided access to a splendid—and usually inaccessible (because the palazzo is a newspaper's headquarters)—balcony overlooking the piazza. Another forgettable exhibit abutted an empty second-floor room with an open window, where we leaned out in awe, realizing that we were looking at, even touching, the Trevi Fountain from directly behind. Despite a thorough search of the Palazzo dei Congressi in the Fascist-built complex at EUR, we never found a sculpture-like convention room by prominent Roman architect Massimiliano Fuksas that we believed was somewhere in the bowels of the place (we found out later it is still on the drawing board). Instead, we discovered and enjoyed painter Gino Severini's massive murals, which decorate one end of the complex. The contemporary art installed at the Swiss Institute was excellent and intriguing, but the real prize was the institute's villa and the views of Rome from four levels. In Rome, such moments come with the territory; they're to be cherished.

FOCUS AND INTENSITY

Once you've tried one or two itineraries in this book, you'll have a good idea of the kinds of things we think are engaging: contemporary art and architecture, Fascism and World War II, wine and jazz, acute observation of detail, good questions and possible explanations, neighborhoods, the everyday, surprises (ancient and modern), Rome's relationship to water, walking and trekking. Now and then we'll find a baroque church irresistible, but only now (Dianne says) and then (Bill says).

We believe in reinforcement and focus. This book was assembled with those values in mind. And to the extent you have your own choices (we've tried to provide lots of those choices), we suggest that you use them to reinforce and focus. How do you do that? One simple technique is to build on what you know. If you've read or seen *Angels & Demons* and think it would be fun to locate some of the sites it mentions, do it (see *"Angels & Demons,"* p. 78). If you've just seen a performance by a musician you admire, buy his or her CD on the spot, or find a record store and buy a CD by that artist—and if you like it, play it often. If you appreciated Richard Meier's "box" for the Ara Pacis (and not everyone does; it is sometimes referred to as the "air conditioner"), put his suburban church (in Tor Tre Teste) on your list. If you enjoyed one of the fifty or more photography exhibitions that dot the Roman cityscape each spring, try another one—or several. Rather than attend an exhibition that includes works from many areas by many artists (for example, on impressionism), choose one that focuses on a particular artist. A show of paintings by Renato Guttuso, an Italian painter of the last half of the twentieth century, opened our eyes to, for us, a new artist. Or choose a narrow period (the 1950s) or a restricted topic (the sculpture of Fascism).

We help by guiding you to places that are more likely to have focused, in-depth exhibitions. But there is much you can do to bring focus and intensity to whatever comes your way. Draw what you see. Strike up a conversation. Photograph the unusual (or the very usual). Write fulsome e-mails to a pal and keep copies. Should you find yourself in an exhibition that's intimidatingly large—where the rooms seem to go on and on—restrict your attention to a small number of items in the show: one or two pictures in a room of eight, for example. Find the festivals in Rome when you're there and try several events (such as dance, foreign cinema, music). No matter what you see or do, find a way to stop and reflect on your experience.

Reinforce and focus. Rather than conquer Rome, let Rome engulf you. Have fun!

ROME
THE SECOND TIME

1

THE WATERS OF ROME

WATER IN abundance. That is one's first impression of Rome, with its hundreds of fountains and thousands of street-corner, hydrantlike *nasoni* running around the clock; the Tevere (the Tiber River—we'll use the Italian) deliciously meandering through its center; the baths of Caracalla testifying to the pleasures the ancients derived from a surfeit of water; and here and there, glimpses of the globe's most fabled water system: the aqueducts.

That first impression isn't wrong, but it is incomplete, even misleading. The romantic view of the aqueducts obscures the fact that they were necessary—that the Tevere and its tributary, the Aniene, did not for long meet the city's water needs—and that they were vulnerable, that Rome could be (and was) brought to its knees by a military force strong enough to sever the aqueducts and cut off the water supply. For all its meandering charm and utility as a commercial avenue, for most of two millennia the Tevere has been either a force of destruction, flooding the city at frequent intervals or, in the twentieth century and today, a boring irrelevancy. Indeed, Rome's relationship to water might be understood as akin to the experiences of Los Angeles, constrained to bring water from long distances to bring life to its desert basin, and New Orleans, a city that tamed the mighty Mississippi only to find it disappearing from view and from the consciousness of its residents.

In this chapter we explore the waters of Rome. We begin with the *Parco degli Acquedotti* (Park of the Aqueducts) on the periphery, where one can best observe and appreciate these remarkable constructions and the link they forged between distant streams and springs and the needy city of Rome. The second itinerary brings the story into the city, where the aqueduct Acqua Paola hugs the Gianicolo Hill to fill one of Rome's great fountains. And we conclude with a journey on the banks of the Tevere, where the river testifies at once to its destructive past and its anomalous present.

ITINERARY 1: ROME AND ITS AQUEDUCTS: PARCO DEGLI ACQUEDOTTI

Today, Rome's water supply flows into the city through aqueducts, just as it did 2,000 years ago. But it was not always so. For 450 years, before Rome was an empire and before Rome had emperors, the city was watered only by springs, wells, and the Tevere. As the city's population increased, and the need for additional sources of water became clear, the aqueduct appeared as a solution. The first aqueduct was built in the fourth century BC, and by AD 226 there were eleven, bringing in more water than the city could use, filling (by AD 410) more than twelve hundred public fountains and sustaining what historian H. V. Morton has labeled the "Cult of the Bath." These monumental structures took their water from a variety of sources. The aqueduct *Aqua* (Water) Anio Vetus, forty miles long and mostly underground, carried water from the Aniene River, near Vicovaro in the Lucretili Mountains, not far from Horace's farm (the remains of which you can see today in this town just beyond Tivoli). Aqua Marcia, fifty-six miles long (six miles of above-ground arches as it neared Rome), was fed by springs near Subiaco, at the base of the Simbruini Mountains; it terminated on Rome's Capitoline Hill.

The Subiaco springs were also the source of Aqua Claudia, which terminated on the *Celian* (Celio) Hill, just above the Coliseum. Acqua Paola, which entered Rome on the Gianicolo Hill, brought to the city the eel-infested waters of Lake Bracciano, to the northwest. (The different spellings—Aqua and Acqua—are customary; the former refers to ancient aqueducts, the latter to "modern" ones built after 1500). As new aqueducts were built, Rome's engineers sometimes put them on top of the old ones, a clever, economical solution to aqueduct building that one can best observe at Piazza di Porta Maggiore, where the holes of Aqua Julia and Aqua Tepula are clearly visible as they ride on top of those of Aqua Marcia.

HOW THE AQUEDUCTS WORKED . . . OR DIDN'T WORK

The aqueducts were a remarkable achievement; it is not too much to say that they allowed Rome to emerge as a great city not once but twice. That some of them still exist and function two thousand years after they were built is testimony to the skills of Roman engineers and builders. In addition, Romans understood and used engineering principles that allowed them to move water uphill when necessary. Most of the time, water in the aqueducts moved downhill by gravity, but knowledge of the principle of the "inverted siphon"—the idea that liquids moving from a higher point to a lower point can go uphill for part of the journey as long as the end point is lower—allowed them to lift water onto Rome's hills.

Even so, the aqueducts were not without flaws and problems. Although lined with special cement, they leaked badly, especially when the structures were above ground. Some of the leaks were intentional, created by watermen (the men, often slaves, who kept the structures in repair) who were bribed by landowners along the route of the aqueducts. In some ways, the economics and politics of Rome's water supply resembled those of twentieth-century Los Angeles, another city that had to bring its water from far away, as depicted in Roman Polanski's 1974 film *Chinatown*.

The Roman Empire didn't last forever, and neither did its aqueducts. They were cut by the invading Goths in AD 537 and then destroyed, with enormous consequences for a city that had grown accustomed to plentiful water. The city's corn mills, driven by aqueduct water, gradually migrated from the Gianicolo to the banks of the Tevere, where rafts moored in the river provided the necessary waterpower. Fountains dried up. Fresh water, now in short supply, became by scarcity "holy water." Over the centuries, Rome's population moved toward the river, creating the portion of the city now described as medieval Rome.

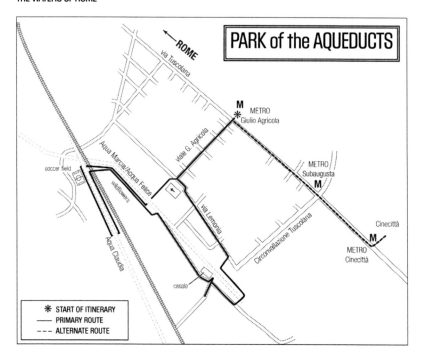

Not only were the aqueducts physically destroyed and rendered unusable, but the knowledge that built them was lost too. That is, until almost a thousand years later, in 1429, at the beginning of the Italian Renaissance, when scholars found a book by Sextus Julius Frontinus, a Roman commissioner of water. His book described in detail where the aqueducts were, how they worked, and how they were maintained. Equipped with this knowledge, a new age of aqueducts began, led by the popes who now governed the city. Renaissance Rome's first functioning aqueduct (and the only one for more than one hundred years) was the restored Aqua Virgo, completed in the late fifteenth century. Acqua Felice followed in 1586, Acqua Paola in 1611, and Acqua Pia Antica Marcia was refurbished and opened in 1870. These four aqueducts (now supplemented) form the core of Rome's modern water supply.

Although Rome's aqueducts are known as massive structures with enormous arches, for the most part they were, and are, underground, usually rising above the surface only in low-lying areas between the lakes, mountain springs, and rivers that provide the water, and the city miles away. *Aqueduct* in Italian means simply a tube carrying water, so any such device is an aqueduct. While we have visions of the gorgeous Roman aqueducts in our heads, sometimes we see simply a concrete or metal pipe; don't let that discourage you. The visually stunning aqueducts indeed are out there, even though they can be seen above ground only in a few places. One is Piazza di Porta Maggiore, not too far from Termini train station, and we recommend a brief visit there. Another, and the best place to see the aqueducts and feel their power, has recently become a city park—the *Parco degli Acquedotti* (Park of the Aqueducts), and that's where this itinerary takes place.

PARCO DEGLI ACQUEDOTTI

HOW TO GET THERE
Take Metro A (Red) to the stop Giulio Agricola. You'll emerge at the intersection of via Tuscolana and viale Giulio Agricola.

WHEN TO GO AND WHAT TO BRING
Go on Saturday or especially Sunday if you prefer more people around; otherwise, go anytime during daylight hours. Take a picnic lunch, a cloth for sitting on the ground, Frisbee, ball, your game of choice. Sneakers will do. This is one place you can wear shorts and not stand out as a tourist.

THE GOTHS
Not far from the Metro stop, further down via Tuscolana and near present-day Cinecittà (the Hollywood studios of Italy, closed to all visitors) is the *campo dei barbari*—camp of the barbarians—where the invading Goths encamped while they laid siege to the aqueducts in AD 537. As you'll see, the Goths knew what they were doing; they had found a place where several aqueducts were above ground and vulnerable.

Today, one sign of the threat of the Goths is the huge cistern of Belisario, constructed in the sixth century AD to store rainwater in case of an

Enormous sixth-century AD cistern in the Villa Medici, now used as exhibit space.

attack on the aqueducts. It is inside and near the entrance to Villa Medici (on the Pincio at the top of the Spanish Steps) and recently has been used as a space for exhibitions (one way to get to see it is to attend an exhibit there). Later, Villa Medici was directly served by an underground aqueduct, Acqua Vergine, whose waters were tapped by a fifty-foot well and a sophisticated hydraulic system employing Islamic technology.

ACQUA FELICE, AQUA MARCIA

From the Metro exit, turn right (southwest) onto viale Giulio Agricola and walk several blocks to via Lemonia, which runs along the park. (At the corner of via Lemonia and viale Giulio Agricola is Caffè Tornatora—a good place to pause if you wish—table service is available at a reasonable additional cost. You can buy sandwiches and drinks here to take in the park.) Cross via Lemonia and enter the park at any convenient place to the right of the modern church. (Ten years ago there was no park as such, only an open, wild space called *Prato della Valle* [valley field].)

Straight ahead you'll see what appears to be one aqueduct but is really two, one riding on top of the other, together moving away from you toward the corner of the park. On the bottom is Aqua Marcia, a fifty-six-mile project with its origins in springs near Subiaco, built in the second century BC; atop it is Acqua Felice. Not of ancient Roman origin, Acqua Felice was built under Sixtus V, an activist pope who managed to have a substantial impact on the city despite a reign that lasted less than six years (1585–90). It was said at the time that Sixtus "would not forgive Christ himself," and the four thousand workers who built Acqua Felice finished it quickly, fearing his wrath. Unfortunately, the engineering was faulty, and when the aqueduct was "turned on," the water sometimes flowed backward. One shudders to imagine Sixtus's reaction. The defect was corrected, and the aqueduct had a successful opening a year later, in 1587. It carried water from springs near the town of Pantano Borghese, fifteen miles to the east, just off via Casilina. You can distinguish the new (that is, sixteenth-century) stones of Acqua Felice from the older *tufo* stones of Aqua Marcia. Beyond the northwestern end of the park, where you're heading, Acqua Felice heads off to Rome riding on either Aqua Marcia or the ancient Aqua Claudia, which you'll see in a moment.

In Rome, where it is underground, Acqua Felice skirts Piazza di Porta Maggiore, goes under Piazza Vittorio and Piazza della Repubblica, and finishes at the Moses Fountain, its *mostra* (showpiece fountain), adjacent to Largo S. Susanna, a block from Piazza della Repubblica (see p. 76). Acqua Felice also waters the *Quattro Fontane* (Four Fountains), the Navicella on the Celian Hill, the Triton Fountain (by Bernini) in Piazza Barberini, and another triton fountain across the street from Bocca della Verità.

AQUA CLAUDIA

As you pass through Acqua Felice at this point, you may see ahead a sign, *Non Dare Da Mangiare Al Cane* (basically, Don't Feed the Dog). Go right and follow Acqua Felice on its left (west) side, heading roughly northwest. Follow the path as far as you can—perhaps one hundred yards— where it heads into the brush and turns left, through some dense cane fields, emerging a short distance from a second aqueduct, Aqua Claudia— which is thoroughly of ancient Rome, built by the Emperor Claudius (hence its name) in AD 52. At the right moment in May, this area becomes a sea

Aqueduct Aqua Claudia: the opening at the top is the ancient water channel.

of cacti and wildflowers—at least twenty-five varieties, according to a friend—including a brilliant display of poppies. Work your way to Aqua Claudia, and through it, just to the other side. Here, in the vicinity of a small soccer field, you'll be able to look up and see the holes through which the water flowed almost two thousand years ago.

THE GARDENER'S STORY

You can follow the path next to Aqua Claudia for a while, but eventually you should retrace your steps through the brush to the space between Aqua Claudia and Acqua Felice. When we visited in 2007, this area housed one vegetable garden after another, each fenced and screened from view by dense vegetation. The origin of these gardens is obscure. A middle-aged gardener told us that his garden and the others were part of a narrow strip of land, owned by a Torlonia prince named Gerini, that ran from Turin in northern Italy to Calabria in the south. He explained that in 1968 he had asked permission of a Torlonia priest to use some space as a personal garden and his request had been granted. In 2003, the commune decided to buy his and the other gardens but lacked the money. In the 1950s, the gardner added, many of the spaces under the arches of Acqua Felice were occupied by prostitutes, but this was no longer the case, except for the occasional *Romena* (that is, a woman from Romania).

No doubt there is much truth to this man's story, but certain elements are apocryphal or incorrect. No such country-long strip of land existed or now exists; Prince Gerini was Marquese Gerini. What seems clear is that the land was part of the Torlonia *tenuta* (a large agricultural land holding); that the gardens did not belong to the commune;

Aqueduct Aqua Claudia on its way to the *Colli Albani.*

and that those doing the gardening are middle-class people rather than transients. Some, at least, might be described as "squatters," who under Italian law can claim a right to the land after occupying it for twenty or more years. In any event, the gardens no longer exist, as we discovered a year later. Given the gardner's story, it seems likely that the commune acquired the funds to purchase the gardens and returned the land to its wild state.

ACTIVITY IN THE PARK—NOW AND THEN

Moving along the path toward the southern end of the park (away from Rome), you are likely to see all kinds of activity, as we did one summer day: bicycling, jogging, soccer, girls dancing with long ribbons, a boy washing a dog, a man and wife singing a song about "La Fontana Trevi"— a not-so-subtle reminder of water's prominence in Roman life. Here, at this end of the park, Acqua Felice gradually emerges from the earth while Aqua Claudia presents a grand stretch of perhaps a hundred arches—lower here than at the other end of the park but more complete and undeniably majestic. Between the two aqueducts is the *casale*—the old manor house of the Torlonia *tenuta*—and between the *casale* and Acqua Felice, stones mark what were once, we suspect, pools for *tenuta* inhabitants. Taking the path that runs alongside Acqua Felice, we noted at our left a lovely girl sunbathing topless and, on our right, further on, a small, four-sided pyramid set on a stone, marking Acqua Felice's presence underground, so that watermen can make repairs.

GETTING BACK

From this point, you can continue toward the hills on any of several paths, or turn around, following Acqua Felice (crossing over it so that it is now on

A stone pyramid marks aqueduct Aqua Felice, here underground.

your left) until it enters the more wooded area of the park, where it skirts via Lemonia. Follow via Lemonia to the church on your left and turn right on viale Giulio Agricola back to the Metro stop, a few blocks ahead.

THE NEIGHBORHOOD

This neighborhood is a dense area of tall, high-occupancy apartment buildings erected in the 1970s, some designed by Rome's best modernist architects. You may find the urban planning here and the different building features of interest. All the streets have names from the old Roman Empire, a harkening back to Rome's past in an area that, except for the aqueducts, could hardly seem more removed from it.

CINECITTÀ AND ISTITUTO LUCE

If you have any energy and enthusiasm left, you can head up via Tuscolana (away from Rome) to look at the outside of, first, *Istituto Luce* (Light Institute, established in the 1920s) and *Cinecittà* (Film City), Rome's answer to locations and production for, respectively, propaganda and Hollywood-style films. Built by the Fascists in the 1930s, both complexes on the opposite side of via Tuscolana are active today. The original Istituto Luce buildings (opened by Mussolini himself, who well understood the value of propaganda) now belong to the municipality, and Cinecittà, with its hundreds of acres and more than fifty buildings, now houses Istituto Luce as well. At one time, these were the hotbeds of cinema study and experimentation. They are still here, awaiting more Italian resources to be poured into its once top-notch film industry. Neither site is open to the public. Istituto Luce has an online archive (in Italian) of more than one hundred thousand films at www.luce.it.

ITINERARY 2: WATER AND WAR—ON THE GIANICOLO

Tracking the waters of Rome along a Renaissance aqueduct, this brief itinerary opens in the city's largest public park, teaches something about the Garibaldi-led attempts to take over Rome from the popes in the nineteenth century, and ends with one of Rome's most beautiful fountains and

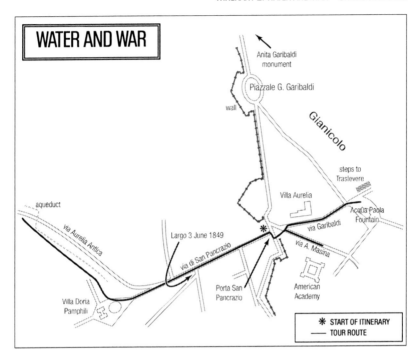

best views. You are in the city, with plenty of traffic and people, but you're not in the prime tourist lines. You can enjoy some of the greenery and views with relatively few others. You also can spend more time here exploring the immense park or walking up or down the Gianicolo (Janiculum Hill). We suggest you bring along a good flashlight.

HOW TO GET THERE

Public transportation is limited to the top of the Gianicolo; even the suggested bus routes recommend a walk uphill of a third of a mile (that is, from the heart of Trastevere). But coming from near the Vatican, you can take Bus 870 up and across the Gianicolo, stopping anywhere for a wonderful view. Catch Bus 870 from Lungotevere in Sassia (in front of the twelfth-century church-hospital complex Santo Spirito in Sassia) just before the large and busy Piazza della Rovere, or on the Centro (toward the historic center) side of the Tevere on corso Vittorio Emanuele II, where

Bus 870 begins and ends (*capolinea*—head of the line) a block before the Tevere (take Bus 64 from Termini to get to Bus 870). You can track your way back using the same bus. Bus 870 runs every twenty minutes, if on schedule, so expect to wait a bit. If you see the small electric circling Bus 115 in Trastevere, it also will take you up and down the Gianicolo.

WHERE TO START

Tempting as it is to plunge into Porta San Pancrazio itself (the big arched gateway to Rome with tempting glimpses of views to come), we suggest you put the porta at your back and take the small, somewhat protected walkway on via di San Pancrazio, almost due west, toward the green opening to Villa Doria Pamphili a few yards down the road (keep the arch in sight at your back, and you can't mistake the route). Crossing over to the villa is no mean feat; take care in this vortex of roads and traffic (drivers may be having a harder time figuring out where to go than pedestrians; hence, this caution).

HERE COMES THE AQUEDUCT

Although the fascinating history of the movement toward Italy's unification in 1870 can be found here, we recommend you head straight for the traces of water; we'll delve into the history as you leave the park. Keep to the right side of the park, past the enormous Arch of the Four Winds (*Arco dei Quattro Venti*) on your left and the Casino Corsini (now *Casa dei Teatri* [House of Theater]) on your right (see *Case* in chapter 6, p. 205). Keep going until you see the wonderful aqueduct that you've actually been following (mostly as a wall containing the park, on your right), but which you haven't been able to see until now.

As you head down (don't stop short), you'll also be able to see where the aqueduct crosses the Old Aurelian Road (*via Aurelia Antica*), which has an uplifting arch that contains a commendation (nicely visible from the park—since you're already high above the road below) by Pope Paul V to himself for constructing this new aqueduct. You also can try to figure out where this aqueduct uses the ancient half-buried arches of its predecessor, *Aqua Traiana* (Trajan's Aqueduct, AD 109).

Aqueduct Aqua Paola as it turns on an arch to cross the Old Aurelian Road.

Aqueduct Paulus (Pope Paul's Aqueduct), or Acqua Paola, was constructed by Pope Paul V (1605–21) of the Borghese family, who was known as harsh and despotic (having been a quiet and retiring cardinal . . . perhaps something about power going to one's head) as well as ambitious about exceeding the civic achievements of a predecessor, Sixtus V. Sixtus V brought in Acqua Felice (see the Parco degli Acquedotti itinerary above). So Paul V decided to revive the ancient Aqua Traiana by bringing in water from Lake Bracciano, a large volcanic lake north of Rome. Acqua Paola began to flow in 1612. Within the modern city limits of Rome you can still find a small brick building (in Piazza di Villa Carpegna) where water is tapped for the Vatican and an eel-trap is used. (We saw this building and scouted about for the aqueduct—mostly underground here, but *non ne vale la pena*—don't consider it worth the effort—simply to see the outside of this building and the bumps in the ground where the aqueduct runs.)

Paul V viewed the new aqueduct as necessary to provide water to the right bank of the Tevere, including Trastevere, the Borgo (near the Vatican), and the Vatican itself. In addition, water was needed for the regions north of the Vatican and on the left bank, including Piazza Navona. The water flowing through the aqueduct you're following feeds many of the finest fountains in Rome. In addition to its *mostra* fountain (which you'll see in a few minutes), it feeds, among others, the fountains in Piazzas Navona and Farnese, St. Peter's and the Vatican, the Fountain of the Amphorae in Piazza dell'Emporio (see the next itinerary), and several fountains in Trastevere (including at S. Maria in Trastevere, S. Cecilia, and Fountain of the Prisoner, as well as the Fountain of the Ponte Sisto, which is described below).

PARK BREAK

Spend as much time in this park as you wish. It has the usual tame park spaces for children and grandmas, some great statues, waterworks, other monuments, and some wilder parts as well. Romans favor it as an exercise area. (Because the park is covered in many guidebooks, we won't describe it in detail here; besides, that would take away all the fun.) The park was laid out in 1650 for a Pamphili prince, a nephew of a pope. A grand villa, Casino dei Quattro Venti, occupied the center, where *Arco dei Quattro Venti* (Arch of the Four Winds) now stands.

HISTORY WAS MADE HERE

As you head out of the park, imagine the villa here, destroyed in the 1849 fight between Garibaldi's forces and the French. In that year, the French arrived to the northwest, up the coast at Civitavecchia, and came along via Aurelia from there (the same road you have just seen running along the park and carrying the aqueduct). The French came to help the pope take back Rome from the Garibaldi forces that earlier had seized the city from the papacy; they took the villa at night with a surprise attack. As the *Garibaldini* (the Garibaldi forces) fought to retake this high land, hundreds fell to their deaths along the path you entered and are exiting. In a particularly bloody battle on June 3, 1849, the villa changed hands more than once. It was finally lost by the vastly outnumbered Garibaldini and fell into French hands. The Garibaldini resisted for three weeks but finally retreated. Among those retreating with the Garibaldini was the Italian nobleman (and revolutionary) husband of American feminist, literary critic, and journalist Margaret Fuller. Fuller arrived in Rome in 1847, joined her husband in the cause, gave birth, and took charge of the nurses at the Fatebenefratelli Hospital on the Tiber Island (see p. 49). The last American to leave Rome when papal troops took control of the city, Fuller would not see her dreams fulfilled. She, her husband, and infant were washed to their deaths in 1850 when their ship was wrecked on their return to America.

Rome would not be taken again for more than twenty years, and then it would be taken from the papacy for good. The successful 1870 approach by the Garibaldini (their breaching of the city wall) was on the opposite side of the city, at Porta Pia, where there is a large statue to them, and the street beginning there is named for the date of their success, 20 September (1870). The piazza as you exit the park is called a *largo* and is named for the earlier fighting on June 3, 1849 (*Largo III Giugno 1849*). The villa was destroyed beyond repair in the conflict; the arch was erected on the spot to commemorate the battle.

Exit the park and head to Porta San Pancrazio the way you came and on the same side of the street. On your left, you'll see another building involved in the 1849 fighting, the Vascello, of which only a floor or so remains. You should also see some arches that tell you you're still following Acqua Paola. Recently several sign boards were posted in Italian and in English around the porta and also at the park entrance to explain some of this history.

GATE TO THE CITY

The porta was originally named Porta Aurelia for the Roman road you have been following that began on this spot, via Aurelia. Also heavily damaged during the 1849 battles, the porta was rebuilt in 1854 by Pope Pius IX (1846–78; his shield features two prancing lions), who was then in control of Rome. Before this, the porta and the wall of which it was a part had been constructed at the direction of one of the great builder-popes, Urban VIII (1623–44). You will note he was a Barberini pope by the bees that are part of his shield. You can see the shields of the two popes flanking each side of the arch, and you can figure out which is which by their symbols (see "Popes' Symbols" on p. 38). The wall started at Porta Portese far below on your right (south) and went to the Vatican. As you can see, the wall remained a crucial part of the defense of Rome as late as 1849.

AMERICAN ACADEMY IN ROME

Passing along the right side of the porta, head straight down the hill on the right sidewalk about one block, along (of course) via Garibaldi. You have been following the course of the aqueduct, now underground. You also are passing by land on both sides owned by the American Academy in Rome (see p. 188). The Villa Aurelia, on the hill to your left, was Garibaldi's headquarters (since reconstructed) when he briefly held Rome in 1849. The American Academy building farther down via A. Masina (the street on your right) was built in 1913 for the academy by U.S. architectural firm McKim Mead & White.

Not too long ago, relics of milling were found here, indicating the ancient Romans operated grain mills, using aqueduct water, on this high hill to serve hundreds of bakers in the city below. Of course, once the Goths destroyed the aqueduct system in the sixth century AD, such activities were forced down to the river.

POPES' SYMBOLS: READING MONUMENTS

Every pope since about 1300 has had his own coat of arms. Entire coats of arms and symbols on them appear on the great building or restoration projects of the popes. Spotting pope symbols is an interesting and entertaining way to discover more about Rome just by looking more closely at the buildings and monuments. Kids may be better than adults at this. Some guidebooks have information on papal coats of arms. Georgina Masson's *The Companion Guide to Rome* has a two-page spread showing the design of each of the coats of arms and giving the family of the pope (which often contributes the main symbol to the coat of arms) in addition to the name the pope takes on ascending to the papacy and the dates of his reign.

Seemingly everywhere around Rome are the bees of the Barberini pope, Urbano VIII (1623–44). The bees can be seen on Porta San Pancrazio (see p. 37). In this itinerary we also see the dragon of Borghese Pope Paolo V (1605–21) both in his coat of arms and used in many different places in the Acqua Paola Fountain. Often the dragon's tail, a symbol of evil, is cut short.

Most of the full papal coats of arms fea-

Bees on this shield mark it as the work of Urbano VIII, a pope of the Barberini family.

A SHOWPIECE FOUNTAIN AND MORE

As you approach the piazza and view, you're coming alongside the back of the large Acqua Paola Fountain (*Fontana dell'Acqua Paola*). You can look through one of the basement windows to see modern waterworks; here's where a flashlight helps. You can also see above one doorway a marble plaque with the word *castello*. Although the word also means castle, in ancient Rome (and, as you can see, in modern Rome) it referred to the distribution points of the water system.

Coming around the front, you won't know where to look first and longest—at the gorgeous view of Rome below you or at the splendid

---

ture crossed keys. These keys, one silver (earth) and one gold (heaven) are a reference to the Apostle Peter's power on earth and in heaven (from the Gospel of Matthew). Another standard in papal coats of arms is the three-tiered tiara, or pope's crown. Benedict XVI in 2005 replaced the tiara with a pointed mitre (a different type of ecclesiastical headgear), causing quite a stir. The crossed keys and tiara are the first signs that the Roman Catholic Church built whatever you're looking at.

Other common symbols are mounds that represent mountains. These appear in a pyramid of three as a part of several coats of arms, including those of Clement XI (1700–1721), Clement XIV (1769–74), Pius VII (1800–1823), and Pius XII (1939–58). Pope John Paul I had five mounds at the base of his coat of arms. Five mounds with a star on top appear over the Colonnade of St. Peter's, here representing Alexander VII (1655–67). Pius XII topped his three mounds with a dove holding an olive branch, an interesting symbol, given his role during World War II. The dove, in Christian symbolism, represents the Holy Spirit. The dove holding the olive branch appears in the coat of arms over Porta Portese, here representing the Pamphili pope, Innocent X (1644–55).

One of our favorites is the upright lion (or rampant lion), part of Sixtus V's coat of arms, which also includes a star, three mounds, and a branch of a pear tree—the last apparently a takeoff on his family name, Peretti (*pera* is pear in Italian). Because Sixtus V was such a prolific builder, all these symbols, and the lion especially, appear in many places, one of which is Porta San Pancrazio.

Those are some clues. Have fun looking for these symbols and what they might have to say about the date of a building or monument and about the builder or restorer, as well as the creativity of his architect.

fountain. Fontana dell'Acqua Paola is a *mostra* fountain (showpiece fountain—generally one such fountain is associated with each aqueduct), signaling the aqueduct's entrance to the city. This was an ancient Roman practice that the popes continued. For this showpiece, the pope imagined everyone in the city (which then was entirely below the fountain) could see his showy fountain. The Acqua Paola Fountain was designed by a well-named fountain designer, Giovanni Fontana, along with Flaminio Ponzio. It used materials from the ancient Roman Forum of Nerva, especially from the Temple of Minerva. The popes also recycled their own buildings; four of the six columns were taken from the facade of the old Vatican basilica. The fountain is based on, and clearly outdid, the Moses Fountain in Largo S. Susanna (see p. 76). The large basin was added later, ringed with marble to keep animals from being watered there. But animals of a human kind apparently found the pool too inviting. Edicts and fines in the 1700s document unsuccessful attempts to keep Romans from bathing in the fountain. As historian Mario Sanfilippo, author of many books on Rome, says, on hot nights there is always someone who throws himself into the fountain, city dweller or farmer, sober or drunk.

FACT AND FICTION

Of course, each showpiece fountain also had to have an inscription with the name of the emperor or pope who had it built. The inscription here includes

references to Lake Bracciano and to the thirty-five-mile trek over the ancient aqueduct, which the pope restored. You also can see on the pope's shield (topped with customary papal tiara and

Aqua Paola Fountain—lovely fountain, lousy water.

crossed keys) the Borghese coat of arms, which include a dragon and an eagle. Your kids (or you) can look for all the places around the fountain where these symbols appear, because the fountain designer clearly reveled in these symbols (see "Popes' Symbols," p. 38).

The inscription above Acqua Paola contains two anomalies that give us pause, even four hundred years later. First, there is a reference to the Aqueduct Alsietino (age of Augustus), an indication that the builders misidentified the ancient aqueduct they thought they were restoring; it was constructed during Trajan's, not Alsietino's, reign. Second, they called the water very salubrious. Unfortunately, this water was not considered tasty or healthy. It generally was used only for augmenting other fountains and for industrial purposes. In fact, the words *acqua paola* are a common phrase among Romans in reference to something not being very good or, in fact, worthless.

TAKE A BREAK: COFFEE OR A GARIBALDI THEME PARK

If you can drag yourself away from this lovely vista, walk back up to the porta and take a break at Bar Gianicolo (the older bar, not the newer one). It's beloved by Romans, and it's customary to sit right on the street—just keep your toes in. You can catch your bus back here, or you turn left and walk across the porta to the street heading up into an opening in the wall. This will take you to the Gianicolo, which has more fine views, often a puppet show, and, as one of our good Roman friends says, a Garibaldi theme park. Don't miss (Di-

anne says) the intriguing monument to Garibaldi's wife, Anita, just over the crest of the hill toward the Vatican (away from Porta San Pancrazio). Look for guns, babies, Anita astride her horse, and more.

A friend enjoys Bar Gianicolo.
Watch your toes.

ANOTHER FOUNTAIN FOR THE HARDY

Yet another alternative is to head down the Gianicolo, following steps (just to the right—as you look at it—of the Acqua Paola Fountain) and streets to Trastevere below. You may wish to stop and pay one more visit to Acqua Paola in Piazza Trilussa, at the head of *Ponte Sisto* (the Sisto Bridge) on the Tevere. There was once a second showpiece fountain for Acqua Paola in the city below, on the left bank of the Tevere, next to Ponte Sisto. It's hard to imagine now, but this fountain was beloved by Romans. It was destroyed in 1879, despite a public outcry, in the building of the big Tevere holding walls (see the discussion in the next itinerary). One protester, Ouida (Louise de la Ramée), called the destruction "an outrage to art and history." In 1883 the city decided to rebuild the fountain. The pieces, however, were so dispersed they couldn't find them all (some had simply been thrown in the large fields near Forte Bravetta—and some may be there still). After many years, the fountain was reconstructed of new and old pieces, no longer part of a building, and now on the right bank of the river in Piazza Trilussa. A second inscription was added to explain away the first inscription that describes the fountain as being on the left bank. Some like the fountain elevated as it is now; Mario Sanfilippo describes it as having the vague flavor of a tombstone.

GETTING BACK

An easy return to the city center from Trastevere is by way of Tram 8, which runs from viale Trastevere to Largo di Torre Argentina. To return to the Center from the top of the Gianicolo, retrace your bus route by taking Bus 870 to its end on corso Vittorio Emanuele II and then Bus 64 to Termini.

ITINERARY 3: THE STRANGE CAREER OF THE TEVERE

Romans as well as visitors to Rome have always loved the city's splendid fountains, demonstrating their affection time and again with late-night dips, sometimes followed by a trip to the police station. The paradigm for playful adventures of this sort is, of course, Anita Ekberg's spirited excursion into the waters of the Trevi in Fellini's *La Dolce Vita* (1960). Only days before we wrote this, four Eastern European tourists in their thirties, having stopped at every bar in the *zona,* jumped into the ever-tempting fountain of the old boat in Piazza di Spagna, then (a big mistake) used a screwdriver to gouge out a piece of it as a souvenir of their fun.

In contrast, the *Fiume* (simply, the river), as the Tevere is usually called, is not, by and large, understood as a site of play and pleasure. There are exceptions, to be sure. One section of the right (west) bank above *Ponte Cavour* (Cavour Bridge) has a year-round floating bar-restaurant, the *Buttatevia Fiume* (loosely translated: go jump in the river). Another section, on the east bank, has a row of elite sports clubs, off-limits to tourists and ordinary Romans. A handful of Romans use the riverside paths to jog or bike, and private rowing clubs dot the river just south of Piazza del Popolo.

PLAY ON THE RIVERBANKS

As spring becomes summer, the island and the banks on either side take on a fairlike quality, with open-air restaurants, soccer games on big-screen projection televisions, and tents with arts and crafts. Recently, American artist Kristin Jones managed to have the portion of the Tevere between *Ponte Sisto* (Sisto Bridge) and *Ponte Mazzini* (Mazzini Bridge) dedicated as "Piazza Tevere," decorating this artistic space with delightful, fantastic versions of the Roman she-wolf, creatures brought to life, actually, by cleaning portions of the *muraglioni* (large retaining walls).

Another activity is a boat trip along the Tevere. There have been various enterprises offering boat rides, most of them ending in failure. The latest is a shortened, somewhat pricey tour of a little over an hour from mid-March to mid-November for €12, running between the Tiber Island (see below)

A summer evening on the Tevere.

and Duca D'Aosta Bridge, with now only three (at one time a dozen) stops where you can board and disembark. Earphone commentary is offered in various languages. A dinner and wine bar cruise are €54 and €35 respectively. Booking at tel. 06.9774.5414 or info@battellidiroma.it (or try www.rexervation.com—and we do mean rex, not res—and click on Bateaux). Again, we emphasize that availability, itineraries, times of these river taxis, cruises, etc., change from year to year. The Web site has an English version: www.battellidiroma.it. Click at the top right.

But all these activities, frankly, don't add up to much—certainly not to the sort of joy that Ekberg experienced as she waded into the Trevi. Indeed, the most famous film scene of the Tevere, from William Wyler's *Roman Holiday* (1953), features a nasty fistfight on an entertainment barge moored below Hadrian's Castle. At best, Romans have to work hard at getting pleasure from the Fiume, or even caring much about it. Although the Tevere snakes along tantalizingly on the map of the city, in most ways it barely exists.

It was not always so. Early Rome was a riverside community, a link to the sea, and the Tevere was where real work was done. It was also a border, a contested space of vigilance and, sometimes, warfare. In this itinerary, we explore the ancient Tevere that was at the heart of early Rome, and we examine the cultural and historical sources of today's curious attitude of detachment.

WHERE TO START
Piazza dell'Emporio (piazza of the emporium or store, referencing this area's ancient Roman history), on the left (east) bank of the Tevere, at the *Ponte* (Bridge) *Sublicio.*

HOW TO GET THERE
The nearest Metro stop is Piramide on the B line. Exiting the station, walk left toward and past the large *porta* (arched gate) and the Pyramid and onto via Marmorata running left, which ends at Piazza dell'Emporio, ten minutes walk ahead. To your left on this route, between via Marmorata and the Tevere, is the neighborhood of Testaccio, once the heart of Rome's working class.

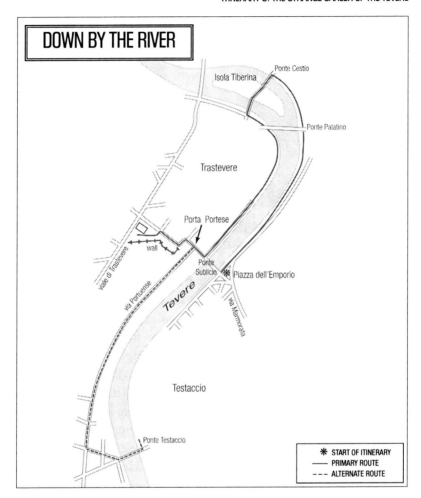

DOWN BY THE RIVER

Ponte Cestio
Isola Tiberina
Ponte Palatino
Trastevere
Porta Portese
wall
viale di Trastevere
via Portuense
Ponte Sublicio
Piazza dell'Emporio
Tevere
via Marmorata
Testaccio
Ponte Testaccio

✳ START OF ITINERARY
——— PRIMARY ROUTE
--- ALTERNATE ROUTE

WHEN TO GO

Sunday, if you want to include the Porta Portese market (closes at 1:30 p.m.) in your tour. Otherwise, any day. The riverbank can be hot and devoid of shade, so you may want to avoid the midday sun on warmer days.

WORKING ROME

Our starting point is the *Fontana delle Anfore* (Fountain of the Amphorae) adjacent to *Ponte Sublicio* (Sublicio Bridge). The fountain was designed by

Fountain of the Amphorae.

Pietro Lombardi and un-
veiled in 1926 (the fourth
year of Fascism); some
consider it Lombardi's
capolavoro (masterpiece),
a designation of some
significance, given that
Lombardi was the official designer for a series of fountains intended to represent the activities and particularities of the nine *rioni* (zones, quarters) of
the city. We will see one of them on this tour.

Although not part of this *rioni* program, the Fontana delle Anfore represents this neighborhood perfectly. The Emporium was ancient Rome's
largest wharf district. Here, workers loaded and unloaded river barges, heft-
ing large jars (amphorae; shaped like the ones on the fountain) filled with
oil, wine, salt, and other products (more than a staple, salt also played an
important role in festival rituals in early Rome). From the downriver side of
the bridge you can see what remains of the old port's transit storage facilities, where goods were kept before being moved into huge storage warehouses in Testaccio. Millennia later, in the late nineteenth century, Testaccio
became a meat-processing center (a de-assembly line for cattle); the pens,
hooks, and blood drains are still visible at the ex-*Mattatoio* (1891, former
slaughterhouse, reopened in 2007 as one of the city-sponsored, large contemporary art galleries, MACRO Future), a few blocks downriver on the
left bank. Exhibits at MACRO Future generally are open from 4 p.m. to
midnight Tuesday–Sunday. (Information in English: click on Eng at upper
right at www.macro.roma.museum, see p. 183.)

ROME'S FIRST BRIDGE

Just a few feet away is Ponte Sublicio. It is a rather ordinary bridge (1914)
by one of Rome's finest modern architects, Marcello Piacentini, whose

work would be synonymous with Italian Fascism. Although the structure is symmetrical, its placement over the river makes it seem asymmetrical and unbalanced, especially when viewed from the right bank. More important, in its earliest incarnation, more than twenty-five hundred years ago, Ponte Sublicio was the first to span the Tevere. It was constructed to facilitate trade between Rome and regions to the north, but there were risks involved. At the time, Rome was a small kingdom governed by kings (the empire and its emperors would come later) and faced the threat of war with the rival Etruscans, whose centers of power were on the other side of the river.

As a defensive measure, Ponte Sublicio was built of wood—indeed, *sublici* refers to the supporting wooden piles—and repaired with wood (even when iron was available), apparently to make the bridge easier to destroy should the Etruscans invade. When war broke out in 510 BC, so the story goes, the Roman Horatius Cocles held the western edge (right bank) of the bridge single-handedly while his compatriots cut it behind him. Horatius then jumped from the bridge and drowned (or swam to safety, depending on the storyteller). The original bridge was probably a bit upstream from this one.

DRAIN DRAMA

Walking upriver on the left bank, you'll soon come across a stairway that leads down to the river. Be prepared for garbage and the smell of urine. This, the left bank, is less trim than the right. Some of the pathways are of dirt, not stone. We have seen burning garbage here. But if you're not faint of heart (and stomach), the "sights" here are worth it. As you

Walking on the wild side of the Tevere.

walk upstream (north), you'll see two carved steers' heads attached to the wall at the right, emblems marking this as once the *Foro Boario* (the Cattle Forum), which stretched from in front of what is now Bocca della Verità. The next "sight" is a small storm drain, its gate festooned with bits of plastic and other detritus. This is the drain for *Circo Massimo* (Circus Maximus, the famous open hippodrome and entertainment venue), although how old the drain is we can't say. The first ferry across the river, connecting Rome and Etruria, was a few yards upstream. As you approach the next bridge, Ponte Palatino, you'll notice on the wall to your right a much larger opening than the Circo Massimo drain—indeed, two openings. The larger arch dates to about 1900, when the banks of the river were redone (more on that later). The smaller opening was created two thousand years earlier, in the late second century or early in the first century BC. According to Rome scholar John N. N. Hopkins, one can date this opening from the stone: the arch is made of Lapis Gabinus, and the wall behind it is of *tufo giallo della via Tiburtina* (yellow tufo from the via Tiburtina), which was not commonly used after the first century BC. This is the outlet for the Cloaca Maxima.

All we have here is a drain, and you can't see any more of it elsewhere; the system, though still functioning, is entirely underground. But the story, as told by Hopkins, is worthy. The Cloaca Maxima had its origins in the sixth century BC, when Rome was a kingdom and the Tevere, for all its commercial benefits, was a nuisance, flooding the city every year and, with the streams and springs in the area between the Palatine and Capitoline hills, preventing construction on some of the area's most precious land—what would later be the Forum. Over a period of many years, the kings of Rome filled in this basin with gravel and other materials, until it was above the regular Tevere flood level. Then, a permanent open-air canal was dug and bridged here and there, channeling the basin's water and carrying it to the river. The work was unpleasant in the extreme, so much so that Roman king Tarquinio il Superbo instituted crucifixion at the construction site in an effort to convince workers that resistance was not an option. According to Hopkins, the Cloaca Maxima was an extraordinary feat of engineering, intended not only to drain the Forum area but also to demonstrate the power of the kingdom.

ROMAN FEARS

You'll pass under the Ponte Palatino, Rome's most dangerous bridge and often referred to as the *ponte all'inglese* (English bridge), because traffic over it uses the English system of driving on the left to allow vehicles to make U-turns over the river. The fragment of bridge on your left is the *Ponte Rotto* (broken bridge), the second bridge to be built in Rome. It was originally called the Pons Aemilius, and some of what you see here dates to the second century BC. It was the key crossing point on the Tevere until the Middle Ages and rendered useless when part of it was swept away by flooding in 1598–99. What's left is a handsome fragment, best seen from the island on a summer evening, when it is illuminated.

As one approaches *Isola Tiberina* (the Tiber Island), it is tempting to imagine the early Romans getting as much pleasure as we do from the fast-moving rapids that power by the east bank. Not so. The Tevere itself was then an object of anxiety and dread. "The Romans," as historian Rabun Taylor explains, "regarded rivers and streams as ominous barriers, perhaps separating the living and the dead." To cross in safety required a "ritual of auspicia" (auspices, an offering of a sort), although some bridges, perhaps including Ponte Sublicio, were considered "magical" and could be crossed without auspicia. Even in modern Rome, Romans eschew having much to do with the river, even though they like other forms of water. Mention being on the Tevere, and they quote a simple Roman saying: "Fall in the Fiume, you die."

ISLAND PAUSE

Early Italians especially feared the fast-moving, roiling waters around Isola Tiberina—so much, in fact, that the island became what Taylor calls "taboo territory." By the first century BC it had taken on cult status, the Temple of Aesculapius becoming a mecca for pilgrims. You may have a different mission at this point in the itinerary: a cool drink and a panino. There's an inviting bar at the center of the island, as well as the 1580s

Fatebenefratelli Hospital (see *"Angels & Demons,"* p. 78). Take the stairway up and relax. Consider reading ahead.

CROSSING THE TEVERE

After your *pausa* (pause), continue across the island to the right bank. Here we found a *pannello* (panel, in Italian and English) explaining the *Ponte Cestio* (Cestius Bridge) you've just crossed and including a superb, and often reproduced, eighteenth-century etching by Giovanni Battista Piranesi that depicts the bustling, organic, thriving riverfront of his day, a riverfront that was part of the fabric of the city.

WHO KILLED THE TEVERE?

Taking the long stairway down to the water and walking downstream, one finds something very different from the perspective offered by Piranesi. The wide promenade, the enormous wall, the large hanging lamps—all are of Victorian vintage, from Rome of the late nineteenth and early twentieth centuries, just about a hundred years after Piranesi's etching. The riverfront we walk along is pleasant enough, despite graffiti and the occasional person sleeping off a hangover. But, except in summer, the Tevere here and along most of its course through Rome is empty, nearly bereft of activity related to its waters, haunted by irrelevance, isolated from the teeming life of the city above. The few posts for tying up boats, the huge iron anchoring rings embedded in the wall, and an old millstone serve as reminders of what is *not* here, what is *not* happening in this space, what the river was but is no longer. What happened?

The Tevere was irrevocably changed by two events in 1870. One was the unification of Italy, and with it, the "Third Rome" that would transcend the Rome of the emperors and the Rome of the popes. Under a new, secular, business-oriented governing class, dozens of papal buildings and a significant section of the Jewish ghetto were torn down and new quarters (*rioni*) were built—Prati, Monti, Trevi, and Ripa (on the right bank here) to provide housing for Rome's rapidly growing population.

The second event occurred on December 28, 1870, when the Tevere once again overflowed its banks, flooding much of the city. For those governing the municipality, the biggest obstacle to Rome's economic development was the unpredictable, flood-prone river, picturesque though it was. If the city were to grow and prosper, if economic life were to be made predictable (the great desire of business leaders everywhere), the Tevere had to be controlled. Proposals to do so date back at least to the early nineteenth century, when great embankments were first suggested and when the ubiquitous Garibaldi suggested diverting the Tevere under Monte Mario (see p. 128).

In 1876, only a few years after the unification of Italy, work began on a plan to tame the Tevere. Over the next fifty years, parts of the river were straightened, eliminating the *curve morte* (deadly curves) that tempted the river to spill over its banks, and other parts were widened. Constrictions, debris, ancient ruins—anything that would impede the flow of water— were removed. Most important was what was built: the *muraglioni* (huge walls) that now guard the banks—fifty-six feet tall, supported by twenty-six-foot-wide buttresses.

In 1900 flood waters as high as those of 1870 brought down three hundred yards of the new right bank wall and a portion of the left bank wall below the Aventine Hill (about where this itinerary began), bringing water into the Pantheon and Piazza Navona and revealing that contractors had made the foundations only six and a half feet deep rather than the twenty-six feet required by the engineering specifications—shades of Hurricane Katrina and the shoddy workmanship on the New Orleans levees. Most of the project—just as you see it here—was completed by 1910; in the 1920s the Fascists completed the work.

Rome had solved its flooding problem and destroyed its river. As historian Sanfilippo writes, "With the revolution on the river, Rome was no longer a river city: the massive buttresses and walls had isolated the river itself."

LOMBARDI'S RIONE FOUNTAIN

Continue walking along the river on this right bank. Dianne thinks it's not so bad and prefers it to the left. It's cleaner, there are bike paths and bikers, and the lovely Aventine Hill churches loom above on the left. Before Ponte Sublicio, where we started our walk along the Tevere (on the opposite bank), head up the wide steps and cross the street to your right, at the light. Fifty feet from the corner (upriver) is another of Pietro Lombardi's fountains. This one was designed to represent the Ripa *rione* (note the Ra RIPA at the top) and to link the Ripa neighborhood with its riverfront past. Its position, however, across one of Rome's busiest streets and separated from the Tevere by the *muraglioni,* effectively isolates the fountain from the river that was its inspiration. Today it can be rather pathetic: often waterless, with its basin holding a Coke can, serving mainly as an obstacle to the scooters that frequently use this sidewalk to bypass the long lines of traffic at the intersection.

FASCIST ENTERTAINMENT AND RECREATION

The next portion of the itinerary has nothing to do with water, but it's very close and *da non perdere* (not to be missed). If you choose, you can continue on through Porta Portese (the large arched gateway) ahead to the Sunday morning market. Otherwise, turn right before the porta, following the tram tracks as they curve left and then right, slightly uphill. The right side has a sidewalk; the left has a sign warning pedestrians of its dangers. Once around the corner, on your left are two significant buildings from the Fascist era. Cross the street carefully to have a better look. The first building is now the Nuovo Sacher movie theater, owned by Italy's most famous living actor and film director, Nanni Moretti (sometimes called the Woody Allen of Italy). The opening scene of his best-known film, *Caro Diario* (*Dear Diary*) (1993), is a classic, featuring Moretti scootering through an early morning Rome of empty streets (see "Cinema," p. 196).

The letters above the entrance describe the building's original purpose: *Dopolavoro dei Monopoli di Stato* (an afterwork center for employees of state-regulated businesses—like tobacco, salt). It was designed by Ettore Rossi and built in the late 1930s. We leave you to decipher the mosaics, especially the figure of the woman at the lower left.

The next building up the street, in the rationalist style, is of even greater architectural significance. Designed by Luigi Moretti (not related to Nanni) and built between 1933 and 1936, the *Casa della GIL* (House of the Italian Fascist Youth, now often referred to as the ex-GIL) was one of several large youth recreational facilities built by the Mussolini regime. The complex provided health services as well as sports facilities (for which there was limited space). This and similar facilities demonstrate how important the physical training of young people was to the Fascist state.

Over the main entrance is the Fascist slogan "*Credere, Obbedire, Combattere*" (Believe, Obey, Fight). On the side of the building, toward the movie theater, are the words: "Necessario Vincere / Piú Necessario Combattere." The translation seems simple—it is necessary to win / more necessary to fight—but the meaning is less clear. One interpretation, focusing on the post–World War I concern that the

A gem of modernism—Luigi Moretti's Fascist youth center.

Italians were not sufficiently committed to combat as a cultural tradition, is that it is better to fight and lose than not to fight. Another interpretation (Bill's) is that the goal of winning is primary, but winning is impossible to achieve without a sufficient commitment to the fight itself.

When we visited in 2008, the building was being restored—and splendidly. A front portion of the interior, now occupied by the province's cultural ministry, was finished and open to the public (housing a free exhibit), revealing aspects of Moretti's extraordinary achievement: a striking second-floor modernist cupola and, on the left side of the main room, a monumental etched map of Italy's African colonial adventures in Libya and Ethiopia, anointed with a bold "M" for Mussolini. If you have time, walk in the parking lot, to the entrance on the side of the building, for a look at Moretti's graceful and sensual spiral staircase.

MARKETS OR MOTORCYCLES

Retrace your steps to Porta Portese. If you're here on a Sunday morning, you'll find the busy and famous Porta Portese market—nearly half a mile of it—through the porta and down via Portuense, which parallels the Tevere. You can get something to eat here too. If it's not Sunday, you will have the opportunity to explore the city's epicenter of scooter, motorcycle, and bicycle accessory (and sometimes sales of the two-wheelers) shops. This is where most Romans purchase their *caschi* (helmets), *bauletti* (the containers on the back of scooters), fancy leather riding suits, and other

SCOOTERS AND CYCLES

Motorcycles and especially scooters (referred to in Italian as *lo scooter* or *la moto*) are everywhere in Rome and with good reason: without them, automobiles would clog the streets and traffic would grind to a halt. Indeed, this happens whenever a good rain keeps the scooters at home.

Scooters are Rome's most efficient means of transportation because of where they can go and what they can do. Under the Italian rules of the road (if not the law), scooters travel between lanes and cars and even use the white line in the center of the road—with caution—because the scooters going the other way are using it too. At traffic signals, scooters work their way to the front, line up ahead of the cars, and when the light changes, use their superior acceleration to race ahead of the automobiles. If traffic is very heavy and backed up, scooters now and then will take to the sidewalk. Most scooters obey traffic signals, but about 5 percent pay no heed, going through red lights to keep Rome's traffic moving. There is no right on red.

Italy has a national helmet law, requiring all drivers and passengers to wear *caschi* (helmets), and all helmets must meet a demanding European standard. Although the law is only about a decade old, it is observed without fail in Rome: unhelmeted riders are immediately fined. Not so in many small towns and rural areas, where teenagers especially often race around without head protection.

Motorcycles, which are shifted manually using the left foot and left hand, are growing in popularity—especially the "crotch-rocket" type, on which the rider leans forward. One also sees a few cruisers, with the rider sitting more upright. All but a very few older scooters shift automatically rather than manually. Most can stop on a dime. As you'll observe, Romans are clever at using their scooters to transport any objects, from potted plants to carpets. Dogs travel between the rider's feet.

Although Chinese and Taiwan brands (especially Kymco) are beginning to have an impact in the Italian market, for now the majority of the scooters you'll see in Rome are either Japanese (Honda, Suzuki, Yamaha [pronounced with an emphasis on the sec-

equipment—mostly new as well as new and used trikes and bikes. (See "Scooters and Cycles," below.)

A FOUNTAIN WORTH SEEING—OR NOT

Near the end of this street is the Portuense neighborhood, centered by the rectangular Largo Ettore Rolli, which suffers from having been overpaved.

The scooter is a liberating technology for many Italian women.

ond syllable, not the first]) or Italian (Piaggio, Aprilia, Malaguti). The Vespa brand, first manufactured in 1946 by Enrico Piaggio and made famous by Gregory Peck and Audrey Hepburn in *Roman Holiday* (1953), is now manufactured by Piaggio, the company descended from the founder.

You can identify some scooters by sound. The small ones with high-pitched engines are two-cycle (*due tempi*) machines; they mix oil with gasoline and spew noxious fumes behind them. Because they pollute, all two-cycle machines but those of historical value—such as the classic Vespas—have been illegal in Rome since late 2007. Most scooters now have four-cycle, cleaner engines, and the trend is away from smaller machines designed just for urban use and toward maxi-scooters of 400, 500, or 650cc that are better suited to traveling. The Burgman 400, made by Suzuki, is very popular, as is the Yamaha Majesty 400 and several models by Honda. New scooters cost from €2,500 to €7,500, but to purchase one you'll need proof of Italian residency.

Scooters may be rented in many places in Rome, but usually only if you have an international driver's license (available in the United States from AAA) with a motorcycle rating (which requires a U.S. motorcycle license). Unless you have experience operating a two-wheel machine in dense traffic (and maybe even if you do, Dianne says), we don't recommend it. Scooter driving in Rome is fast, demanding, and not for the faint of heart.

Here you'll find the last of the fountains on this itinerary and one of the most unusual in Rome. Completed in 2000, it was inspired by the ideas and designs of neuropsychiatrist Massimo Fagioli. Bill likes its playfulness, its creativity, and the archlike form that hints of the ancients; Dianne thinks it's too awkward for words. For her, the only saving grace to walking this far is the gypsy market in the piazza on Sunday mornings and perhaps glimpses of spaces of ancient gardens (popes' and Romans' and others') and industrial detritus. One more compensating benefit, she says, if you're out on any day other than Sunday, is the delightful newer restaurant *La Vecchia Stalla* (The Old Stall), open every day except Saturday lunch and Sundays, in the walls lining via Portuense, at No. 86 on your right (tel. 06.5834.0075). As to that fountain, you decide—that is, if you've made it this far.

What one can say, with some confidence, is that there had to be a fountain of some sort here. Without it, the piazza would have been incomplete, and Romans would have felt its incompleteness and missed the water. The river as a marker of the city is gone, gone for good, we think—a necessary tragedy, one might say—but the fountains remain, testifying to the deep Roman attachment to the life-giving liquid that flows from the hills.

Find a bar and order a bottle of water.

GETTING BACK

From the "bowls" fountain, cross via Portuense and head for the Tevere, a block away, straight ahead. Cross the river on *Ponte Testaccio* (Testaccio Bridge), which will put you directly in back of the old slaughterhouse (*l'ex mattatoio*). Turn left for fifty yards, then right on via Aldo Manuzio, which will take you back through Testaccio to via Marmorata. Turn right to Porta San Paolo and, nearby, Metro B (Piramide). Another possibility is to catch a fairly frequent bus right on the "bowls" fountain piazza, Bus 170, which circles it. It will take you across the Testaccio Bridge, along the Tevere to Piazza Venezia, up via Nazionale to Termini (Station).

2

THE NAZIS IN ROME

Why was Rome called an "open city" in 1944? What side was Italy on during World War II? What happened when Hitler came to Rome?

Italy's role in World War II has puzzled many people, including us. There appear to be few signs of this war that ravaged the peninsula, unless you look for them. But once one starts looking, the traces of the war are there, and they are fascinating.

This chapter offers three itineraries, each designed to introduce key elements of Germany's relationship with Rome in the prewar and war years while also highlighting Fascism and other intriguing layers of Rome. To assist in understanding the itineraries in this chapter, we offer a brief setting.

THE SETTING

The Axis alliance that joined Italy and Germany as World War II combatants was forged in 1936, when Italy and Germany united in support of the Franco dictatorship in Spain. It was further strengthened in September 1937, when Benito Mussolini traveled to Berlin, and in May 1938, when Adolf Hitler came to Rome. The German invasion of Poland that launched the war in Europe was sixteen months in the future. But

Germany had only recently absorbed Austria, and there was anxiety across the Continent about the Führer's intentions, especially if he found a strong and aggressive ally in Mussolini's Italy. A year after Hitler's visit, in May 1939, Italy and Germany signed a ten-year "Pact of Steel," agreeing to reorganize Europe and to cooperate economically, politically, and militarily. The die was cast.

Mussolini and his Fascist regime had come to power in Italy in 1922, when King Victor Emmanuel III, with the support of many of the nation's leading political figures and other elites—all obviously influenced by the sight of forty thousand of Mussolini's black shirts marching toward Rome—invited him to form a new government. The king was not alone in hoping that Mussolini would cut the legs out from under the socialist movement in the North, provide the leadership that seemed to be lacking under a liberal parliamentary system, and restore honor to a nation damaged by its indecisive participation in the Great War. Fascism appealed to veterans and to a broad spectrum of the middle class, including professionals and white-collar workers, many of whom found work in the growing state bureaucracy. Mussolini's power grew in 1926, after an attempt on his life; thousands of black shirts gathered in Piazza Colonna in Rome's center to call for the execution of the eighteen-year-old would-be assassin, and Pope Pius XI announced that the Italian leader's narrow escape from death was "a new sign that Mussolini has God's full protection." A critic of Fascism coined the word *totalitarianism* in 1923, several years before the Duce consolidated his power by suppressing the democratic unions and silencing opposition newspapers. Although Mussolini was a dictator, until the mid-1930s he was widely praised by American journalists, who saw him as a great leader and an exceptional person.

On the domestic front, the Mussolini regime followed a patchwork of policies that did little to modernize Italy or help its people through the Great Depression of the 1930s. Fascism generally favored big business and basic industries such as steel and chemicals. Under a system called "corporativism," Fascism brought together business, Fascist-controlled unions, and the state in a series of cartels that controlled production, prices, wages, and marketing while failing to make industry more efficient or more competitive. Outside the cities, Fascism pursued land reclamation (with some success in the Pontine marshes, but little elsewhere) and ruralization, a failed effort to keep Italians from moving off the land (see "Standing Water: Conquering Malaria," p. 60). It also supported large landlords over share-croppers and peasants and largely ignored the impoverished South, where malaria remained widespread. Unlike Germany and the United States, where the Great Depression brought unemployment insurance and old-age assistance, Italy under Fascism moved backward, destroying the mutual aid associations that had in the past helped the elderly and the unfortunate. Women also fared poorly under Fascism; they were discouraged from work-ing and were expected to serve the nation by having lots of children.

Fascism was more aggressive, if not more successful, in foreign affairs. In 1935–36, Mussolini tapped a wellspring of Italian nationalist sentiment by invading, conquering, and annexing Ethiopia in search of a new North African empire that would recapture the imperial glory of ancient Rome. Later in the decade, Italian armies invaded Albania and, in 1940, Greece. Although many U.S. officials remained convinced that Italy could be per-suaded to remain outside the war Germany had declared against Britain and France in 1940, these hopes proved naive. On June 10 of that year, Mussolini's Italy joined the conflict. "The hand that held the dagger," said President Franklin Delano Roosevelt in response, "has stuck it into the back of its neighbor."

War came to Italian shores in July 1943, when British and U.S. troops invaded the island of Sicily and took its largest city, Palermo. A long cam-paign between the Allies and the Italian army seemed to be in the offing. Then an extraordinary event took place. On July 25, Mussolini was sud-denly removed from office, and by early September a new Italian govern-ment had signed an armistice with the Allies, effectively withdrawing the country from the war. At this critical juncture, German troops flowed southward into the peninsula, replacing Italian forces so rapidly that the Allies were unable to take advantage of the changeover. What happened to the Italian army is evidence of a deeply divided nation. Many soldiers

continued on page 62

STANDING WATER: CONQUERING MALARIA

For centuries, the arrival of spring in Rome was greeted with consternation, especially when it brought winds from the Pontine marshes or from the Tiber River Delta. The concern was for malaria, sometimes called "Roman fever," a disease whose scientific name derives from the Italian (*mal aria*, bad air), and so strongly identified with Italy that it was frequently referred to as the "Italian national disease." "The Roman Campagna," wrote novelist Émile Zola, "is a desert of death that a dead river crosses and that forms a belt of sterility encircling Rome." Daisy Miller, Henry James's American protagonist in a novel by the same name (1877), dies of malaria after spending the evening at the Coliseum, understood then as a place where one could easily contract the disease.

The anxiety that came with the approach of summer was certainly warranted, although the theory prevailing in the 1870s—that the bad air that caused malaria was a product of miasmatism, a poisoning of the air caused by vapors rising from wet earth—was false. So, too, was the idea that the province of Lazio was somehow unique; in the 1880s, only two of Italy's sixty-nine provinces were unaffected by malaria, and an estimated twenty-five million people were infected, including many rural peasants in the south and center of the country.

It is widely believed that the singular accomplishment of the Mussolini dictatorship was the eradication of malaria. But it isn't true. The battle against malaria began much earlier, in the nineteenth century, when a series of experiments carried out by the Rome School of Malariology proved the miasma theory wrong. By 1900 most scientists understood that malaria was a blood disease transmitted by the anopheles mosquito; that mosquitoes proliferated in areas where there was standing water; and that quinine, properly administered—that is, taken every day—could either prevent the disease or cure it. The last of these was the basis for the first national crusade against malaria. It began in 1904 and focused on using quinine to prevent people from getting the disease. There were problems. Peasants distrusted the doctors who told them to take the drug or, if they had malaria, only took it long enough to rid themselves of the symptoms. Landlords and farmers resented paying quinine taxes. Nonetheless, the public health stations and school education programs that were at the heart of the effort had a major impact, cutting the death rate from malaria from 490 per million in 1900 to 90 per million twelve years later.

These gains ended and were rolled back during World War I, and by the time of Mussolini's March on Rome in 1922, malaria was back with a vengeance. Once he had consolidated his power, the Duce turned to the Pontine marshes and malaria, determined to use the swampy, largely uninhabited area directly south of Rome (between the mountains and the sea) to demonstrate the awesome transformative powers of the new Italy. Beginning in 1929 (the year of the U.S. stock market crash), the Fascist government drained the marshes with a series of trenches and canals (one called the Mussolini Canal), installed huge pumps, constructed rural health stations for the dispensing of quinine, built hundreds of screened houses and five major cities from scratch (including Littoria or, roughly translated, *Fascistville,* renamed Latina after the war), and resettled the new province of Littorio with immigrants from the Veneto region who were soon engaged in intensive agriculture.

The work was "finished" in 1939 and trumpeted as a great Fascist victory. Yes, malaria rates declined dramatically in the new Littorio. But the regime cared little about the thousands of construction workers who contracted malaria; did nothing about malaria in other regions, including the South (that is, Naples and south), where the problem was most serious; and in its educational campaigns, defined malaria as a self-inflicted disease brought on by ignorance—a classic case of blaming the victim. Moreover, the regime's imperial ambitions and, in 1940, the turn to war sealed the fate of the Littorio project. Deprived of resources, malaria rebounded. Soon after they occupied Italy in late 1943, the

This poster proclaimed the Fascist regime's National Campaign Against Malaria with Mussolini's words, "This is the war we prefer."

vengeful Germans shut down the pumps and blocked the drainage canals, flooding thousands of acres with a mixture of fresh and salt water that proved an ideal breeding ground for the most dangerous species of mosquito. When the people of the Littorio returned in 1944, after the Germans had left, they were the victims of a two-year malaria epidemic caused by an act of biological warfare.

Malaria was not finally and fully defeated in Italy until 1962, the culmination of twenty years of spraying with DDT, a chemical now banned because of the harm it does to the ecosystem. The first spraying of the Pontine marshes was actually carried out by U.S. aircraft on June 5, 1944, the day after the Allies entered Rome.

Based on Frank M. Snowden, *The Conquest of Malaria: Italy, 1900–1962* (New Haven: Yale University Press, 2006).

We recommend traveling in the Pontina and visiting the Fascist-built planned cities such as Latina, Sabaudia, and Pontinia. The last, a small town, has an informative (mostly in Italian but with lots of photos and charts) museum of malaria (open Monday–Saturday 9 a.m.–noon and Tuesday, Wednesday, Friday 3–6 p.m., but ask at the library; these days and times aren't trustworthy) and an exciting regional market on Friday mornings. Pontinia has a hotel and restaurant on the edge of town (as a local informed us, and we agree, "only one, but it's good"), Hotel Ares, www.hotelares.it—in Italian only; tel. 0773.86.8132; info@hotelares.it.

simply went home, to civilian life. Others fought alongside the Germans—either voluntarily or under some degree of coercion. Still another group joined the Allied cause. Many others joined with angry civilians and became partisans (*partigiani*), carrying on a campaign of guerrilla warfare against the German occupying forces and the Italians who cooperated with the Germans. It was a period of bitter division among Italians, and memories of it color national politics and personal relationships to this day.

The Allied campaign against the German army went slowly, stalling for many months at the Gustav line, about seventy miles south-southeast of Rome, where German forces held a critical position at the abbey of Monte Cassino, high above the city of Cassino—eventually the site of one of the bloodiest and most controversial battles of the war. An attempt to outflank the German forces with a sea landing at Anzio (just an hour from Rome by car) also stalled, with American troops under Maj. Gen. John P. Lucas unable to move beyond a narrow beachhead.

During these difficult months, between September 1943 and June 1944, Rome was occupied by German troops. Hoping to save the Eternal City from destruction, the Axis and Allies agreed Rome would be an "open city"—that is, a demilitarized zone that would not be bombed by the Allies (generally, but not entirely, respected) and not used by the Germans as a staging area (not respected at all). Many Romans found the situation unbearably inhumane and dishonorable, as they faced starvation and humiliation at the hands of the brutal and arrogant occupying Germans and their Italian Fascist supporters. A small but significant minority engaged in acts of sabotage and violence in an effort to make life difficult for the Germans and, they hoped, to foment a general uprising in the city. Rome, writes historian Robert Katz, "would be a city of spies, double agents, informers, torturers, fugitives, hunted Jews, and hungry people."

The military stalemate eventually was broken, and Rome fell to the Allies on June 4, 1944. Fleeing to the north, German forces offered only minimal resistance. To celebrate the occasion, and to deliver what he had promised to his mother, an American soldier of Italian descent climbed onto the balcony of Palazzo Venezia, where Mussolini had once spoken to cheering throngs and, in Italian, he mocked the Duce's gestures and movements, clenching his fist and shouting, "Death and destruction to Mussolini and all his Nazi masters!"

ITINERARIES IN BRIEF

Each of the following three itineraries is designed to fill a good portion of a day, with the first likely to spill over into a second day.

Itinerary 4, centered in the area of the Pyramid, evokes Hitler's 1938 visit to Rome and the resistance to the occupation of 1943–44. It also deals significantly with Fascist-modernist architectural styles, two historic cemeteries, Rome's empire-driven relationship to the sea, and with an Ostiense neighborhood in the process of transition from commerce and industry to hip cafés.

Itinerary 5, centered in the via Veneto area of Rome where the Germans established their headquarters, also deals significantly with Fascist monumentalist architecture. It concludes with a church Dianne just can't resist.

Itinerary 6 begins with a surprise bomb attack by resistance fighters against a column of troops on via Rasella, not far from the foot of via Veneto; continues with a trip to the German SS headquarters on via Tasso; and concludes with a journey to the Fosse Ardeatine, where the German high command, in reprisal for the 33 SS who had died up to that point in the via Rasella bombing, killed 335 Italians in cold blood. Together, these events constitute one of the most important chapters in modern Italian history.

ITINERARY 4: HITLER AND THE GERMANS COME TO ROME

HOW TO GET THERE

Take Metro B to the *Piramide* (Pyramid) stop. Turn right on the platform and go up the steps and through the gates. Follow the signs for Piazzale dei Partigiani. Walk outside, up the stairs, and to the right toward the Ostiense train station, where the itinerary begins.

WHEN TO GO

The best time is Saturday morning and early afternoon, when the flea market and the Porta San Paolo museum are open.

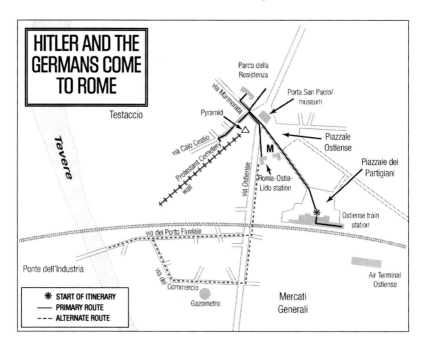

HITLER AND MUSSOLINI: THE MEETING AT OSTIENSE

The stage for the Rome meeting was the Ostiense train station, where Hitler's train arrived on May 3, 1938, after darkness had fallen. The German entourage included Hitler, Joseph Goebbels, Rudolf Hess, and Joachim von Ribbentrop. King Victor Emmanuel III—a diminutive man, shorter and thinner than Hitler—was there to greet them, and so, of course, was Mussolini and dozens of dignitaries and thousands of ecstatic Italians, no doubt thrilled that their country was finally at the center of world affairs. There was much bowing and posturing, Fascist salutes all around—a real show, ably parodied in Charlie Chaplin's 1940 film *The Great Dictator*. (The Fascist salute, also known as the Roman salute because of its origins in ancient Rome, was required in state offices and public schools beginning in 1925, and in 1932 the salute was officially designated as the substitute for the "bourgeois" handshake. The *passo Romano*, a vigorous, stiff-legged marching style, was instituted in February 1938, just months before Hitler's visit. According to Mussolini, it was of ancient Roman, rather than Nazi, origins.)

The Ostiense Station, brilliantly lit for the occasion, had been designed and built just for events such as this, but architect Roberto Narducci's design was not completed until 1940. What Hitler saw was something very similar to what you see today, but he saw a temporary station with a permanent appearance on a grand scale, with very high ceilings, huge and elegant cone-shaped hanging lights, enormous columns of travertine marble, and (to Hitler's left as he stepped into the exterior portico) a huge eagle, symbolic of the Third Reich.

It is hard to imagine the king and Mussolini taking the time at this juncture to show their guests the mosaics that covered the floors of the outer concourse (indeed, they may not have been laid), but it is a fascinating set of images, echoing those in the ancient Roman port city of Ostia Antica. From left to right (as one faces the station), the mosaics tell Italy's story, including the earliest contacts with the Greeks (panel 1); the mythical founding of Rome in 753 BC, with the twins Romulus and Remus nourished by a she-wolf (panel 3); the Roman Empire, featuring conquests in Africa and Dacia (Romania) (panel 7); the age of discovery

The dramatic portico of Ostiense Station, where Adolf Hitler arrived in 1938.

(panel 8); the pope, St. Peter's, and a sailboat, the last perhaps a reference to Ostia, Rome's link to the sea (panel 9); and, joining Italy's past and present, a naked Roman demonstrating the Fascist salute, surrounded by the eagles and swords that betoken a proudly aggressive, warlike people (panel 11).

Enter the station and proceed to the platform. Walk left for about seventy-five yards to get a good look at the four-story railroad building in the center of the tracks. With its rounded front and light, overhanging cap, it's a classic of mid-1930s streamlining, the architectural equivalent of the streamlined trains that graced the Ostiense Station and were a favorite subject of poster artists in the decade. Across the way, in the distance, you'll see the arches of prize-winning Spanish (and longtime Roman) architect Julio La Fuente's Air Terminal Ostiense (1990), intended to serve people arriving from the airport at Fiumicino. It was never used for this purpose, however, and is virtually empty. Down the platform in the opposite direction, note the panel that sticks out from the wall. It reveals what was once here—a ten-foot statue of *Dea Roma,* Goddess Rome (there's a picture of it)—and what you can't see: the elaborately decorated Presidential Room, its militaristic tapestries carried out for the occasion of Hitler's visit.

Exit the station. Take yourself back to that May evening. Imagine Hitler and King Victor Emmanuel III (the pairing required by protocol), climbing into a horse-drawn carriage for the journey to the royal palace, leaving Mussolini to follow. The carriage proceeds along a course of bricked streets: down the new viale Adolfo Hitler to the *porta,* right on viale Aventino, past Circo Massimo, onto (then) via dei *Trionfi* (victories), between the Arch of Constantine and the Coliseum (a road closed today), down the (then) via dell'*Impero* (Empire) through Piazza Venezia and up to the royal palace on the nearby Quirinale Hill, the route illuminated by hundreds of torches, the Coliseum ablaze with torchlight, every tree "aglow" according to one report, guards everywhere. It seemed as if everyone in Rome had turned out for the event (and that, in fact, was the premise of Ettore Scola's 1977 film *Una Giornata Particolare* (*A Special Day*), set on May 3, 1938, and featuring Marcello Mastroianni (as a homosexual) and Sophia Loren (as a housewife) as the only two residents of the massive apartment complex on viale XXI Aprile who do *not* participate in the celebration (see Itinerary 8, p. 112).

TODAY, SERVICES AND A FLEA MARKET

If you're following this itinerary on a Saturday or Sunday, between 9 a.m. and 8 p.m., you may want to take a few minutes to explore the underground *mercatino* (antique and flea market), which is marked by signs just outside the station. This is a decent one, with dozens of tables covered with jewelry, household items, Fascist publications and broadsides, old postcards, and clothing. The station itself has been recently remodeled and has a bevy of services, including a grocery store, bar, and cafeteria.

ART AND THE PYRAMID

Exit from the station again into Piazzale dei Partigiani, and head back toward the Metro station on your left. Between the Metro station and the Pyramid, on a small island amid the traffic of Piazzale Ostiense, is a significant piece of modern art: silhouettes cut from massive pieces of iron plate. A 1995 plaque marks the sculpture as a political work of opposition to the twentieth-century's barbarous acts, from the racial persecutions conducted by Hitler and Mussolini, to the train bombings of the 1970s, to the more recent attacks on "nomad" camps. The colored emblems on the backs of the silhouettes—symbols used by the Nazis—represent persecuted groups: the yellow star stands for Jews, the red triangle for gypsies, the pink triangle for homosexuals, and the blue triangle for the stateless, those lacking citizenship.

Friends experiencing modern political art in Piazzale Ostiense.

You'll find a discussion of the Pyramid in any guidebook. Built as a tomb to Caius Cestius, who died in 12 BC, this Carrara marble–covered structure gleams anomalously two thousand years later in one of Rome's busiest traffic circles. (If you're using buses, you'll see references to stops as "Caio Cestio," the Italian version of the name of the Pyramid.)

VIEW FROM THE PORTA

Cross to the imposing arched gateway of Porta San Paolo to the right of the Pyramid, using crosswalks and extreme care; seven streets merge here. Porta San Paolo is now named for the important basilica a mile or so away, San Paolo *fuori le mura* (St. Paul's outside the wall). It once was named Porta Ostiense, because the via Ostiense (road to Ostia) went through it on its way to Ostia on the Mediterranean. On the back side of this wonderfully intact third-century AD *porta* (or gate to the city) is the entrance to the Museo di Porta San Paolo (open Tuesday–Saturday and the first and third Sundays of the month 9 a.m.–1:30 p.m. and also 2:30–4:30 p.m. on Tuesday and Thursday). In this delightful, free museum you can wander among the many levels of a fortification built more than seventeen hundred years ago, look through gun holes, and imagine boiling oil being poured through the slots. From the ramparts of the museum, you have a marvelous view of the immense double piazza—Piazza San Paolo to the north and Piazzale Ostiense to the south—of the seven converging roads, and of the meaning of this transportation hub. From this vantage point, you can see long stretches of the wall built by Emperor Aurelian in the third century AD, the second set of walls around the city and the most intact. The Aurelian wall defined the city of Rome for fifteen hundred years. Even as Rome's population dwindled from almost one million to less than fifty thousand in part because of the many sacks during the Dark Ages, the Romans kept this wall intact as a real as well as a symbolic effort to maintain their city. Also inside the museum are models of Roman port cities, statuary and frescoes from nearby tombs (note the birds and peacocks symbolizing the soul), and more.

RESISTANCE IN 1943

Exiting from the museum, a few feet down the path you'll come across a rectangular monument with an inscription that will bring us back to the twentieth century: "In memory of the glorious fallen [*caduti*] who in defense of liberty sacrificed themselves in Rome from September 1943 to June 1944." The dates are those of the German occupation of Rome, and the place you're standing was, for three days in September 1943, the scene of intense fighting between German troops and the Italian "resistance." In July 1943, Mussolini's regime had come under increasing pressure as the Allies invaded Sicily and even bombed some areas of the city not far from the Center. In a remarkable turn of events, Mussolini was removed from office and replaced by a government led by Marshal Pietro Badoglio, which announced on September 8 that Italy had negotiated an armistice with the Allies. Most Italians celebrated, and most soldiers in the Italian army simply went home. In contrast, German troops moved rapidly to occupy Rome, a distasteful prospect for most Italians. Armed resistance to the occupation led by groups of Italian soldiers and armed civilians began immediately around the Pyramid, the Porta San Paolo, the Protestant cemetery, and other sections of the city.

Getting across the street to your left (as you face the small monument and the *porta*) is not as dangerous as being a resistance fighter, but it isn't easy, either. A successful crossing will bring you to the edge of the *Parco della Resistenza dell'Otto Settembre* (Park of the Resistance of 8 September). It is a space of contradictions and ironies. On the one hand, the park's siting and contours (a somewhat sunken center) and its towering, brooding pines make it an appropriate place for memory and reflection.

The three-sided monument, which you'll see on the left soon after you enter, is mostly about the contributions of the Italian military to the resistance. It notes the 87,000 Italian soldiers who died liberating Italy from the Germans, the 80,000 soldiers who fought in partisan (resistance) brigades, and the 590,000 members of the FF.AA (Italian armed forces) who were imprisoned for their refusal to serve the German occupation.

On the other hand, the park was created under Fascism. Its small marble benches are the same as those that appear in other parks of Fascist origin. The back side of the post office, a Fascist landmark, dominates the park's southwest side. And close inspection of the amphora-shaped fountain at the park's center reveals SPQRs alternating with *fasci* (bundles of rods or sticks with an ax blade), both symbols identified with the Fascist regime. (The amphora is also a reference to the pots brought by ancient vessels up the Tiber into nearby Testaccio and the disposal of which created Monte Testaccio, the hill you see close by to the west; see p. 46.)

You can take a brief respite at the very Roman, mostly outdoor and covered Café Du Parc.

POST OFFICE–DEFINING ARCHITECTURE

Rising up along the southwest side of the park is the back of an imposing modernist post office, a fitting demarcation of the Fascist-designed park. Built in 1933–35 by winners of a competition, the post office was opened by Mussolini as he proudly faced two other icons of Roman history: the Porta San Paolo and the Pyramid. (See the discussion of the uses—in Fascist times and today—of the new post offices in Piazza Bologna [see p. 98], viale Mazzini, via Taranto, and Ostia Lido.) Round the post office to the front to understand its modernist, rationalist structure. The architects that served the Fascist state (after 1932, one had to be a party member to work on state projects) were not of one mind about what sort of architecture would best represent Fascist ideals. One group of modernists, led by Giuseppe Pagano and including Mario De Renzi and Adalberto Libera, designers of this post office, understood Fascism as a forward-looking, business-oriented movement best repre-

Ostiense post office (1933–35), Fascist architecture at its best.

sented by an architecture that emphasized functionality and simplicity. Another group, led by Marcello Piacentini, preferred to see Fascism as building on the strengths of Imperial Rome, and therefore best represented by an architecture that commented on those Roman roots and emphasized, above all else, monumentality. Mussolini (who made most of the decisions about what was built) was of a mixed mind, and hence Rome has many buildings of both types. After 1936, however, after Italy invaded Ethiopia and announced its intention to acquire an empire, the Piacentini view was increasingly dominant.

Inside (open Monday–Friday 8 a.m.–7 p.m. and Saturday 8 a.m.–1:15 p.m.), you can see (among the many intricate features of the building) the wonderful play of light created by the elliptical center ceiling; the shape is meant to remind us of the Diocletian stadium, now Piazza Navona. The bent plywood chairs are new, but they work here because that chair style was developed and popularized in the 1940s and remains a touchstone of midcentury modernist design. Note: you can't take photos in post offices in Italy (see p. 98).

THE SWEETEST CEMETERY

From the post office, cross again the busy via Marmorata (you might exercise more care if you remember Spaniard architect Gaudí was killed by a streetcar in Barcelona), to the first street before the Pyramid, appropriately named via Caio Cestio. About fifty steps from the Pyramid is the entrance on your left to the Protestant (variously called non-Catholic or *acattolico*) cemetery (open Monday–Saturday 9 a.m.–5 p.m.; last entrance 4:30 p.m.; €2 donation requested). The cemetery has been spruced up recently and has excellent directions and tablets in Italian and English that will lead you to often-visited spots. The old section has marvelous views of the Pyramid. You'll also see tombs and monuments to Romantic figures, such as English poets Percy Bysshe Shelley (1792–1822; only his heart is here) and John Keats (1796–1821) and others of both trivial and important note, such as the last man to have a dinner party on the Palatine (Charles Andrew Mills, d. 1846); the nineteenth-century beauty Rosa Bathurst (d. 1824), swept away after falling with her horse into the flood-swollen waters of the Te- vere; and Antonio Gramsci, the Italian intellectual and activist who was tortured and died in 1937 in a Rome hospital, under police guard, after spending a decade in Fascist prisons. Shelley wrote about this cemetery: "It might make one in love with death to think that one should be buried in so sweet a place."

A few steps past this cemetery is the British Military Cemetery, the bur- ial place of more than four hundred British troops who were killed in and around Rome during World War II.

MORE COMMEMORATION OF RESISTANCE, THE PYRAMID, AND THE CATS
Heading out of the Protestant cemetery, retrace your steps back to the Pyramid and around to the other side of it. On the wall to the left of the Pyramid are several plaques. One in English commemorates U.S. and Canadian armed forces. To the left, a 1990 plaque is about the role of women in the September 1943 resistance. In the center, the top plaque notes the "German invaders" while the bottom one refers to the "nazi- fascist barbarity."

Seeing the inside of the Pyramid is impossible without a guided (and infrequent) tour. The best vistas of the outside are from the Protestant cemetery where you just were and from the large and charming cat grounds accessible via the gates just to the left of the Pyramid. These grounds are open 2:30–4:30 p.m. each day. A contribution to help the cats is requested.

GETTING BACK OR GOING ON

You can end your *giro* (tour) here, have lunch in any one of the trattorias around Porta San Paolo, and catch the Metro at the Piramide stop back to any location (see "One More Piece of Fascism," p. 76, before you head down into the Metro). Or take a break and head into an interesting section of the city that is transforming from industrial-commercial to residential-retail.

ROME CONNECTS TO THE SEA

To pick up your walk again from the gates to the cat grounds at the Pyramid, head across the street toward the lovely early-twentieth-century electric train station that takes Romans to their beloved beaches (the Roma-Ostia Lido line). Built in 1924, this restored and still heavily used (especially on weekends and the many holidays) train station was designed by the same Piacentini who did the post office. Here he reflects more the nineteenth than the twentieth century. Covering the high walls and ceilings are G. Rosso's captivating seaside-themed art *nouveau* graphic designs that recall modern Ostia (the seaside town) as well as Ostia Antica (the ancient Roman port). This train line was part of the Fascists' design to build Rome southward and westward to the sea, rather than to the north and east, as most city planners had expected. On the walls are photos of the station in 1924 and explanations of how it reflected the latest in modern designs, such as platforms serving two directions, the use of reinforced concrete for the first time in the overhangs, and recessed tracks that allowed the passengers to step right into the cars. On a wall to the left you will see a plaque quoting verse by Gabriele d'Annunzio, a significant Fascist poet with broad appeal. The poem, "Beyond the Sea," harkens back to ancient Rome to underline the imperialist goals of modern Rome.

CHANGING—AND INDUSTRIAL—VIA OSTIENSE

Exit the station and proceed along the wide, busy boulevard just to the right of the station (as you look at it). This is the important via Ostiense. A 1970s *Blue Guide to Rome* describes this street as "broad uninteresting [and passing through] . . . a depressing part of the town. It is not recommended to walkers." We disagree. It's bustling and fascinating, even if, as is the case for many transitional areas, a bit grungy. Don't hesitate to walk under the train overpass. Then take the next right along a street the 1970s guide would no doubt be appalled to find us recommending: *via del Porto Fluviale* (street of the river port). Take this past old warehouses and manufacturing buildings, some still in operation. Examples are Saccheria Sonnino at No. 45—a sack, twine, and tarp manufacturer, now specializing in "Camping" equipment—and at No. 67B—an enormous fresh fish market (*Pescheria*). Just beyond these, you'll find an iron bridge crossing the Tevere. Built as a train bridge in 1863 (note the pylons with their capitals intact), it was rebuilt as an iron car-and-truck bridge in 1923 to handle the increasing industrial traffic from the Ostiense area. Its official name is *Ponte dell'Industria* (Bridge of Industry); unofficially it's called *Ponte di ferro* (the iron bridge). Your vistas across the river are of the dense Marconi neighborhood, with high-rise apartment buildings dating mainly from the 1970s. Directly across the bridge on the right is a large flour mill and pasta factory (formerly Molini e Pastifici Biondi) that has been converted into apartments while maintaining much of the historical industrial features.

To the right of the bridge is our last stop on this walk that recognizes World War II, the touching monument with ten bronze heads in relief: "In memory of the 10 women killed by the nazi-fascists 7 April 1944."

Turn back on via del Porto Fluviale and take the first accessible street on your right, via del Commercio. On your right, at and around No. 13, are the beautifully converted general warehouse build-

The tallest *gazometro,* a landmark of modern Rome.

ings, now government offices. Just before them (Nos. 23/25) is the deeply colored goldenrod river customs house, Dogana Porto Fluviale, a sign that the Tevere remained an important commercial thoroughfare well into the twentieth century. Ahead is the unmistakable skyline of the *gazometro* (gas meter)—actually *gazometri,* since there is a large one and several smaller ones. These feathery buildings of iron were built in the 1930s to be useful but also monumental in signifying Italy's rapid industrialization. They showily carried gas and represented both the gasworks (now "italgas") and electrical works in this industrial part of town. The *gazometri,* which ceased operation in the early 1970s, are now essential parts of the city's skyline, and there have been protests to make sure they are kept intact and are illuminated.

Your trek along via del Commercio takes you into Piazza del Gazometro. You can turn back left here along via Ostiense. First look across the street at the remains of the general market, *Mercati Generali,* built from 1913 to 1924, now being converted to other uses, including part of the University of Rome. You may choose to continue walking out (right) via Ostiense another ten minutes. On your right, don't miss (Dianne says) the museum at Centrale Montemartini (via Ostiense, 106)—the former electrical works (built from 1910 to 1912, ceased operations in the 1970s) beautifully displays, in and around the enormous electrical machinery, much of the Roman statuary owned by the city. Open Tuesday–Sunday 9 a.m.–7 p.m. (until 2 p.m. Christmas Eve and New Year's Eve), closed Christmas, New Year's, and May 1. Admission €4.5. Information is available in English (click on Eng at upper left) at www.centralemontemartini.org.

HIP CAFÉS COME TO OSTIENSE

Heading back toward the Piramide Metro on via Ostiense, you will come across several hip bars and restaurants: *doppiozero* (double zero) at the north end of Piazza del Gazometro; on the right side of via Ostiense, at 99, *Mangiafuoco* ("eat fire," also the name of Pinocchio's puppet master), a restaurant passing itself off as a "wine bar"; at 95, *Caffè Letterario,* which, as its name suggests, has a small library and hosts other events in addition to offering food and drink. These give you some idea of the changing ambience of the via Ostiense neighborhood. Feel free to take a well-deserved rest in one of these.

ONE MORE PIECE OF FASCISM, THEN GETTING BACK

Head back to the Piramide Metro stop. Before you go down to the trains, take a look to your left as you enter the main station entrance. It's the sign for the toilets. If it's open, go through the glass doors. Here you'll see one of the best Fascist bas-reliefs in the city. When we first came to Rome, one passed the relief while walking down to the trains (and it had an ad pasted below it showing women in skimpy outfits—quite a contrast). Then the sculpture was positioned on the way to the toilets; now even that doorway seems to be closed. One day no doubt this piece of art will return to its glory, but its shabby treatment tells a Roman story: so many wonderful sights not properly cared for and preserved.

Now we'll let you go.

ITINERARY 5: THE NAZIS AND FASCISTS IN CENTRAL ROME

GETTING THERE AND MORE

We begin at Largo S. Susanna (adjacent to the much-maligned Moses Fountain). To get there, take Metro A to Piazza della Repubblica. Walk out of the piazza to the left (west) one long block to Largo S. Susanna. (Just before the largo is Piazza S. Bernardo, with, on the right, Santa Maria della Vittoria, the church containing Bernini's famous Santa Teresa in ecstasy. It's in all guidebooks and worth a look, Dianne says, to determine what kind of ecstasy or to refresh your recollection of a famous scene in Dan Brown's *Angels & Demons*). The church is open daily 6:30 a.m.–noon and 4:30–6:30 p.m. (see "*Angels & Demons*," p. 78). Take the left fork out of Largo S. Susanna, via Leonida Bissolati.

WHEN TO GO

Most of this itinerary is outside or consists of peeks into buildings (such as hotels) that are always open. If you want to take a look in the church suggested at the beginning of the itinerary, Santa Maria della Vittoria,

see its opening times on the facing page; for the church at the end of the itinerary, Santa Maria delle Concezione see p. 82 (closed Thursdays). Also note that San Carlino (the church recommended in part 1 of Itinerary 6 below) can be added at the end of this itinerary; see its opening hours at p. 87.

VIA VENETO: *LA DOLCE VITA*

First, here's a little background on the famed via Veneto. For most Americans, and no doubt for most Italians, via Vittorio Veneto is less a real street than an image, the one presented by Federico Fellini in the 1960 film *La Dolce Vita*. The film stars Marcello Mastroianni as Marcello, a playboy journalist who spends his evenings and nights amid the opulent, sexualized, alcoholic decadence of Rome, epitomized by the café life on via Veneto, searching for meaning in life but finding only boredom and unhappiness (see chapter 6, p. 197). The film had its counterparts in other

77

Western countries, including the United States, where the boom years of the 1950s had created the impression of a society given over to the ephemeral pleasures of consumption. Today, the upper portion of the street, with its

ANGELS & DEMONS

Fans (*tifosi*) of Dan Brown's best-selling Rome-based novel *Angels & Demons* (2000) will be pleased to learn that several of the major settings of the book are on or near the itineraries or sites recommended in this book.

The Pantheon, where protagonist Robert Langdon's Rome saga begins, is just steps from the entrance to Hotel de la Minerve, whose rooftop bar is featured in chapter 7 (p. 227).

Santa Maria del Popolo (and the *porta* next door), site of the Bernini-decorated Chigi chapel (Brown's "First Altar of Science"), is at the beginning of our tour of restaurants in the Flaminio district (see "Around the Block in Flaminio," p. 214). If you go to the Villa Medici, one of the academies we feature in chapter 6 (p. 190), you'll also be only six hundred yards or so (and nice ones at that, Dianne says) from the church.

The itinerary "The Nazis and Fascists in Central Rome" begins and ends with *Angels & Demons* locations. Santa Maria della Vittoria, home to Gian Lorenzo Bernini's Santa Teresa in ecstasy and the site of Brown's "Third Altar of Science," is near Largo S. Susanna (see p. 76) and not, as the novelist claims, at Piazza Barberini (also on our

tour). For those who may not recall, Bernini is Brown's historical villain, cast in the novel as the sculptor of an anti-religious, anti-Catholic cult known as the Illuminati. Piazza Barberini, briefly described by Brown, contains two delightful Bernini sculptures and the Hotel Bernini (now Hotel Bernini Bristol, constructed in 1943). At novel's end, Langdon and Vittoria Vetra found the Hotel Bernini the appropriate place to consummate their relationship, but the hotel's rooftop bar did not make our list of the best such places (rooftop bars, that is). The rooftop management reserves the prime seating area overlooking the piazza for diners, relegating bar patrons to the back; even so, we enjoyed a drink there, and an *Angels & Demons* devotee might find it irresistible.

Finally, the itinerary "The Strange Career of the Tevere" follows a course across *Isola Tiberina* (see p. 49), where Langdon is pulled from the roiling waters of the Tevere, a closeup view of which is on the itinerary too. Langdon is treated by the staff of the island's 1580s Fatebenefratelli Hospital (as was one of the authors) and helicoptered (Langdon, not the author) to more adventures.

ritzy chain hotels and glassed-in sidewalk cafés, is there to remind us only nominally of Marcello's story. A plaque just up the street from the Grand Palace Hotel commemorates the film.

FASCISM BUILDS ITS WALL STREET

Today's itinerary is about another, older via Veneto, the one built by Italian Fascists and, for a time in 1943 and 1944, occupied by the German high command. If you followed the directions above, you've taken the left fork out of Largo S. Susanna and you're on via Leonida Bissolati. The street was widened in the 1920s/30s, when most of the buildings were constructed, with the intent of creating a Fascist-style Wall Street to be occupied by corporations and the government entities serving them.

The first building worthy of note is the one with the big Banca Carige sign on top. It was built between 1938 and 1947 (the sources disagree) as the Fiat Building, and the name *Fiat* is still above the huge, Fascist-style doors in big squarish, modernist lettering. Appropriately, the frieze at this end of the building is mostly about transportation, although a cow and a tractor provide a hint of the agricultural economy; Fiat makes tractors as well as cars. (In 1993, Bill was pulled aside, questioned, and asked for various documents by men in suits when he was seen taking photos in the area. Apparently there is or was some important government office just to the right, and security forces were concerned that he was photographing the big wigs [*i big* in Italian] with some dastardly plan in mind.)

Further down via Bissolati, the enormous INA (*Istituto Nazionale delle Assicurazione*—National Insurance Institute) has a similar feel, with massive doors centering two friezes, each of a ship—the symbol of the risk-prone seaborne commerce that at one time was the main business of insurance companies. Designed by Ugo Giovanozzi, it was completed in 1927. At the far end of the building, columns in brick offer a hint of ancient Rome.

Just ahead, at the intersection of via Bissolati and via Veneto, the *Banca Nazionale del Lavoro* (National Workers' Bank, 1936) is solid and reassuring, as banks had to be in those days (and these days), when many people preferred to put money under their mattresses rather than entrust it to vulnerable institutions. Its designer, Marcello Piacentini, was the most prominent and prolific of Fascism's architects (see the index for more of Piacentini's works), and his considerable talents are displayed here in the elegant loggias of the upper floor, the long marble-framed windows, the complex horizontal-style brickwork, and the graceful statues that decorate the building's corner. From time to time, the interior of the bank—its offices and meeting rooms and hallways filled with the bank's extensive art collection—is opened to the public for guided tours. Not to be missed if you get the chance.

AND WHAT WERE THE WEALTHY ITALIANS DOING?

Crossing via Veneto in front of the American Embassy (which is disgracefully and clumsily barricaded), we find two sites of interest as we make the bend in the street. At No. 70 is the site of what was then the *Albergo degli Ambasciatori* (Ambassador Hotel, 1926), now the Grand Hotel Palace (not to be confused with the earlier Hotel Ambassador Palace at No. 62). It is another Piacentini masterpiece, this time a collaborative effort with Emilio Vogt. The huge columns of travertine are another reminder of Italy's Roman past, as is the top-floor loggia, crowned by Nino Cloza's bronze statues. Worthy, too, are the more visible art deco lights, shouldered by beguiling ladies. Step inside as well and ask to see, or walk into, the Salone Cadorin to the left of the entrance. On its walls are the frescoes of Guido Cadorin, the Venetian painter and friend of Fascist poet Gabriele d'Annunzio. They date to the 1920s and offer a glimpse of the life of the wealthy in that era who seem oblivious to the Fascist politics from which they are benefiting. The figures depicted were real people, including Piacentini. You can also have something to eat and drink here, although it's not on the economic side. A bottle of wine costs about €50, but at certain times of day you'll get a nice buffet with that, and, as in all of Italy, there are no additional taxes and a €5 tip is more than sufficient.

THE GERMAN HIGH COMMAND

We've seen the Fascists and Italian rich enjoying themselves on via Veneto. Now enter the Germans. The Nazi high command in World War II, once the Germans took over Rome in the fall of 1943, moved into the Excelsior Hotel a bit farther up via Veneto on your right (across from the Grand Hotel Palace). Completed in 1908, Otto Maraini's Excelsior reflects Rome's desire to imitate Paris. The French and baroque influences exhibit themselves, for example, in the charming (if unaesthetically small) cupola and garland flourishes. From here one can imagine the Germans holding forth over the entire business district of Rome, with a grand vista down via Veneto to the entire lower part of the city. They turned their backs on the Fascist-style build-

Headquarters of the German general staff during the occupation of Rome.

ings, putting themselves in a strategically better position and perhaps in an architectural style that seemed more familiar to them. Today the hotel is a Westin.

It was in this fancy building that the Germans made their cold-blooded decisions to murder 335 Italian men. The reason for this act of reprisal occurred only a few blocks away, and the gruesome story of attack and revenge plays out in the next itinerary.

If you want a break now, you can have a drink or snack in the Doney café or another of upper via Veneto's somewhat imitative *La Dolce Vita* sites. You will also find English-language newspapers and magazines (such as *Wanted in Rome*) in the newsstands here.

BACK TO THE FASCISTS

As you head back down via Veneto, taking the curve right around the Grand Hotel Palace, you enter the heart of Fascist monumentalism, a place redolent with the intimidating power of the Fascist state and its major institutions. At via Veneto, 89, the facade of Carlo Braggi's INA

The massive entrance to what was the Ministry of Corporations under Fascism (1932).

Building manages to mix the grandeur of Fascism with neoclassical flourishes. But the building wants us to know that it is a Fascist structure; it announces it was built in the sixth year of Fascism (AN VI, 1928; see "Fascist Numbering System," p. 85), and its ideological origins are present in the *fasci* on the keystone of the arch. Nine large arches—one of Fascism's key symbols, linking the movement to ancient Rome and its empire—line the facade.

Next door is the Ministero delle Attivitá Produttive (also known as the Ministry of Corporations or the Ministry of Industry). Designed by Piacentini (again) with Giuseppe Viccaro and opened in 1932, it is a bulky, glowering, menacing structure—the Darth Vader of Fascist architecture—built with travertine marble and blocks of *tufo,* the durable golden brown volcanic rock first used by the Etruscans. We leave it to you to enjoy interpreting the frieze above the door and the amazing cast bronze door panels by Giovanni Prini. What social values are depicted here? What can one learn here about Fascism?

CHURCH STOP (DIANNE SAYS)

We're headed next to a small street on the other side of Piazza Barberini, at the bottom of via Veneto. As you make your way there, be sure to stop in the church of the Capuchins, Santa Maria delle Concezione, at the bottom of via Veneto, where it meets Piazza Barberini. Don't miss the crypt to the right of the stairs, on the sidewalk level, as well as the lovely Bernini "bee" fountain just beyond it. The crypt is open daily from 9 a.m. to noon and 3–6 p.m. except Thursday. Don't miss Bernini's Triton Fountain in the piazza either. The Capuchins, of

Fascism had its muscular side. A panel on the door of the Ministry of Corporations illustrates Fascism's homage to laborers.

course, gave their name to the favorite Italian coffee drink: cappuccino. The Capuchins are so named because of their big brown hoods (the *cappuccio*) they wear over their heads, just like the big foam tops on cappuccinos; hence the name (and for the Capuchin monkey as well). You'll also hear Romans call for a *cappuccio* as often as they do for a cappuccino.

GETTING HOME, IF YOU WANT TO GO NOW

The next paragraph begins Itinerary 6. It's so close to where you are now that we recommend walking the first part of Itinerary 6 at the end of Itinerary 5. Conceptually, however, the next paragraph begins a new itinerary. If you want to head home now, catch the Metro at Piazza Barberini and start Itinerary 6 by heading to Metro A's Barberini stop at the beginning of your next touring day. If you have stamina to spare, keep reading into the next itinerary.

ITINERARY 6: ATTACK AND REPRISAL— A STORY OF PARTISANS AND NAZIS

This itinerary should start with a new day and carry you through the attack, torture, and reprisal, but it makes sense for you to see the site of the attack while you're close to it and save the rest of the story for another day. Either you're doing this at the end of Itinerary 5 or at the beginning of Itinerary 6. The three parts to this itinerary are referred to as via Rasella, via Tasso, and the Fosse Ardeatine, the three main locations.

GETTING THERE

If you're starting your day rather than ending it with this first part of Itinerary 6, take Metro A to the Piazza Barberini stop. Once you have done this first section (via Rasella), take Metro A to the San Giovanni stop for the second section (via Tasso). The complete itinerary requires a couple of bus or Metro rides, and the last part is at the end of a bus ride of twenty minutes outside the city walls, each way. An integrated all-day ticket, BIG, for €4 and coordination of times are advised.

WHEN TO GO

You can go to via Rasella (see map for Itinerary 5) at any time. The prison site (via Tasso) may be open only in the mornings (closed Mondays and August), and the Fosse Ardeatine should be open until about 3:30 p.m. (Monday–Friday), one hour later on Saturdays and Sundays. The catacombs near the Fosse Ardeatine are closed Wednesdays and in February. See all opening times below. You may be able to check the via Tasso museum opening times through an e-mail to biblioteca@viatasso.it. The recommended church stop in the first part of the itinerary is San Carlino, closed to visitors on Sundays; see opening times below.

PART 1: VIA RASELLA

Take the street just to the right, as you face it, of the cinema, *via Quattro Fontane* (Four Fountains). You'll see placards telling you about the fabulous Palazzo Barberini, its heritage and art collection (worth seeing another time), but you're headed for the second street to the right, via Rasella, a long, narrow street of high buildings on each side, pitching downhill. It was here, on March 23, 1944, that a small group of young, committed, idealistic partisans carried out a brazen attack on the German occupying force. Their target was a column of SS police, numbering about 150 and three abreast, that had been observed marching up via Rasella—a narrow, quiet street with few shops and little foot traffic—with Teutonic regularity. Two of the partisans (there were perhaps a dozen directly involved), a physicist and his wife, had fashioned forty

FASCIST NUMBERING SYSTEM:
HOW TO DATE A BUILDING

The Fascists, being no slouches when it came to appropriating anything significant relating to the ancient Roman Empire, picked up on the Romans' numbering system. They used Roman (of course) numerals and dated their works—anything from publications to schools—from what they considered to be the most important year of the beginning of the Fascist government, the Mussolini-led March on Rome in 1922.

Often the dating is clear: Anno XVI means Year (*Anno*) 16, the sixteenth year after 1922, or 1938. Sometimes Anno is simply abbreviated as A. For example, in the photo here, there's a gate with ironwork in the form of A XIII for the thirteenth year of

Elegant iron gate of the Fascist era. E is for Era, F for Fascist, A for *Anno* (year), VIII for the eighth year of Fascism (1930).

Italian Fascism (again, starting from the March on Rome in 1922). So we know construction was completed in 1935. In some cases you also will see the Roman numeral accompanied by the letters EF standing for *Era Fascista* or Fascist era.

pounds of TNT into a bomb with a fifty-second fuse, to be started when the column turned the corner from via Boccaccio and headed up via Rasella. The bomb was hidden in a municipal rubbish cart, which was positioned in front of Palazzo Tittoni at No. 156. Although the building was chosen primarily because it was semi-abandoned, in the 1920s it had once been home to Mussolini, who, according to one biographer, used the premises to sexually assault a steady stream of female visitors.

Standing next to the rubbish cart, Rosario Bentivegna, in the uniform of a city street cleaner, used his pipe to light the fuse as the German column turned the corner, then walked up the street and around the corner onto via Quattro Fontane, where Carla Capponi, his lover, was waiting to cover him with a raincoat. Writes Robert Katz:

[The explosion] rocked the entire block and could be heard throughout the center of Rome. . . . Two dozen men were blown apart. They fell in puddles of blood. The rubbish cart and the steel case inside it disappeared. Shrapnel whistled through the street. It pinged on German helmets and sliced and chopped through human flesh. Dying and wounded men fell to the ground. They lay groaning among parts of arms and legs, in many cases their own. . . . Hunks of concrete were chopped from as high as thirty feet out of the facades of the buildings across the street from Palazzo Tittoni. . . . A hole of about thirty cubic feet was blown out of a stone wall.

Down at the corner of via Boccaccio, three partisans tossed mortar shells and escaped through the tunnel leading to via Nazionale. Another group fired on the German police with pistols. Twenty-six died instantly, another sixteen—eventually—of their wounds. In a scene that would prove prophetic, one of the first German officials to arrive at via Rasella could think of nothing but revenge; his first thought was to blow up every house on the street. Notified of the attack, Hitler called for a reprisal that would "make the world tremble." It did.

Via Rasella, where a partisan bomb killed forty-two Germans.

Years ago there was a plaque here, and you could see the bullet holes. Now virtually every trace of this event has been erased, save for one vague sentence well buried in the placards on Palazzo Barberini.

CHURCH DETOUR

Before going on to part 2: Via Tasso, of this itinerary, head farther up via Quattro Fontane, to the four fountains for which it is named, and stop inside Francesco Borromini's gem of a church on the south corner (across the street and on the right), San Carlo alle Quattro Fontane, sometimes called San Carlino ("little" San Carlo), because it's small and sweetly designed (see the map for Itinerary 5 above). It was considered revolutionary when built in the mid-1600s. It's open from 9 a.m. to 1 p.m. Monday–Saturday and from 4 p.m. to 6 p.m. Monday–Friday. If you've seen Santa Maria della Vittoria and the Bernini statue in the prior itinerary, you can compare the two great seventeenth-century rivals, Bernini and Borromini.

PART 2: VIA TASSO

TORTURE AND REPRISAL

In reprisal for the partisan attack in via Rasella, the Germans rounded up or emptied out of prisons 335 Italian men and killed them in caves outside of town, the *Fosse Ardeatine* (the Ardeatine Caves). We'll see the German SS prison, where they tortured men and which they cleaned out to help make up the 335 men to be killed, and then the caves themselves, making this one of the saddest and most emotionally compelling tours you can take in Rome.

GETTING THERE

Take Metro A to the stop at San Giovanni in Laterano. Once you emerge from the San Giovanni Metro stop, you will see the immense Lateran church of San Giovanni, the administrative church for the Vatican for most of its centuries and home of the popes prior to the 1309 move to Avignon. Unless you want to go in the church (not one of our favorites), keep walking to your right without crossing the piazza, past the *Scala Santa* (Holy Stairs; the tradition is for pilgrims to crawl up these stairs on their hands and knees), then jog right and turn left onto via Tasso. Note: You also can take the prior Metro A stop, Manzoni, which lists the museum as a sight; we prefer the route starting at San Giovanni.

BACKGROUND

This street and its buildings couldn't look more normal. But here, at via Tasso, 145, was the Nazis' political torture prison. The rooms the Nazis occupied and in which they confined their prisoners have been kept as the Historical Museum of the Liberation (*Museo Storico della Liberazione*); open Tuesday–Sunday 9 a.m.–12:30 p.m. and Tuesday–Friday 3:30–7:30 p.m., closed Mondays, major holidays, and in August; however, these times can vary, and you are more likely to find it open in the morning.

Begin at the reception area on the ground floor, where you can pick up a flyer available in English that briefly describes the museum and the contents of each room. Admission is free, but we suggest a donation of €5 per adult.

THE CELLS AS THEY WERE IN 1944

The prisoners were kept in the jail cells you begin to see on the first floor (Italian usage; in U.S. usage, it's the second floor—and so listed in the English-translation flyer), just as the Germans left this prison on June 4, 1944—the wallpaper, the walled-up windows (*finestra murata dalle S.S.*). In all these rooms, even without a knowledge of Italian, you can feel and see the lives and deaths of Italians who were former war heroes and ended up fighting and dying as partisans, of Italians who volunteered to carry out fatal missions behind the lines, of Italians who fought to prevent the Germans even from entering the city at a location we've already seen—Porta San Paolo.

Cell 1 held the greatest number of prisoners, and many here ended their lives at the Fosse Ardeatine, as the Germans rounded up Italians and prisoners to kill in retaliation for the attack on via Rasella. Hence this room is a monument to them and has a picture of the Fosse, which you will see later. In a glass case in the middle are the last letters of men about to die. Several patriots are honored here, with a focus on those who were war heroes in World War I and those who were tortured and kept silent. A bulletin on Paolo Petruccio explains that he made contact with an advancing Allied army and asked to return behind the lines. He parachuted into Rome, made contact with partisans, organized student demonstrations against "the Nazi-Fascists," was arrested, and ultimately was killed in the Fosse Ardeatine. Items recovered from his body there are displayed. Maurizio Giglio (information displayed to your right) was associated with the U.S. Fifth Army. He went behind the lines

Once a bricked-up prison cell in the SS Headquarters on via Tasso, this room in the museum now documents the horrific German retaliation at the Fosse Ardeatine.

with a radio transmitter and was assimilated into the "pseudo" Italian Republic. He collected information until he was arrested, tortured, and died in the Fosse Ardeatine. Romualdo Chiesa (information on the wall opposite the door, in the left middle section) fought at Porta San Paolo, where he instructed workers and students in obstructing German troops marching into the city.

Cell 2, the isolation room, keeps in place the engravings the prisoners made with nails, leaving prayers and notes. One says, "I leave all to Claudio." Another says, "Ultimo Canto" (last verse): "Forward Italy, that the sacrifice of so many children already has saved you; leave mother, fiancée, these aren't important, because you [Italy] live."

On the second floor (third, U.S. style), Cell 11 contains posters urging Italians to collaborate. On the far wall, several posters show offers of *lire* (Italian currency) to anyone who would provide information to the German command in Rome. On the left wall, a four-part poster begins: "Rebels: This Is Your End."

In Cell 13, just to the left of the door, in a small glass case are the four-pronged nails partisans used with great success against German convoys. Blacksmith Enrico Ferola made them by the thousands in his Trastevere shop until he was caught, tortured, and killed at the Ardeatine Caves. This cell also has a photo of partisans on Monte Soratte (about twenty-five miles north of Rome) with English and American former prisoners.

JEWS IN ROME

On the opposite side of this floor, down the hall is a room (Room 1) on the deportation of the Jews from Rome in mid-October 1943, about a month after the Germans occupied the city. The Jews in Rome's ghetto had understood immediately that the German occupation spelled disaster for them, and some had taken guns and headed for Porta San Paolo in a desperate attempt to keep the Germans out (see "Jews in Rome: A Brief History," p. 91.)

On the board at the left, below the picture, the caption states, "The Biondi family with three of their six children. The entire family was

THE JEWS IN ROME: A BRIEF HISTORY

What is known of the Jewish experience in Rome suggests how unlikely it is that the horrific scene played out at the Tiburtina train station (see p. 109) would have happened if the Germans had not occupied Italy. The Jewish community in Rome was the oldest in the Western world, dating to the second century BC. For fifteen hundred years the city's Jews prospered. Although most had ordinary jobs in the skilled and unskilled trades, some rose to prominence as physicians, merchants, and bankers. The Rome ghetto—the forced concentration of Jews in the Portico d'Ottavia area, where Jews were systematically deprived of their property and their access to trades, and forced to listen to sermons designed to convert them to Christianity—was created in 1555 by Pope Paul IV.

With the defeat of the Vatican army in 1870, the ghetto walls were torn down. Nonetheless, a majority of Rome's twelve thousand Jews—after centuries of discrimination an impoverished, mostly illiterate, devout community—continued to live in the old ghetto area or just across the river in Trastevere, even as the Fascists took power. Some Jews joined the Fascist Party and/or embraced Italian nationalism, and many others felt comfortable and secure with Fascism, under which they continued to enjoy the freedom to worship and work. As a result, the devastating racial laws of 1938 and 1940, which severely restricted Jewish access to most trades and professions, came as a shock to Rome's Jews. These laws seemed to be more a product of Italy's expanding military relationship with Nazi Germany than any deeply embedded Italian anti-Semitism.

When Mussolini was dismissed in July 1943, the city's Jews rejoiced, convinced that the worst was over and that Rome would soon be liberated. Even the German occupation, although hardly welcomed, was not at first understood as a desperate situation; the Germans seemed to care less about Jews than about rounding up Italian soldiers; the Allies would be there any day; and there seemed to be no awareness of the systematic extermination of the Jews in Germany and Eastern Europe.

This uneasy calm was shattered on September 27, 1943, less than three weeks into the German occupation, when the head of the SS in Rome, Maj. Herbert Kappler, demanded 50 kilos (110 pounds) of gold from the Jewish community in Rome. Failure, it was learned, would result in the deportation of 200 Jews to Germany or the Russian front. The Jews complied. Still, a curious optimism reigned. "Everybody talked about the pope," remembered a Jewish woman who survived, "about how in Rome the Germans would never do anything." On the morning of October 16, the Germans raided the ghetto and other Jewish areas, arresting more than 1,250 Jews, including almost 900 women and children. From that moment, no Roman Jew was safe.

Based on Alexander Stille, *Benevolence and Betrayal: Five Italian Jewish Families Under Fascism* (New York: Penguin Books, 1991).

Italians celebrate as the Allies finally take Rome in June 1944.

deported to Auschwitz and never returned." At the right, in the upper photo is "the flag of the Hebrew Brigade Flies in Via del Tritone, June 1944." A newspaper recently reported that the Hebrew Partisan Brigade flag flew on Liberation Day (April 25) 2007 for the first time since the war. In the hallway leading to this room on the right are the "secret German orders" relating to the deportation, the prison records of Jews killed in the Fosse Ardeatine, and a chart explaining the colored symbols that various categories of "undesirables" were required to display (see p. 67).

PART 3: THE FOSSE ARDEATINE

Emerging into Rome's usual bright sun from these rooms, it is hard to imagine what the neighbors to this plain yellow building must have heard and ignored. Head back up via Tasso to its end and turn to your right to the piazza tucked behind the church of San Giovanni. Bus 218, heading right, on the corner of Piazza Porta San Giovanni and the wide via Amba Aradam that opens right, will take you to the Fosse Ardeatine. You also can reach this site using the Archeobus. Using Bus 218, the stop you want should be the tenth and is called Fosse Ardeatine. It drops you right at the site.

We can't do more than lead you to this site. It is an on-site memorial to be felt, not read.

CATACOMBS

You may wish to coordinate this trip with a visit to a burial site more than fifteen hundred years older: the catacombs of San Callisto. They are just

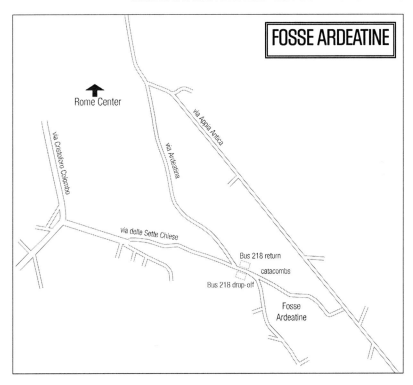

across the road from the Fosse Ardeatine, even though the address is on via Appia Antica. Open 9 a.m.–noon and 2–5 p.m., closed Wednesdays and in February, €6 admission.

GETTING BACK
You can take a bus back on either via Ardeatina or via Appia Antica.

3

BEYOND THE WALL

Life and Community in a Twentieth-Century Suburb

For most tourists, Piazza Bologna (pronounced Bo-lone-ya) is off the beaten track, and rightly so: it houses no great monuments of the "must see" variety to which first-time visitors understandably gravitate. The area has its good restaurants, although not many, and hotels close to the piazza are few. Even so, the *zona* (district) offers a variety of attractions. Chief among them, perhaps, is a clean, prosperous, bustling neighborhood populated mostly by Italians and uncluttered by tourists, where English is seldom spoken, even if it sometimes appears on restaurant menus. Shopping is good here. The area also offers an attractive and complex municipal plan, built around two very large fine piazzas—Piazza Bologna to the north and Piazzale delle Provincie to the south—and marked, especially on the east side, by streets that curve around Piazza Bologna and intersect the diagonals coming from it, providing the kind of mysterious, spatial complexity that one expects from Rome but which is often thought to exist only in the Centro.

Because it was constructed, mostly from scratch, in the 1920s and 1930s, visitors to Piazza Bologna can expect to experience, in addition, something of a time warp, as building after building reflects the values and sensibilities of that fascinating era, among them community, modernism, and, as we shall see, a good dose of Fascism. Mussolini lived close by, and his home is on one of the walks; so is the writer and playwright Luigi Pirandello's; and the place where more than a thousand of Rome's Jews were herded onto a train headed for German concentration camps.

Moreover, the area's reputation for right-wing politics extends beyond the Fascist era and into the 1970s, when right-wing groups carried out attacks on the Left and on elements of the establishment. Writer Fulvio Abbate recently described Piazza Bologna as the "neo-fascist epicenter" of Rome in the 1970s, a claim based on murders carried out by the leader of the Armed Revolutionary Nuclei (NAR), Francesca Mambro (b. 1959), who lived in the pleasant apartment complex you'll visit on the first tour (p. 110) and who, with other members of the NAR, frequented Penny Bar, just down the street on via Pavia from the area's main market. In one of the many contradictions that characterize Rome, the area is also home to a large Jewish community.

GETTING THERE AND WHEN TO GO

Very easy. Take Metro B from Termini. Follow the signs for Rebibbia. Get off at the third stop: Piazza Bologna. After going through the gates at the top of the escalator, turn right, then take the left fork and follow the sign "via Lorenzo il Magnifico." You'll emerge on the south side of the piazza. Like most Italian neighborhoods, this one is a lot more interesting when the stores are open, and most are closed from 1 p.m. to 4:30 p.m. and on Sundays. If you're planning a morning walk, we suggest you arrive and begin your walk before 11 a.m. For an afternoon experience, time your arrival before 5 p.m.

ITINERARY 7: PIAZZA BOLOGNA: THE ARCHITECTURE OF MODERNISM AND FASCISM—AND SHOPPING

FIRST THINGS FIRST

If you haven't had your morning coffee, or you want a second cup, we suggest you begin at Bar Meeting Place (that's what the sign says outside). It's just ahead of you, on Piazza Bologna, going counterclockwise at the intersection of via Michele di Lando. Like most Italian businesses (and unlike

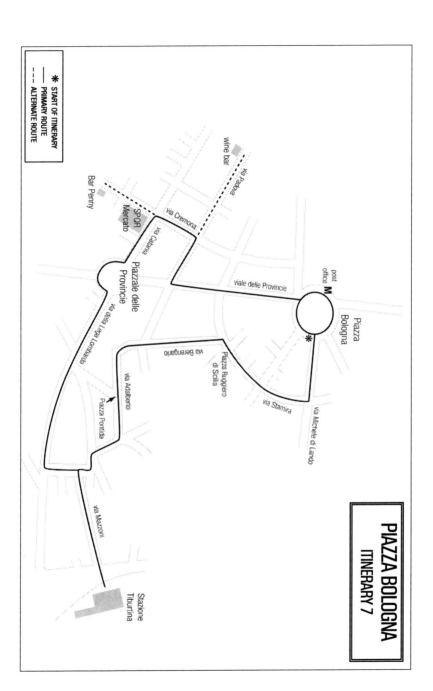

PIAZZA BOLOGNA
ITINERARY 7

START OF ITINERARY
PRIMARY ROUTE
ALTERNATE ROUTE

wine bar
via Padova
via Cremona
Bar Penny
SPQR
Mercato
via Catania
Piazzale delle
Provincie
viale delle Provincie
post
office M
Piazza
Bologna
via della Lega Lombarda
via Berengario
Piazza Ruggiero
di Sicilia
via Stamira
via Michele di Lando
via Adalberto
Piazza Porlida
via Mazzoni
Stazione
Tiburtina

Bar Meeting Place, Piazza Bologna.

American ones) the bar is on the ground floor of an apartment building, in this case a lovely modernist one with curving balconies (an apartment on the fifth floor of this building, overlooking the piazza, would cost well over a million euros). Bar Meeting Place is at once shiny and superficially new and also quite old and a bit austere. You'll be served briskly, efficiently, and often entirely by men (all very Italian) (see "How to Order Coffee," p. 99).

A FASCIST POST OFFICE

When you've finished your coffee, continue around the piazza counterclockwise to the big white building on its northeast side: the post office. With its curving convex and concave surfaces and a top that reflects the Fascist (and worldwide) fascination with flight, the structure has an organic quality associated with one strand of modernist architecture and quite different from the monumentalist modernism of Piazza Augusto Imperatore in the Centro, for example. The Piazza Bologna post office was one of four built by the Ministry of Transportation and Communication, an agency of Mussolini's Fascist government, in the early and mid-1930s (the others are on via Marmorata [see p. 70], via Taranto, and viale Mazzini). This building was designed by Mario Ridolfi and Mario Fagiolo, who won a design competition for the building, which opened in 1935. Today, the partially covered steps serve as an evening gathering place for the area's young people.

You'll get a better sense of what this building meant to the regime that built it—and to contemporary Italians—when you step inside. But first a warning: don't try to take any pictures. In fact, put your camera away before you go near the entrance. In 1993, Bill made the mistake of taking pictures inside the via Taranto post office, the one mentioned above. He was immediately ushered into an upstairs office and questioned about his intent, perhaps with the thought that the photographs were a first step in the planning of a criminal act, and threatened with confiscation of his camera. Not fun.

The interior of the building was modified in 1976, a time of deep concern about possible terrorist attacks. During that renovation, the curving glass ceiling was hidden by panels and the clerks were enclosed in the glass cages you see now. Still, the interior remains suggestive of Fascism's ideals and values. Inside, you'll find a yellow box, at which customers press one of four buttons to get a letter and number for the type of service they require. The chairs are for the long waits that are expected and perhaps for summoning the fortitude to deal with the (usually) hostile or indifferent clerks—all of them with good state jobs and substantial pensions (a status

HOW TO ORDER COFFEE

Ordering coffee (or anything else) in an Italian bar can be intimidating. In most Italian coffee bars, the first step is to approach the *cassa* (cashier), tell the man or woman behind it what you want and pay for it. You'll get a paper receipt, or *scontrino,* that you take to the bar. Put a ten- (euro) cents piece on top of it (that's your tip) and place it on the bar. When you catch the barista's eye, tell him or her what you paid for: for example, "due caffè Americani" (two American coffees, made from espresso, in a big cup, with added water) and "due cornetti" (the truest translation of *cornetti* is croissants, but *cornetto* covers the general Italian morning sweet roll or pastry). While you're waiting for your coffee, move a few steps to your right and tell whoever is there which *cornetto* you want, pointing if necessary.

Most Italians eat their morning meal in a hurry, standing at the bar. The joy to this is watching the *baristi* (or, as English-speakers would say, baristas)—whose call, response, work of making coffee, loading the dishwasher, and preparing food is a kind of performance art. But in some places, like Bar Meeting Place in Itinerary 7, if you like, you can pick up your cup and *cornetto* and sit down at one of the tables in the back. Because you haven't paid for table service, you also should take your cups and saucers back to the bar when you leave.

SHOPPING FOR REAL ESTATE, JUST FOR FUN

Even if you're not interested in buying or renting an apartment, it can be entertaining to see what's on the market. Every neighborhood has its real estate offices, which post signs describing the properties, often giving the rental cost or sales price. A rental is an *affitto*; an apartment for sale is *in vendita* or *vendesi* or *vendite*. You'll need some help figuring out just what is being offered; see the list of the most common terms in the next column.

Advertisements often include a measure of the apartment's size in square meters (mq). Fifty mq (about five hundred square feet) is a small apartment; seventy-five mq is medium size; one hundred mq is large. Because Italians generally don't like being on the ground floor, apartments on that level are usually a bit less expensive (the higher the better, and more expensive if there's an elevator). Recall first floor (*primo piano*) is the second floor in American terms. *Terra* is the ground floor. *Nudo* in an ad refers to "bare ownership," in which the buyer will not have immediate access to the property. Instead, the purchaser must wait for the current occupant to die. To give the potential buyer some idea of when that might happen, ads for *nudo* apartments also include the age (in years) of the current occupant. Apartments offered *nudo* are, of course, discounted. You may recall the story of the Frenchman who bought a *nudo* from a 90-year-old French woman. She lived to be the oldest person recorded in history, dying at 122 and outliving the man.

COMMON REAL ESTATE TERMS

ingresso	entrance, entering hallway
doppio ingresso	two entrances
salone	living room
soggiorno	living room
camera	room, usually a bedroom
camera da letto	bedroom
cameretta	small bedroom
camera di servizio	bathroom
servizio	bathroom
cucina	kitchen
cucinotto	kitchenette
cucina abitabile	eat-in kitchen
ripostiglio	interior storage room
terrazzo	terrace
balcone	balcony
giardino	garden (meaning it's on the ground level)
cantina	small storage room in the basement
box, box auto	enclosed parking place
posto auto	parking space for a car
ascensore	elevator
portiere	the building has a doorman or "super"
ampio	large, ample, as in *ampio salone*
ristrutturato	restructured, redone inside (that's good)
da ristrutturare	not redone inside (needs work, "to restore")
luminoso	lots of exterior light
condominio	condominium
signorile	classy, elegant
terra	ground floor (not as desirable, cheaper)
semi-interrato	partly below ground (undesirable and cheaper yet)

described by the word *statale*)—whose main goal seems to be to explain to customers why they're in the wrong line, have the wrong paperwork, or the window is closing in front of them. Still, the basic message of this room is that, for the Fascists, post offices were major community institutions with a variety of public functions, including the payment of bills and taxes.

INTO THE NEIGHBORHOOD (AND SHOPPING)

After you leave the post office, continue around the piazza counterclockwise, turning at the Bar Bologna sign, and go down the right side of the treed boulevard viale delle Provincie. If the weather is good (and the police haven't been scaring them off recently) the street will be lined with *vu cumprà* (an Italian version of the sound of the non-native-speaking vendors asking if you want to buy their wares—*vuoi comprare?*)—immigrant vendors selling sunglasses (a good deal), purses (knockoffs of whatever the year's current high fashion is and also quite reasonably priced), and caps (the latest fashion is a pre-frayed green "Fidel" look, signaling the rise of Latin American leftist movements and, arguably, some empathy for them among Italians).

After two short blocks, just past the corner with via Reggio Calabria, you'll see shops a few steps below street level. At No. 52 is Il Giardino Fiorito (the flowering garden), a small but well-stocked *bomboniere* store. Here is a mesmerizing array of *bomboniere*—small and sometimes intricate items (a silver charm, a small toy) enclosed in a specially designed bag or box and given to guests at significant events, such as weddings, birthdays, anniversaries, graduations, or first communions. The wedding bomboniere always include a few pieces of confetti—that is, Jordan almonds (they appear twice in *Lo Sceicco Bianco* [*The White Sheik*, 1952], Federico Fellini's directorial debut, featuring newlyweds on their honeymoon in Rome). Don't hesitate to step into this store. It advertises on wedding sites as "a breath of Soho in Rome." Bomboniere stores are also good places, we've found, to buy gifts for the folks back home. The objects often have a Roman theme, the almonds are tasty, and the bomboniere (in the little bags or boxes) can be made to order—customers select the type of lace, ribbons, decorations, size, and quality of almonds. Likely someone will be making them up in front of you.

After another regular block, you'll come to the cross street, via Padova. Turn right and a few doors down—in appropriate weather—you'll see the tables for Snack Bar, also known as Caffè Yang, owned and operated by a young Chinese man named Yang. Across the street from Caffè Yang you'll notice a police car astride the entrance to a building, often with two persons inside. It's part of a police presence, particularly on via Padova, designed to protect the Jewish institutions that are prominent in the area—in this case, a school. A Jewish food shop on this block is another lingering sign of what must have been a substantial Jewish community. (If you continue up via Padova three short blocks, you will find *uve e forme,* the wine bar described in chapter 7, "Wine Bars," p. 225.)

THE IMPORTANCE OF NEW SIDEWALKS

Turn left at the corner onto via Cremona, where in the morning you're likely to find a well-regarded Sicilian selling vegetables from a small white truck and announcing his presence in a voice that we, when we were living five floors up, once used as our alarm clock. Take a moment to examine the sidewalks at this intersection, which are new (2006) and typical of the *municipio* in which Piazza Bologna is situated. With their high curbs and, at the corners, metal posts, the new sidewalks are designed to give added protection to pedestrians and, perhaps most important, to keep cars and trucks from driving onto the sidewalks, especially at the intersections, a custom that, prior to the new construction, sometimes cut off pedestrian access to the street. The new paving stones, and the obvious effort made in this area to keep the sidewalks and streets neat and clean (by Roman standards), reflect the middle-class character and aspirations of the area's residents. They have made this choice, and it is important to appreciate that it is just that—a choice. Rome's twenty decentralized *municipi* (municipalities, but in an American city they would be called wards or council districts) have control over where and how their allocations are spent. One might decide to repave the streets; another to open a social center for older residents, improve garbage collection, or hold a series of concerts for young people. The two hundred thousand people who make up the area around Piazza Bologna have decided, at considerable expense and in lieu of some other projects, to upgrade the public walkways.

Via Cremona has a couple of businesses of more than ordinary interest. On the right, at No. 52A, is another bomboniere store. This is a one-woman operation, and often she's making the bomboniere in the middle of the store. A blizzard of objects fill the store's windows. Across the street at Nos. 55/57 stands Enoteca Romana, a superb wine store (*enoteca*, derived from "wine" and "box," is a term for a store, usually a wine store) run by an engaging and knowledgeable couple, the Salises, who will help you find just the right bottle for any occasion. Around the next corner and to the left, a few stores down on via Catania, Giampiero not only sells excellent hand-made fresh pasta but (if you speak Italian) will tell you that the pasta you've just purchased should be kept refrigerated in a plastic bag (or not), that it should be served with a plain sauce, and how many pieces will be eaten by a Roman.

SPQR MERCATO

Across the street, occupying all of a block, is a huge indoor public market. The lettering above the great glass doors states *SPQR MERCATO*. *SPQR* is the acronym for *Senatus Populusque Romanus* ("the Senate and the people of Rome"), and *mercato* is the word for "market." *SPQR* was used on the shields of the Roman legions and now is on the coat of arms of Rome and therefore on everything from manhole covers to buildings. The Fascists, in their omnipresent effort to tie Fascism to the first Roman Empire, marked almost all their public buildings with *SPQR*. Like many other institutions in this neighborhood, this market building was constructed to facilitate food buying for the

Inside a Fascist-era market.
Don't touch the fruit!

concentration of people moving into what was then a new neighborhood. This type of market substitutes for the smaller outdoor markets more common in the older sections of Rome—and some in the newer ones as well. The building is institutional Fascist, using the ubiquitous Roman brick and reinforced concrete. More striking to the eye is the cavernous interior, colored by food, objects, and people. By now, in addition to fresh fruits and vegetables that are all sold in more or less permanent stands, there are permanent stands of all types around the inside walls of the market, selling everything from meats to housewares, from flowers to packaged foods.

WOMAN WITH A GUN: LUNCH WITH FRANCESCA MAMBRO AT PENNY BAR

You can't really have lunch with Francesca Mambro. She's been in prison since 1982, when she was tried, convicted, and given a life term for her role in a series of politically motivated murders carried out with other members of the extreme right wing. Mambro has been allowed since 1998 to spend some time beyond the walls of the Rebibbia prison (the Metro has a Rebibbia stop). But she would probably not return to Penny Bar, still standing at the corner of via Pavia (which runs next to the SPQR market on this itinerary) and via Sisco, two blocks south of Via Catania, where you enter the market. There, in the late 1970s, she and her right-wing friends spent long afternoons talking, eating, drinking, and perhaps planning to kill. The outdoor tables remain as inviting today as they were then. Order a coffee or panino and read on.

Francesca Mambro was born in Rome on April 25, 1959. She lived with her mother (a housewife), her father (a public security officer who died in 1979), and three younger siblings in an idyllic, villagelike, "gated" public housing project off via Adalberto (see p. 110). At age fourteen, she joined the *Fronte della Gioventù* (Youth Front), a youth organization associated with the right wing, and at eighteen she was standing beside Stefano Recchioni when he was shot and killed by Carabinieri (the Italian elite police corps). "From that day on," she recalled, "I swore I would never be unarmed."

Beginning in 1979, Mambro became a significant player in the violence-ridden years of the late 1970s and early 1980s—the *anni di piombo* (years of lead, referring not just to bullets but to the impact on Italian society). She joined Valerio Fioravanti and other right-wing radicals in a series of violent and often deadly political actions, usually with other

SHOPPING ETIQUETTE

As is the case with many other small businesses in Italy, one is expected to be a faithful customer, to buy produce, for example, at only one or two stands. (Similarly, once you've done some business at Enoteca Romana, it would be untoward to be observed carrying wine from another vendor.) In the market, customer loyalty is rewarded with better service and better produce. The variety of foods is large, with green beans, for example, being sold straight from the farm or cleaned and clipped by women sitting in front of you at the market. Artichokes, in season (roughly mid-April through late May), are available in many varieties of sizes and readiness,

members of NAR (*Nuclei Armati Rivoluzionari*/Armed Revolutionary Nuclei) or the Rome section of FUAN (*Fronte Universitario d'Azione Nazionale*/National University Action Front). In March 1979 she placed a rudimentary bomb outside the windows of the *Circolo Culturale Femminista*/Cultural Feminist Center in the exclusive Prati section of Rome. In May 1980 she participated in the killing of policeman Franco Evangelista and magistrate Mario Amato. In September 1980, with others, she assassinated the head of an extreme right-wing group, apparently for betraying the movement. In March 1982, Mambro was wounded and arrested during an assault on a bank in Rome. In 1985, while in prison, she married fellow radical prisoner Fioravanti; they had a child in 2001. Mambro and Fioravanti were also charged and convicted with participating in the August 2, 1980, bombing of the Bologna train station, which killed eighty-five people—although they have consistently denied involvement in that particular crime, and today most commentators believe in their innocence related to that tragedy.

Penny Bar, whose ambience you may be enjoying at this moment, occupies a strategic location, between the middle-class Piazza Bologna neighborhood and the University of Rome, in the 1970s a spawning ground for extremist views of every political persuasion. Across the street, in via Siena (an extension of via Sisco) was the local seat of FUAN. The organization's library was housed in an apartment on via Poggioli, a few blocks to the southeast, closer to the university. The Rome group was organized informally, its members united by a desire to carry out military actions against the Left—and, one might add, by their fondness for the tables at Penny Bar.

from large untrimmed ones in the open air to very small, trimmed ones in water. Outside the market are stands selling clothes, CDs, and whatever is the current fashion.

Let yourself go in trying to buy some things that look appealing or good; you may have to push a little to keep from being pushed out of the way to get to the vendor. Whether at markets or for the opening of renovated public buildings, Italians don't take the concept of queuing up. They just crowd in. It's not considered obnoxious and, sometimes—if you're looking for a seat at a soccer game and the row appears full—the Italian willingness to press against one another can be very welcome. In the fruit and vegetable wars, you may have to join them, or you will be frustrated and ultimately defeated. A word of advice: don't touch any food, or at least without asking a simple *posso?* (which means "may I"). Know that, as a general rule, vendors do not want buyers touching the food; it's just not done.

Take a few moments on the steps of the market to absorb the ten-story, block-long bank of apartment buildings across the street. It's this kind of density that creates the area's vibrant street life. And the building's curved iron railings are of a type common to the 1930s. For a look at a bar frequented by political radicals in the 1970s, turn left and go around the corner and up via Cremona (see "Woman with a Gun," p. 104). Or turn to the right from the market steps and continue downhill toward the piazza just a block away.

PUBLIC ART AND MODERNIST ARCHITECTURE

In the center of the piazza, practically inaccessible because of the heavy traffic, is an awkward concrete sculpture/waterless fountain in the modernistic style, with curving walls of concrete and brown tiles. It was constructed in the late 1990s as part of then Mayor Francesco Rutelli's *Progetto Cento Piazze del Comune di Roma* (One Hundred Piazzas Project), that is, to renovate one hundred piazzas in the city. If you can reach the sculpture (we don't necessarily recommend you do so), you would find that each of the surrounding posts represents an Italian city, and that the posts are grouped by province, signifying *Piazzale delle Provincie*.

The Jolly Theater: Fascism meets Hollywood.

Continue around the piazza counterclockwise, past Bar Stendhal (a community institution that keeps late hours), and follow the street just to its left, via della Lega Lombarda. In two short blocks you'll arrive at via Giano della Bella and one of the area's most interesting intersections. Have a seat on a bench and take in the *multi-sala* (multi-screen) Jolly Theater. With its corner angle pieces and porthole windows (echoing the heyday of ocean liners and referencing the first-century tomb of Roman baker Marco Virgilio Eurisace Fornai in Piazza di Porta Maggiore) and concave front and convex "awning," it's a treasure of Hollywood-style high modernism. Our friends Massimo and Chiara live just five minutes away (you'll see their building in just a few minutes) from the Jolly but refuse to attend, because the theater is owned by the one of the wealthiest men in Italy, right-wing media mogul and many times prime minister Silvio Berlusconi.

Looking across via della Lega Lombarda, note the steplike building on the left (1929–30) and the rounded one to its right (1926–28). Both were designed by Innocenzo Sabbatini (the rounded building with Giorgio Guidi), and despite their impressive appearances, both were designed as *case popolari*—that is, as public housing for working-class people. The stepped building was developed by the *Istituto Case Popolari* (ICP), a long-standing government agency taken over by the Fascists in the 1920s. This building houses eighty-nine apartments of two and three rooms and features a triangular central courtyard with six stairways. The stepped design is common today in sunny climates and in some big cities, like New York, where stepping is actually required by law to bring light to city streets. The building is well known among architectural historians and critics for what

107

Tram barn as work of art.

some describe as a futuristic design.

The other, rounded building is significant both for what it shows and what it hides. Its facade on via della Lega Lombarda, with its neoclassical uniformities and complexities and its circular balcony, suggests a villa for the wealthy rather than housing for workers. The back reveals the apartments, in this case accessible along long, shared galleries of a sort that one identifies with New Orleans but seldom sees in Rome, whose residents prefer more private spaces.

The red building on the corner to the right is at once an ATAC tram barn (1937) and a work of art. Its exuberant, futuristic overhang brings to mind Eero Saarinen's Dulles Airport terminal outside Washington, D.C., and Rome's Termini Station, whose cantilevered entrance, the work of a group of architects, was completed in 1951. An incipient preservationist movement is beginning to make small noises because there's a possibility distinctive architecture like the ATAC tram barn will be demolished; the area currently is slated for big development.

ENGLISH-STYLE PUB, SOCCER ON THE BIG SCREEN

Continue on via della Lega Lombarda, now on the tram barn side. Follow the decaying wall on your left to the shopping center down the road. Despite the available parking, we can be grateful that brutal concrete structures of this sort have not had much appeal to Romans. But we're not here to critique the architecture. The attraction is up the stairway on the second floor: *Vecchio Franklin* (Old Franklin), an English-style pub. Here, on a Sunday afternoon at 3 p.m., or on a weekday evening if the team is playing in the European cup, you can have a pint of beer, and lunch if you like, while watching the Rome soccer club on a huge pull-down projection screen or on one of several smaller sets. You can just show up, or you can make a reservation (a *prenotazione*) a few hours in advance in person or by phone. If you have a reservation, you'll arrive to find your name on a piece of paper on the table chosen for you. Consult any newspaper for the team's schedule and game times.

STAZIONE TIBURTINA: SCENE OF THE CRIME

Exit the shopping center at the opposite end and turn left. Follow that street for a short block, then curve right and work your way through Largo Mazzoni and onto via Mazzoni, with the hotels on your left and the bus depot on your right. Make a right turn and cross the street under the elevated highway, entering *Stazione Tiburtina* (the Tiburtina train station) under the clock (to the right of a McDonald's). When inside, keep straight (a slight jog right is required) to "Binario/Platform 1." Once on the platform, turn left and look at the plaques on the station wall. One says:

> Think . . . that here this happened . . . Primo Levi . . . the 16th of October 1943, more than 1,000 Roman Jews, entire families, men, women and babies, were taken from their homes, guilty only of existing, from this station, held in sealed train cars. The 18th of October they were deported by the Nazis to extermination camps. Sixteen men and only 1 woman returned. Their memory is that of all the deported Romans—Jews, politicians, military men, workers—an eternal warning, everywhere, that similar tragedies need not ever be revisited. The City of Rome and the Jewish Community of Rome, 16 October 2000.

To the left of this marker is a second one to Michele Bolgia, described as an "innocent victim of the ferocious nazi-fascists, glorified as a martyr at the Fosse Ardeatine. His co-workers and friends at the Tiburtina Station want to commemorate his name in this marble. 8 September 1946." (On the martyrs at the Fosse Ardeatine, see p. 92.)

Although the first plaque seems to suggest that Italian writer Levi, a native of Turin, was among those taken at the Tiburtina Station, his own journey to Auschwitz began at a converted prisoner-of-war camp at Fossoli, near Modena, in the province of Emilia-Romagna. Levi lived to describe the scene at nearby Carpi, where he was struck and kicked by SS who were putting Jews on the train. There Levi spoke briefly to an Italian policeman who was standing guard: "Remember this, and remember that you took part." The policeman replied, "But what else can I do?" Levi answered, "Be a thief. It's more honest." Levi's extraordinary account of a year in a Nazi killing center was published in English as *Survival in Auschwitz: The Nazi Assault on Humanity* (1960).

FASCIST PUBLIC HOUSING, 1928

To exit the station, retrace your path under the elevated highway, on via Mazzoni, and farther past a small grassy mound, a park, on the right. Take the first street to the left of the park, as it curves upward (on your right), to via Matilde di Canossa. The first street left is via Adalberto. Go uphill on it to the small piazza, Piazza Pontida, which has a trattoria on the left and a pub on the right, adorned in late spring with a spectacular display of bougainvillea.

Move to the gate on the right, the main entrance to a complex of apartment buildings, apparently designed by Sabbatini (see above) as *case popolari* and completed about 1928. Massimo and Chiara, our friends who refuse to view films at the Jolly, live with their two children in a small apartment in the complex, which has been converted to condominiums. If you walk in, the *portiere* (doorman, or "super"), whose office is the green door on the left, will want to know your business, and he might—or might not—allow tourists to walk around. Nonetheless, there is much to be seen and learned from the gate. The uneven stone walls that line the paths and stairways lend a rustic tone that helps one to shut out the industrial and commercial life just steps away. To the far right, note the communal drying space. It is available to the residents of the only building in the complex that does not have a drying area on the roof. The most important feature is straight ahead: a round, low-walled play area. Here, children kick a soccer ball or run around with squirt guns, supervised by chatting parents sitting on the wall or watched by more distant eyes from the windows above. Fascist ideology emphasized community, family, and children—lots of them—

and nurturing, enclosing constructions like this one reflected those values and made them seem within reach. The romantic feel of these environments is captured in the delightful 1993 feature film by Leone Pompucci, *Mille Bolle Blu* (A Thousand Blue Bubbles—the name of a popular 1960s song), set in the summer of 1961 in a *case popolari* complex.

A FASCIST SCHOOL BUILDING

Step back out of the gate and continue uphill on the street on which you entered the piazza, via Adalberto (not the similarly named via Ariberto to your right); via Adalberto takes a curve to the right and becomes via Berengario as it crosses via S. Ippolito. Keep on this street to the intersection after the one with via S. Ippolito. You now enter Piazza Ruggiero di Sicilia. The building to your left is one of the neighborhood's gems. It consists of two schools: on the right, the *Scuola Elementare Fratelli Bandiera* (Bandiera Brothers Elementary School); on the left, the *Scuola Media Charlie Chaplin* (Charlie Chaplin Middle School). Bandiera Brothers is a reference to brothers Attilio and Emilio Bandiera, sons of a high official in the Austrian navy, who were shot in 1844 for their participation in the nineteenth-century movement for Italian unification known as the *Risorgimento*

The complex surfaces of Fascist modernism.

(resurgence; see p. 36 for some history of this movement). Both schools were renamed after Mussolini fell from power. This is especially obvious with the middle school. Chaplin, the American movie star of the 1930s, made fun of Hitler's fantasies of domination in the film *The Great Dictator* (1940). Taken as a whole, the building might be understood as a combination of horizontal elements characteristic of the Piazza Bologna post office and the more vertical lines (and features) of Berlusconi's movie house. The flagpole stand on the upper right is a dramatic feature. You can date the building if you walk up the steps to the elementary school and look up and to the right and left. There, you'll see the familiar *SPQR* and the *fasci,* symbol of Fascism, and below A XIII, indicating construction was completed in 1935 (see "Fascist Numbering System," p. 85).

TRATTORIA DA ENRICO

Take a right turn from where you entered Piazza Ruggiero di Sicilia (straight ahead, the left fork, as you stand on the steps of the school facing out) and proceed up the slight upward grade on via Stamira. The first full cross street is via Lorenzo il Magnifico; cross it, continuing on via Stamira. At the next full cross street, via Michele di Lando, turn left. Half a block up via Michele di Lando, on the left side, is "una buona trattoria qui vicino" (as in the question perhaps most often asked by tourists, "C'è una buona trattoria qui vicino?"—is there a good inexpensive restaurant near here?). This is, indeed, a good one. It's called da Enrico. It may be the best trattoria in the zona.

When you exit or pass da Enrico, continue along via Michele di Lando; half a block more and you are back at Piazza Bologna. *Ciao a tutti!*

ITINERARY 8: IN THE PARKS, ON THE STREETS, AND IN THE HOMES OF THE FAMOUS, IF NOT RICH

This second itinerary begins with a large loop through the dense upper-middle-class neighborhood buildings behind the Piazza Bologna post office and toward its end offers a refreshing walk through Villa Torlonia, one of Rome's recently spruced-up city parks and the opportunity to tour

Mussolini's home. This itinerary, perhaps a bit long on city blocks, includes stops for children and lovers of the outdoors. It offers a detour to the astonishing complex of church, mausoleum, and catacombs honoring Saints Agnese and Costanza, a wonderful opportunity to see early Christian Rome without the crush of tourists. Both Villa Massimo (on the loop but not always open) and Villa Torlonia illuminate the changes World War II brought to Rome.

WHEN TO GO

For timing, consider that Villa Torlonia basically is open all day (nonstop). The other grounds and buildings you may wish to enter will not be open generally between 1 p.m. and 4 p.m. Avoid Mondays.

HOW TO GET THERE

As with Itinerary 7, take Metro B to the Bologna stop. Start in front of (facing) the post office.

Head to the street along the left side of the post office, via Ravenna. Follow on the right sidewalk of this bustling street through Largo Ravenna and continue as the street curves slightly to the right. (Note: To head straight to Villa Torlonia, keep on this street, which becomes via A. Torlonia, for about five blocks, where it ends at the large cross street, via Nomentana. A left turn here will put you twenty feet from the main entrance to the park, with its gates again on your left. Go to the Villa Torlonia section below.)

ON THE WAY TO VILLA MASSIMO

To follow the loop to Villa Massimo and beyond, instead of proceeding all the way to via Nomentana and Villa Torlonia, take the fourth street to your right after the post office, viale di Villa Massimo. Just before you turn, note the smaller park across the street to your left. This is a lovely park for children and adults alike, and we return here toward the end of this itinerary. You'll also find some nifty wolf-headed street fountains (*nasoni*) in this neighborhood (see "Drinking Fountains: Nasoni," p. 116).

Turn right from via Ravenna onto viale di Villa Massimo and head to Villa Massimo. As you continue on this viale, pause to look across the street at No. 39. Built in 1934/36, it's a fine example of Fascist-period modernism in residential buildings.

WHERE THE MIDDLE CLASS LIVES

Shortly after No. 39, you'll come to a piazza, appropriately titled Largo di Villa Massimo. On your right is the villa itself, the site of the German Academy in Rome. Before you enter the villa grounds, look around the largo, itself a library of styles. To your left, clockwise, is the often-seen Fascist monumentalist building, likely built for the middle class. Next is a more modern-looking building but in a neoclassical, even Italianate design, and finally a classical neo-Renaissance design with modest flavors of beaux arts. Likely all three were built at the same time.

VILLA MASSIMO: A STORY OF THE TWENTIETH CENTURY

As your eyes complete the sweep around the largo, they come back on your right to Villa Massimo, built in 1913 by a German architect (see "What's in a *Villa* or *Via?*" p. 121). It's fifty-fifty that you can get inside the grounds of Villa Massimo. Find the list of buzzers (the *citofono*) on the wall to the right of the great entrance gates and push the top left one, *portineria* (doorkeeper). The office hours are 9 a.m.–1 p.m. and 2–5 p.m. on Sunday–Thursday and 9 a.m.–1 p.m. on Friday. There's often an exhibit, so ask to see it and you'll be in. Once inside, you'll see that the buildings and grounds, like the largo, display a variety of Italian styles and forms: Roman countryside, classical (ancient) Roman design, baroque elements, and sculptures taken from the catacombs around nearby via Nomentana. (An excellent Web site, www.villamassimo.de is available with lots of history, but only in Italian and German.)

Villa Massimo was built on the site of a large vineyard owned by the royal Massimo family, thousands of acres of open agricultural land. To help German artists obtain higher status in world and Italian art circles, a fabulously wealthy German coal baron and art patron, Eduard Arnhold, contributed substantial funds for the classical building inside the villa walls, including ten artists' studios, landscaping, and fellowships for the artists. The institute, which achieved its patron's goals in its early years, today serves the same purpose of promoting German artists (expanded to musicians and architects, for example, and to artists born in other countries working in Germany).

In the years since 1913, the villa tells the tale of twentieth-century Rome. A relative of the patron managed the institute beginning in 1927. During Hitler's 1938 visit to Rome, however, this "Jewish management" was deemed inappropriate, and the man was dismissed. Moreover, Arnhold's name was removed from all plaques and documents around the institute. In 1943, German airmen used the villa as their social club. After the war, Rome rented the studios to its own artists, who had been pushed out of their customary via Margutta studios by Americans willing to pay high rents in the Centro. In 1956 the villa returned to the control of West Germany, and the dismissed Arnhold relative again became director of the academy housed there.

AND MAYBE A PARTY

An ideal way to see the villa is available if you are in Rome when the academy is hosting a big party. There are several each year, including open studios in April, "white nights" in September, and final presentations of the fellows in November. The German Academy throws a great party, complete with wine and food. The au currant term in Rome for these openings with extras is *vernissages* (see p. 185).

HERE'S TO THE TAX MAN (AND LUNCH)

Outside the villa, resume walking in the direction you've been going, on the continuation of viale di Villa Massimo, which is now the northern section of via Giovanni Battista de Rossi. Take this one long block to the next

DRINKING FOUNTAINS (*NASONI*)

Can you drink the water? Our answer, yes! and please do! The ever-present *nasoni* or street fountains of Rome are one of the best ways to beat the heat and act like a real Roman.

The constantly flowing water of Rome is a hallmark of the city. There are some three hundred of these "big nose" fountains in the streets and parks of the old walled center of Rome and some two thousand throughout the entire city. Also called *fontanelle* or little fountains (*nasone* or "big nose" is the affectionate and more commonly used Roman term; *nasone* is singular; *nasoni* plural), the *nasoni* first sprung up in the city after unification in the 1870s. The earliest designs featured a dragon as the spout. Others use the city's trademark she-wolf. There are fancier ones as well, for example those made of travertine marble, put up in the 1920s and 1930s. Some of the travertine fountains remain, mostly in parks and the Olympic Village area. But we like the plain ones best.

If you look closely, in most *nasoni* you'll see a small hole on top of the spout. By placing your finger against the flowing water and cutting it off at the end of the spout, you'll produce a drinking spray from the hole—just step back and keep your clothes out of the spray. Trial, error, and a sense of humor help in perfecting your drinking technique.

We don't recommend drinking out of the larger fountains, where the water often is simply recycled. And once in a great while you will see a sign *non potabile*—that is, NOT drinking water.

We find it fascinating to watch Romans use their *nasoni*—not just for drinking, but also for washing scooters and cars; supplying

large piazza, Largo XXI Aprile, as it intersects the large viale XXI Aprile (the largo and street are named for the date determined to be the birth of Rome, April 21, 753 BC).

You can't miss the monument to the Guardia di Finanza (basically, a statue to the tax man) in the middle of the largo. The statue makes sense here, because in front of it (across viale XXI Aprile) is a large building occupying more than a block and named Caserma Piave. This building originally housed the academy to train the Guardia di Finanza. They have an even larger building in back now, if you want to go back there (along the left side, via F. Nardini) to see more monumentalist Fascist buildings. An interesting sidenote on the Guardia di Finanza is that a special division of this government agency tracks down stolen artworks and attempts to

local vendors with water for plants, vegetables, and cleaning; filling up bottles that may appear on a restaurant table.

The *nasoni* are not without controversy. Some question if the constantly flowing water is a waste in the global effort to conserve resources. Rome's utility authority (ACEA) says no; the water flowing through the *nasoni* clean out the system and keep water from being stagnant and from producing disease.

The *nasoni* have been the subject of papers, designs, blogs, photography, and even local poetry. Pictures and designs of *nasoni* appear on many Web sites. You can even find *nasoni* in the city center through some satellite-based sites, such as www.colosseo.org/nasoni. The sites with something of interest and the poetry are all in Italian. So if you don't read the language, just enjoy the water.

Interlocking rings on this *nasone*, located in the *Foro Italico,* identify it as of 1960 vintage, the year Rome hosted the Olympic Games.

retrieve them (including the Aphrodite statue, for the possession of which the former curator of the Getty Museum in Los Angeles was on trial in 2007 in Rome).

If you want to stop now or later for lunch or dinner, there's a popular and appropriately named local trattoria, al Monumento (da Giulio), on the side of Largo XXI Aprile you entered (Largo XXI Aprile, 6/8, closed Sundays; tel. 06.4424.5328).

SITE OF CINEMA

Head across viale XXI Aprile at the largo and go left one block. Looking up, you realize you are at the corner of one of Rome's enormous apartment building complexes from the Fascist era. At viale XXI Aprile, 1–29, these buildings contain more than four hundred apartments and originally had seventy stores and a cinema on the ground floor, and a dance hall beneath it. The number of stores is much reduced, and a supermarket has replaced the cinema. Magnificent features of the complex's architecture still can be seen, particularly if you go inside one of the courtyard entrances. The ten-story stairways marked by rounded glass illuminate both the inside and outside of the buildings and their courtyards.

This enormous complex was the setting for a 1977 film about Hitler's 1938 visit to Rome.

The complex was the site of the award-winning 1977 Ettore Scola film *Una Giornata Particolare* (*A Special Day*). In the film, the heroine, played by Sophia Loren, stays home and strikes up a friendship with a homosexual neighbor, played by Marcello Mastroianni, while her Fascist-leaning husband goes off to celebrate Hitler's 1938 visit to Rome (see chapter 2, p. 64, for a tour of Hitler's visit to Rome).

By the time you arrive here, the B-1 addition to the Metro B line may be completed (if not, there's a lot of construction here), and you can take the Nomentana stop to quit or start again another day.

To continue on the main itinerary, retrace your steps to Largo di Villa Massimo outside Villa Massimo and go to "Architecture (More) and Literature" just below the next short section describing the detour.

A DETOUR TO EARLY CHRISTIANITY

For those with the stamina to add several blocks to this itinerary (now about half completed), Dianne recommends continuing on viale XXI Aprile along the apartment complex two blocks to the wide via Nomentana. Cross it and turn right. In about 150 feet at No. 349 is a pair of small columns, an unassuming entranceway to the courtyard of the church of Sant'Agnese *fuori le mura* (outside the walls) and the Mausoleum of Santa Costanza. This is a marvelous complex outside Rome's center, including a courtyard bathed in peace, greenery, and light, and catacombs more than three stories below. (Open generally 9 a.m.–noon and 4–6 p.m.; closed mornings on Sundays and religious holidays, and on Monday afternoons; last tours of the catacombs thirty minutes before closing; €5 for the catacombs.) Very helpful here is a standard guidebook that covers this area outside the city's old walls, such as Georgina Masson's *A Companion Guide to Rome*. When it's completed, you can take the Annibaliano Metro stop on the B-1 line behind the church complex to head home or to easily return to Piazza Bologna. To regain the itinerary, retrace your steps back to Villa Massimo.

ARCHITECTURE (MORE) AND LITERATURE

Continue past Villa Massimo, taking the street that angles right at the largo, in fact a continuation of via Giovanni Battista de Rossi, on which you've been walking. There are buildings worth noting at No. 12 by the same two architects who did the modernist residence at viale di Villa Massimo, 39—this one is sixteen years later (1950–51); at No. 20, built in the late 1930s and featuring open loggias on the highest floor, evoking the Roman Empire; and at No. 9 a concrete-inspired building that has echoes

A medical building of the neo-Brutalist school of architecture (1970).

of the neo-Brutalism school of modern architecture. This last structure, a medical building, was designed in 1970 by a prominent Rome architectural firm headed by Piero Sartogo (whom we met by chance at a *vernissage*; see p. 186); he told us the building recently has been placed on the historic structures list and should be in line for a facelift.

GLIMPSE INTO THE LIFE OF A NOBEL-WINNING PLAYWRIGHT

Turn right at the corner with the concrete building, onto via Antonio Bosio. The second main entranceway on your right at No. 13/B-15 comes just after

Pirandello slept here.

a plaque to Nobel Prize–winning Italian writer Luigi Pirandello. One of his plays, *Six Characters in Search of an Author* (1921), scandalously received at the time, is now considered a masterpiece. The courtyard has become a carpark, and the rustic fountain nonfunctioning, the entire scene an example of unrestored building and grounds. Pirandello ("I am a fascist because I am an Italian") lived in this house for the last three years of his life and died here in 1936. His apartment, including his studio and other artifacts, has been preserved and feels untouched since the day he died.

WHAT'S IN A *VILLA* OR *VIA* (THE NAME)?
READING THE LANDSCAPE

Villa means a freestanding, reasonably sized house, but it also means a whole landholding. The rich and famous lived in villas, that is, lots of acreage surrounded by high walls and enclosing many structures. Like Villa Massimo, Villa Torlonia began life as rural (outside the city walls) vineyards, in this case owned beginning in the late seventeenth century by the notable Pamphili family. So Villa Torlonia is really the whole park, not just one building. The main building is called a *palazzo*—meaning a large building, not a palace—or a *casino,* which is really a decorative term for a large house. No one building in Villa Torlonia is called a *villa.* In contrast, in Villa Pamphili, the largest city park, several of the buildings inside the *villa* (park) are villas (buildings). Same with Villa Borghese.

Via/viale are words for "street." *Piazza, piazzale* are words for "circle." Most viales are larger than vias, most piazzales larger than piazzas, but not always. Rome's viales (in Italian, *viali*) are a product of the city planning tradition of Turin (deeply influenced by Paris's boulevards), imported to Rome when it became the capital in 1871.

Some of this *viale* and *piazzale* likely is just pretension. And then there's a *largo*—usually smaller than a piazza and more rectangular than round—and a *vicolo*—definitely a small street, even an alley.

This house was on the very edge of Rome when Pirandello lived here, and his view from his bedroom terrace was unimpeded to Villa Torlonia, almost unimaginable now. You can get this glimpse into the life of a reasonably well-off author in the 1930s from 9 a.m. to 1 p.m. Tuesday–Friday. Go to the third floor (second, in European custom) and ring the buzzer at the closed doors where you see "Istituto di Studi Pirandelliani. . . ." (www.studiodiluigipirandello.it has an abstract of the site in English; scroll down to find it.) A bonus is that the first two floors are occupied by the Bureau of Measures, with historic weighing instruments on display.

FINALLY, THE WAY TO VILLA TORLONIA

Villa Torlonia is close by. Go back to via G. B. de Rossi, turn right onto it and take another right where it dead ends on via Torlonia. You're one block from the corner of via Torlonia and via Nomentana, the latter one of ancient Rome's seven great consular roads. Taking a left at via Nomentana, the park entrance gates are immediately on the left.

TURNING A DERELICT SPACE INTO A PUBLIC PARK

Villa Torlonia is an impressive city reclamation project. Until a few years ago, it was at best derelict and used by derelicts. You can still see signs of that in some of the unrestored parts of the park. The villa—consisting of thirty-three acres of land and at least ten structures—is named for a wealthy banking family of French origins that supervised the land's transformation in the early 1800s by the most famous Rome architect of his time, Giuseppe Valadier. The villa is a cacophony of buildings, building types, and landscape.

WHEN TO GO AND HOW TO BUY TICKETS

Three of the main structures are restored as museums, and each requires a ticket for entry. You'll want to go when the museums are open. They're closed Mondays and January 1, May 1, and December 25; generally (and these can change) they open at 9 a.m. and close at 7 p.m. from April through September, at 5:30 p.m. in March and October, at 4:30 p.m. from November through February, and at 2 p.m. on Christmas Eve and New Year's Eve. The ticket office closes forty-five minutes earlier than the closing times. A full-price ticket for entrance to all the museums is €6.5 (www .museovillatorlonia.it; click on Eng at top left for a limited English version).

Pay for your tickets at the ticket office just to the right of where you entered before you head off to the buildings. We recommend the audio guides in English, because the attendants in the buildings are unlikely to speak much English, and most explanatory material is only in Italian. Or just wander the villa grounds. In any case, you should be able to pick up a free map, with opening hours in English, at the ticket office. If the ticket office is out of maps, try one of the other museums in the park, even if you don't buy a ticket for them.

The vistas are lovely—from classical buildings, to faux Roman ruins, to unrestored theaters. Of particular note is the commanding Casino Nobile (also called Palazzo Nobile), the large central building directly in front of you as you come through the gates (ticket required). It is mainly Valadier's design, with obelisks in front and back, and palm trees replanted as they were. This building for eighteen years (1925–43) was the family home of Mussolini, his wife, and their five children at the nominal rent of one *lira* per year. Mussolini's jazz musician son, Romano, remembered playing here and that there was only one bathroom. Il Duce had his photo taken many times in the villa, while riding horses, for example, and in other masculine-looking activities. He kept a second home in Palazzo Venezia in the Centro, with his mistress.

After the Allies entered Rome in 1944, Casino Nobile was occupied by British and American troops, who basically trashed it, scratching graffiti into the walls to express their disrespect of the Fascist leader. The Allied military left the building in shambles; time and disuse came next; whole floors caved in. Only sixty years later has this example of early-nineteenth-century architecture been restored to its former beauty. Depending on your tour, you also might see the bunker Mussolini created from the Jewish catacombs under the villa. Unfortunately, the catacombs are not open for either visits or study. They are considered dangerous due to toxic air quality.

Two other buildings of note are Casino dei Principi, the neoclassical smaller building to the right of Casino Nobile, and up a small rise and to the left of Casino Nobile, *Casetta delle Civette* (little house of the owls). Casino dei Principi is open (with a ticket) during (frequent) exhibitions. Casetta delle Civette (ticket required) is a large building in Swiss cottage style, last remodeled in the early twentieth century. It is considered a hallmark of the "liberty" (not *libertá*, simply "liberty" in Italian) style, that is, art nouveau. It was, and continues to be, full of stained-glass windows (in the liberty style) and spaces for stained-glass study. Many owls appear in the glass designs, hence the name.

TO REFRESH YOU AND YOUR KIDS

Keep heading down the hill, opposite from where you entered the villa, with all three of the major buildings just described at your back, and you will see the *Limonaia*—or lemon place, which is now a large bar and

The Limonaia, Villa Torlonia.

restaurant. Attached to the Limonaia is the *Villino Medievale,* or little medieval house—again, neither little nor from the Middle Ages but a replica, built in the early 1900s when the medieval style (with its towers and parapets) was popular. Technotown is now housed in the "little medieval house." It's open for younger folks aged eleven to seventeen. For €5, a teenager can play computer-assisted educational games. As you go into Technotown, note the two quotes on the wall. One is from U.S. blues great B. B. King: "The beautiful thing about learning is nobody can take it away from you." The other is from French intellectual Claude Levi-Strauss: "A scientist is not the person who gives the right answers, but he who asks the right questions."

TO CONTEMPLATE ON THE WAY WAY OUT

The combination of Mussolini, fake ruins, a replicated medieval house, quotes from B. B. King and Levi-Strauss, and more—where else can one find this combination (or should one say mishmash) of culture? Enjoy it . . . and proceed out the park exit in back and left of the Limonaia— through the kids' playground. You're on via Siracusa. Take it to the left. Your next left takes you onto viale di Villa Massimo (you were on it earlier, farther down). Continue on viale di Villa Massimo and you'll come across the small park mentioned above.

A SMALLER RESTING (AND EATING AND DRINKING) PLACE

This smaller park, which runs along viale di Villa Massimo, between via Siracusa and via Ravenna, is another nice resting point. The bar-restaurant *Bistrot dei Pini* (bistro of the pine trees—and you can see why it is so named) is immediately on your right. Near the entrance to the park on this street, in front of the Bistrot, you'll see a plaque that states the park is named for Saigon-born French intellectual Marguerite Duras. Part of this park is for kids—children's playground equipment and rides.

THE WAY HOME

To complete your excursion, take a right at the next street ahead of you, at the other end of the park. This street is via Ravenna, where you were a few hours ago. Retrace your steps back up a few blocks to Piazza Bologna. Metro B should take you anywhere you want to go.

4

GETTING AWAY INSIDE ROME

WHY GET away? Rome can be irritating. The Centro, especially, is noisy, dirty, and crowded, and even in comfortable neighborhoods, like Piazza Bologna and Appio Latino, one cannot escape the Italian drivers for whom the human form is an object to be narrowly missed, the horns of angry motorists blocked by a double-parked car, or the whine of the *due-tempi* (two-cycle) scooters, many of them still on the roads, spewing clouds of effluent. The subways can be so crowded at rush hour that it is physically impossible to squeeze one's body on board, and sometimes the next train is just as full. A ride down via Nazionale on the popular but jammed Bus 64 requires constant vigilance—not to figure out when to get off, but to hold onto your wallet. Sometimes it's just too much.

PARKS AND PARKS

Getting away inside Rome isn't difficult. A glance at any map reveals huge green spaces, most of them available to the exhausted tourist: Villa Doria Pamphili (on the west and in chapter 1, p. 34), Villa Borghese (center north), and Villa Ada (north). All are presentable immense parks, and all offer a place to stroll. And all, we think, are a bit boring (Bill says), perhaps too normal and pleasant (Dianne says) to provide the kind of stimulating, renewing, getting away your authors favor.

Rome has two kinds of parks. One consists of the landscaped and more-or-less (often less) trimmed-up villas, once home to the super-rich, where mothers with strollers, elderly couples, and men in business suits seem equally to belong. These parks are for "walking." The other kind of park is scruffier, more primitive, less visited by the hand of man, seldom by mothers with children and corporate CEOs. These parks are for walking too, but also for "hiking." Imagine New York's Central Park before landscape architect Frederick Law Olmsted dressed it up in the 1860s.

AND NEIGHBORHOODS

A few of Rome's neighborhoods also offer an escape from the city's intensity. One of the quietest is Appio Latino. You can enter that neighborhood via the railroad overpass at Piazza Zama, and within a block or two you'll feel like you're strolling the streets of a small town. Stop for coffee at Fruit Bar (owned by a Ukrainian and her husband), with tables outside, on via Macedonia. The area's quiet shopping street is one block to the east, through the small piazza.

THREE ITINERARIES

The itineraries in this chapter offer a different sort of getting away, something more adventurous than a stroll through Appio Latino, more ambitious than a promenade on the wide avenues of the Borghese Gardens or the Villa Ada, though we don't deny that each of those contains its treasures and occasional surprises.

ITINERARY 9: MONTE MARIO

The tallest peak in the urban Rome zone, at 450 feet, Monte Mario has been the site of human activity for thousands of years. Ancient foundries operated here as long ago as the first century AD, and modern versions continued in use until the 1960s. Within the past decade, much of Monte Mario has been set aside for park use, and the vast acreage (150 hectares) incorporates several paths, none of which forms a good loop because of all the private and public land and buildings interspersed with park land. But there are several good paths and much to see, including some of the best vistas of Rome. You can spend one hour here or several.

HOW TO GET THERE

Take Metro A to Ottaviano-San Pietro (St. Peter's) and then Bus 30 or Bus 271 to Piazzale Maresciallo Giardino—about five stops. There are some accesses to the park that are locked. So don't give up. We recommend the one due west of Piazzale Maresciallo Giardino. Do not head up to your right on via di Villa Madama (now the seat of the Ministry of Foreign Affairs, displaying a frustrating if efficacious practice of the Italians to turn beautiful buildings into impenetrable government offices; Prime Minister Silvio Berlusconi welcomed President George W. Bush here in June 2008). Skirt the via Gomenizza back of the piazzale. You'll have to cross the busy

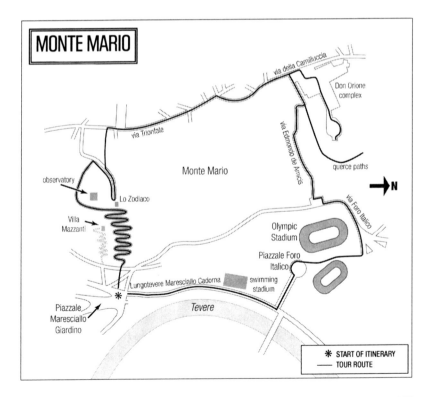

street, with merging and diverging traffic. We recommend you do it in sections, near where the roads diverge (at least the drivers slow down to under 50 mph here), and you'll spot the open gates just past the terracotta-colored building owned by the ACEA utility monopoly.

An alternate, or additional, path begins at the park gates a few yards beyond the entrance described above. This path goes to Villa Mazzanti, an 1870 villa appropriated by the government and now hosting government offices devoted to city nature ("RomaNatura"). Helpful pamphlets and information (mostly in Italian) are available here.

WHEN TO GO AND WITH WHOM

Go any time, bearing in mind the park gates are unlocked at 7 a.m. and locked at 6 p.m. from October through February, at 8 p.m. in March and September, and at 9 p.m. from April through August. We enjoy these paths and recommend them, but if you go beyond the first jaunt, we caution you only to take those children (and perhaps adults) who can stay on a very straight and narrow path without wavering for ten minutes or so at a time, perhaps children twelve and older; it's not the steepness of the climb that will get you, it's the cars. We recommend not walking alone, although we've seen solitary walkers here. We have never had a problem in this park, but there are parts of it that are quite solitary, and there have been reports of crime in all these parks. By contrast, we think this park is a winner for courting—and from what we've observed, we're not the only ones who think so.

FOLLOW THE YELLOW BRICK ROAD

The path we've started you on begins with a large panel map of the park that outlines its many paths. The current path is made up of gold-colored stones, probably *tufo*. Americans might find the path a bit ragged and unkempt, but by Roman standards, it's not bad (that is, a weed whacker—a rare sight in Rome—and garbage crew are in here regularly). There are plenty of benches and rustic wood fences that remind us of the nineteenth-century desire to see nature, as long as it's tamed (*natura domata*; see p. 177).

You'll see a panel (in Italian) on the history of human development on Monte Mario, with photos of some of the foundries and descriptions of the many fossils found in the rocks here. About one million years ago, Rome and its environs were submerged. See if your kids can find some of these mollusk fossils while they walk.

After about fifteen minutes you'll see more panels, some on geology, flora, fauna (sorry, these are all in Italian, but for those with expertise in these areas, the photos, pictures, and Latin names provide some useful information). One panel shows there are seventy species of birds as well as other fauna you and your children can look for. And there are views of the Colli Albani, including its highest peak, Monte Cavo (see p. 155), which you already may have hiked or plan to. You also may debate which Monte—Cavo or Mario—wins the satellite-tower competition. About five minutes more and you'll have your first view of St. Peter's dome and the Gianicolo Hill behind it. The neighborhood of Prati stretches out below. To the left are the shell-like roofs of Renzo Piano's Parco della Musica (see page 199), with the ritzy Parioli neighborhood above it. And much more. Take your map of Rome!

The path now spreads out into a larger park, with plenty of ostentatiously necking lovers ignoring the magnificent views. Here's a place to watch the drop offs if your children are with you. Just follow the path, down through a larger, flat park area and out the gates to an asphalt road (there are no shortcuts here; believe us, we tried them). Take a hairpin right out of the gates and walk up the road. You'll see a sign (you may have seen one of the many of these, and we translate, leaving you to decide its accuracy: "Parco di Monte Mario—here nature is protected and watched over").

BEST VIEW IN (OR OF) THE CITY?

A few yards up the road on your right is the Fascist-era observatory, now closed to visitors (and replaced by a new public observatory in EUR, the Fascist-built suburb about eight miles south of Rome's center, which we highly recommend to you), and then the road ends (the paths are closed off on the left by a military installation—unfortunately a common ending to many Italian paths). A welcome end, however, is the restaurant, café, bar

Lunch for all at Lo Zodiaco.

complex, Lo Zodiaco (the zodiac). Here you can sit down (assuming you're willing to buy something, a juice or coffee will do) and enjoy the views, which are stunning. Your kids can play on the bucking broncos or try the videogame machines. On a clear day, looking just slightly left, you'll see in the distance the Monti Lucretili. Among those mountains is the highest summit (at four thousand feet) near Rome: Monte Gennaro. In urban Rome, you see the districts Flaminio and Parioli, Piano's Parco della Musica, the Tevere (the arches of Ponte Milvio ahead on the left), the Centro Storico (historic center) across the Tevere to your right, and Prati on the near right as well. There are telescopes for fifty (euro) cents here and more lovers. It's not for nothing the name of the little path here is vialetto degli Innamorati—little way of the lovers. Lo Zodiaco has a piano bar at night and jazz on some evenings; you may wish to plan a return trip by car or taxi.

GETTING BACK FROM HERE

Without a lot of pauses and at a leisurely pace, you should arrive at Lo Zodiaco thirty-five or forty minutes after you begin this itinerary. If you have small children with you, we recommend you retrace your steps back down the path and call it a day.

INTO THE NEIGHBORHOOD

If you're ready to go on, go back down the asphalt road until you come to the pine grove on the right. Take the well-worn path through it, down the small steps on the right, and out the high old arch, stopping on the sidewalk, cautious of the busy via Trionfale in front of you. Take a right up via

Trionfale. Cross to the other side at a light and continue. Forte Mario should be on your right, but the broad, open park there doesn't give any access to it or any views (thank you, Italian military for keeping these to yourself, Dianne says). You'll also see a stone plaque explaining that the street numbers now will indicate the meters from the dead center of Rome, Campidoglio. So you'll see, for example, numbers in the 5000s. Take the right fork when you see No. 6006 on your right, and you're now on via della Camilluccia. These streets, Trionfale and Camilluccia, are extremely fast and busy and often without sidewalks on either side. Hence our caution about children (and it's not over yet).

DON ORIONE

At the next cross street, via Edmondo de Amicis, cross over to the complex kitty corner from where you've come. The medical and meeting complex Don Orione has fascinating buildings inside. Enter the complex at via della Camilluccia, 90, and head around the first building on its left. You'll be in a courtyard-piazza with a statue of the Don and a quote from him—"Sempre curvo sulle necessitá del prossimo" (I always bend to the needs of my neighbor)—words consistent with the appearance of the sculpture. On the building opposite you'll find *fasci* and a reference to A XIII, the thirteenth year of the Fascists, or 1935 (see "Fascist Numbering System," p. 85). Go right and straight back. Don't ask anyone. Just go there. Here you'll see a graceful, curving one-story building covered with small tiles. Begun in 1933 as a heliotherapy (sun therapy) center, this complex was designed by Enrico Del Debbio as a place for gathering and shade for the Fascist boys' group, Balilla, and at one time it was connected

The graceful curve of a Fascist youth center (1933).

with the *Foro Italico* (the "Italian Forum," the site of Mussolini's sports forum and the 1960 Olympic Games; see below) at the bottom of the hill. One has to use some imagination to picture the boys doing physical exercises here. A tall reflecting gold statue of the Madonna takes away one's eye from the Fascist complex. You can't get too close to the Madonna and the magnificent view she must command. All ways out are gated here; you'll have to turn back now.

DOWNHILL

Retrace your steps to the nearby intersection of via della Camilluccia with via Edmondo de Amicis. Take the latter street downhill for a few hundred yards. Just as it curves right, take the stone path–road at the left, which skirts the hill. As this path arrives at the front of the hill, more or less below the Madonna, a panel describes a short circular trail below, in the cool *querce* (oaks). This is a delightful trail for nature lovers, shaded and solitary. Starting to the right, the trail is obvious except for one place, early on, where the trail turns sharply back and to the left just before a small clearing. If you arrive at the fence, retreat through the clearing and look for the opening. We thought there might be a trail all the way down the hill, and there could be. But the downhill side of the loop is well fenced, and the only opening in the fence—the only way down—was a small, wood-framed "door," leading right through the front yard (bright-colored bins and clothespins) of a squatter's home, complete with chimney, built

into the hillside. No one appeared, but we decided not to enter this space.

Returning to the top of the loop, retrace your steps down the hillside path to via Edmondo de Amicis. Follow it down-

A side trail among the oaks.

hill, watching the cars and doing your best to stay on the narrow sidewalk to the left. At the T at the bottom (about ten minutes), go through the small piazza and left on via Foro Italico, walking on the left (careful—there isn't much of a shoulder, and the cars are shooting out of a tunnel at high speed). At the light (five minutes on), press the button to stop the traffic and cross over to the Stadio Olimpico (Olympic Stadium), entering the stadium grounds through the bright yellow open barricades (signs of new security measures after the killing of a policeman at a soccer game in Italy in 2007). Relax.

THE STADIUM

Stroll along the side of the stadium, at your right. The original stadium on this site was built in the 1930s during the Mussolini regime. In an effort to keep the stadium in harmony with nature and reveal Monte Mario behind it, much of the seating was below ground. The stadium was rebuilt for the 1960 Olympic Games and again in the 1990s, when the tentlike cover and other features were added. At some point in this process, Monte Mario was eclipsed by a much taller stadium. Although architecture critics don't much like the current version, the rounded stairway towers are impressive. Today, both Rome teams, Lazio and Roma, use the stadium. In very broad terms, Lazio is the team of Rome's upper and middle classes; Roma of the working class and of those with more liberal political views. Serious younger fans sit in the cheaper seats at the ends of the stadium—the *curva sud* (south curve, that is, the end zone) or the *curva nord* (north curve). To keep fights from breaking out during the game, the home team fans occupy one curve, the visiting fans the other. Frequent signs warning fans of prohibited items (but usually present)— torches, smoke bombs, fireworks, studded belts, flagpoles, and glass items—suggest how dangerous the stadium can be on a Sunday afternoon.

FORO ITALICO

As you clear the end of the stadium, you'll be in the heart of the *Foro Italico,* designated the *Foro Mussolini* when the project was unveiled in 1927. Architect Enrico Del Debbio (see above, Don Orione, p. 133) was given

Foro Italico.

the job of overseeing the design of this modern complex devoted to sports. The *Stadio dei Marmi* (Marble Stadium, to the left of the Stadio Olimpico), the Piazzale del Foro Italico, and the pink terracotta buildings you'll see as you make your way toward the river were all part of that project. Foro Italico was the first of the three immense Fascist building projects in Rome, along with EUR and the university (near the Piazza Bologna area in chapter 3). The cultural framework of Fascism, its imperial goals, and its relationship to sport are laid out in front of you here. In addition to the Marble Stadium, look at the mosaics (evoking Ostia Antica, ancient Rome's heritage, see p. 73) on the ground. You'll see designs by some of Fascism's best architects and artists (including Luigi Moretti), showing Fascism's and ancient Rome's imperial conquests. Don't miss the obelisk, currently in restoration to display the large "MUSSOLINI" spelled out on it; the large marble blocks that were written confirmations of Italy's twentieth-century conquests up to 1943, including blank ones for the conquests that never came; and the swimming building with its gorgeous 1930s mosaics. We'd like to say that your typical Rome guidebook gives you information on this spectacular demonstration of twentieth-century Italian history, but few of them do. There's simply not much information available in English. Someone who clearly appreciates the mosaics in the swimming building offers some good information via the Web site http://mosaicartsource.wordpress.com /2007/01/28/foro-italico-pool-mosaics-men-mosaic-artist-angelo-canevari -rome-italy/.

If you've wound your way through *Foro Italico* and come upon the obelisk and swimming building, you're almost at the river and on the street Lungotevere Maresciallo Cadorna. *Lungotevere* means "along the Tevere" or along the Tiber River, and you'll be walking next to the river here.

GETTING BACK
Turning south (right) on Lungotevere Maresciallo Cadorna, you're just minutes from Piazzale Maresciallo Giardino, where you started and where you can catch Bus 32 or Bus 271; take it about five stops to the Otta- viano–San Pietro stop of Metro A to get home. If you walk on the river- side of this street, you can get a glimpse of the private sports clubs that line the Tevere, which are normally not seen from the streets above.

ITINERARY 10: ON THE BANKS OF THE ANIENE

How do we come up with these things? This itinerary developed when Bill had the bright idea of hiking along the banks of Rome's second river, the Aniene—the great waterway that flows from the Lucretili Mountains—to its end, where it empties into the Tevere just to the north of the grand and luxurious Villa Ada. We never made it. Close—maybe two hundred yards from the Tevere—but no cigar. We moved from the luxury of Villa Ada, with its running tracks, gelato stands, and kids' playgrounds, across the six-lane fast-moving via del Foro Italico. When we turned around, we were on via *Foce dell'Aniene* (mouth of the Aniene), a dirt road (on the map, but . . .) running off the via del Foro Italico. We passed a junkyard for autos and scooters, dwellings—some would say hovels—made of scrap materi- als, tin and corrugated iron, one with a friendly offering to "ring the bell." Dogs, children, hanging laundry, smells of food cooking. Quite perma- nent "homes." Around a bend, in thickening vegetation, a small railroad underpass, nearly full of garbage and trash. Bill went through; Dianne held back. A boy on the trestle saw her and warned in Italian, "Signora,

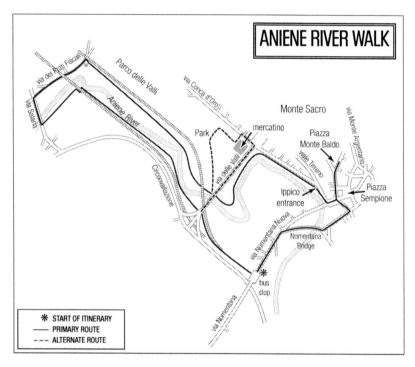

ANIENE RIVER WALK

* START OF ITINERARY
— PRIMARY ROUTE
- - - ALTERNATE ROUTE

don't go there." She stopped. What he saw, or couldn't quite see, made this the end of this particular journey: dense vegetation, a crowded cluster of shanties a level below those we had just passed. These also were made of scrap materials, including wood and plastic sheeting, with a narrow path through them. To get to the Tevere, we would have to pass through this village—no doubt home to poor immigrants, certainly illegal, perhaps dangerous. Rest assured, this is not on the tour.

HOW TO GET THERE

You can take several buses up via Nomentana. Bus 90 begins and ends at Termini, runs every ten minutes most of the day, and goes far north on this large street. Via Nomentana becomes via Nomentana Nuova, the main drag out of town going northeast (two thousand years ago one of the original Roman consular roads that went then to Nomentum, now Mentana). Get off at the first stop after the bus crosses the large bridge over the

Circonvallazione Nomentana, a very busy multilane inner-city expressway. This is three miles but only the seventh stop. Not far from the bus stop, and walking in the same direction, you'll come upon a small triangular park on your right, where the old via Nomentana deviates on a right fork from the busy via Nomentana Nuova. (This park is mentioned in the opening pages of Pier Paolo Pasolini's *A Violent Life* [1959, English translation 1968], the classic commentary on the angry young men growing up in shanty villages in via dei Monti di Pietralata, in the valley of the Aniene River, just upriver from this itinerary.) Enter the park on via Nomentana.

WHEN TO GO

Any day but Thursday, when one of the access roads is closed. And the flea market on the walk is closed from 1 p.m. to 3 p.m. on weekdays. If you're more comfortable with people around, go on a Saturday or Sunday.

THE NOMENTANA BRIDGE

Not far ahead (on old via Nomentana in the small park) is the Nomentana Bridge, one of the city's lesser-known treasures. Dating to the late second or early first century BC, it was built of stones from the Etruscan settlement at Gabii (about ten miles out of Rome) and faced with travertine marble. Despite many changes—the latest of them in the fifteenth century, when the crenellated forms at the top were likely added—the bridge has an undeniable elegance and authority, and the late-medieval touches give it a look different from that of Rome's other bridges. The more ephemeral presence of today's young people is revealed in the combination locks and chains that have been placed around one of the span's fence posts, a new custom signifying undying love—in the case of the one we saw, of Manuel and Giorgia (etched into the lock itself). Ponte Milvio, over the Tevere in the center of Rome, has hundreds of these locks and chains, following a popular teen romance (*I Want You* by Federico Moccia); there's also an online way to show your love through these locks, www.lucchettipontemilvio.com (click on *Entra* and then Photogallery for photos).

Astride the Aniene, one of the city's two most vital rivers, it is not hard to imagine the role the bridge played in the economic life of ancient Rome and the surrounding area. Confirmation of the importance of the bridge as a crossing point comes just a few yards after the bridge, on the left, where a great trough connected to a standing water fountain–spigot (*nasone*; see "Drinking Fountains (*Nasoni*)," p. 116) suggests that large numbers of animals must once have watered here. The terracotta building across the way, now Pizzeria *Ponte Vecchio* (old bridge), undergoing renovation, has the look of a travelers' way station, although obviously of relatively recent vintage (maybe five hundred years old instead of two thousand).

We don't usually report on graffiti, but the walls in this area bear some revealing pieces. One, on the electrical box on the terracotta building, reads: "Fedayn Roma / Noi siamo immortali (we are immortal) / Bin Laden is the king." On the next wall to the right, closer to the bridge: "Contro la sistema (against the system) / la gioventù si scaglia (youth throws itself) / Boia chi molla (swine who refuse to fight) / E il grido di battaglia (and the cry of battle) / Adol. [Hitler] is my friend." Note: On the left of this "poem" was a swastika. The phrase "boia chi molla" is a standard neofascist line, dating to the 1970s, now frequently used by soccer fans.

CITTÀ-GIARDINO ANIENE

Continue on this road, bearing left, to Piazza Sempione, which sits at the base of the Monte Sacro neighborhood. The curious assortment of buildings that grace this piazza is most of what remains of *Città-giardino Aniene* (City Garden Aniene), one of two planned communities constructed by the *Istituto Case Popolari* (ICP, Institute for Popular Houses, or a type of subsidized housing for lower- and middle-income workers) in the 1920s. The other, more elaborate and better preserved, is Garbatella, a recommended stop on Metro B. But there is enough left here to give us a sense of what the Fascist government, planner Gustavo Giovannoni, and architect Innocenzo Sabbatini had in mind. The style of the development is sometimes referred to as *barocchetto,* or late Italian baroque (the original Italian baroque is seventeenth century), and the overhanging balconies and tower structures seem to us to derive from the medieval, to which has been added a touch of playfulness.

The use of medieval iconography in Città-giardino Aniene reflects the desire of the planners to establish a cohesive community; that is, because medieval communities are today understood to have been places where people knew each other intimately, to the modern mind, "medieval" connotes "community." (The faux Villino Medievale in the Villa Torlonia also evokes these values; see p. 124.) Concerned about the corrosive effects of urbanization and industrialization on community life in the early twentieth century, Città-giardino's planners looked backward to the medieval village for inspiration. They also placed this (then) lower- (mostly) income community *lontanissimo* (very, very far) from the city center and ran utilities out here for the first time to accommodate this location/dislocation.

According to an often-told story about the area, the great Latin American patriot and liberator Simon Bolivar took his famous oath to liberate his native Venezuela from Spanish colonial domination atop Monte Sacro on August 15, 1805. Indeed, Bolivar himself described the place as "Monte Sacro" in an 1824 letter, and his teacher, who was present, describes the "magnificent view" from the "Sacred Hill." Nonetheless, the most recent scholarship suggests that the actual site was the Palatine Hill, where the view more closely corresponds to the ancient marvels that Bolivar had mentioned in his speech. The view from Monte Sacro, a small hill far from the center of old Rome, is rather ordinary.

In contrast, there is little doubt that Monte Sacro was a hotbed of resistance activity during World War II, especially during the German occupation. One resistance group included Italo Grimaldi, whose butcher shop was in Piazza Sempione. Grimaldi was arrested on December 23, 1943, and executed one week later, at Forte Bravetta, after a brief inquiry. Another group, consisting of young men in their teens, was formed around the *liceo* (high school) Orazio. As boys, they had a small beach on the Aniene, near the old bridge you've just seen, and a swimming group called "I caimani del bell'orizzonte" (Crocodiles of the Beautiful Horizon). The center of the Monte Sacro resistance was Il Villino Rainelli (the Rainelli Villa) in via Monte Argentario (two short blocks from Piazza Sempione, walking northeast), where political discussions were the order of the day, and where Paul Laufer, a Jewish dentist who had fled persecution in

Austria, was in hiding. The Nazis conducted more than one *rastrellamento* (roundup) in Monte Sacro; some of those caught were killed at the Fosse Ardeatine (see p. 92).

If you have a desire to explore further, head up via Gargano into Piazza Monte Baldo, visible ahead. Above the arch in the piazza is a sign, "Istituto per le Case Popolari." The *Scuola Elementare* (elementary school) Don Bosco (about 1930) that dominates the piazza is also worth a look. And around the corner to the right, just a few yards up viale Adriatico, is a gem: an enormous arched entrance—surely the largest arch we have ever seen used for this purpose—apparently leading to some of the original *case popolari.* Go in and have a look (see "The Arch: From Rome to St. Louis," p. 143).

DOWN BY THE RIVERSIDE

Eager to get on with your hike? Retrace your steps to Piazza Sempione. Turn right at the piazza and right again, before the bridge, on viale Tirreno. A few yards ahead on the left at No. 13 is *Circolo Ippico* (horse-riding center), closed Thursdays. One should be able to enter the path below through a city-provided park, but none appears open at this time. (We tried some other paths and ended up walking into the shanty settlements; so we don't recommend you repeat this experience.) Walk down to the horse-riding center, amid the terraced plants and flowers, and either go directly to or ask for the *sentiero* (path), which you'll find on your

left. We talked with the management here, and they are happy to let people come through their facility to the path. Follow this path as it twists and turns along the riverbank. After about ten

Enter here to access the right bank of the Aniene.

minutes, you'll come to a fence with an opening. Horses would have to stop here, but you go through, bearing right. Walk under the large highway bridge.

THE ARCH: FROM ROME TO ST. LOUIS

The Romans were great builders, in part because they learned to support structures of great weight—the aqueduct is a good example—by using the form of the arch. Critical to the arch form was its keystone, the irregularly shaped piece in the center that held the arch together and allowed it to do its work of distributing weight downward. Under the emperors of Rome, large and elaborate ceremonial, triumphal arches represented the power and reach of the empire and provided spaces where its military victories and territorial acquisitions could be celebrated.

The Fascists who took control in 1922 knew this history, and they used the arch to link the expansionist glory of ancient Rome to the imperial ambitions of the Italian nation. The arch signified Italy's emergence as a great power, building its own empire in North Africa and becoming a major player in European and world affairs. When Italian aviator Italo Balbo returned in 1933 from a dramatic flight that had taken him and a squadron of aircraft from Orbetello (on the Tyrrhenian coast) to Chicago and back, Mussolini rewarded his fellow Fascist with the ultimate expression of the gratitude of the Italian Fascist state; together, they marched through the Arch of Constantine.

Dozens of posters from the 1920s and 1930s used a double arch to suggest not only the country's new imperial ambitions and its glorious Roman past but to represent Mussolini, whose initial (M) was presented as a set of two arches. When Mussolini and the Fascist state prepared to celebrate the twentieth anniversary of Fascism (1942) and its ambitions for empire by constructing a new development between Rome and the sea (now EUR), it was understood that the centerpiece would be an enormous arch.

Although the arch for E42 (*Esposizione* [Exposition] 1942) was never built, many designs were offered. One of them, a poster by Fascist architect Ludovico Quaroni, seemed to closely resemble the design that Eero Saarinen presented in 1948 in a competition to design a monument to represent American national expansion under President Thomas Jefferson, who had purchased a huge tract of western land from France. When *Life* magazine raised the similarities in 1948 after Saarinen won the competition with the arch that was finally completed in St. Louis in 1966, some people wondered if Saarinen had copied his arch from Quaroni's, and even if the American arch was in some way "Fascist."

YOUR CHOICE

At this point you have a choice:

Route A takes you farther downriver and back on the other side, so that in about forty-five minutes you'll be just across the river from where you are now, and in about one hour you'll be near the starting point of this itinerary. While mostly a pleasant and interesting riverside walk, this route has about eight minutes of travel on a rather narrow sidewalk next to fast-moving traffic—not recommended for those with small children.

Route B turns right at this point, up through an urban park, past a large, permanent outdoor market, then back to via Nomentana Nuova on the bike path across the river from where you are now. Using this route, and provided you don't shop, you'll return to a point near the start in about thirty minutes.

ROUTE A

Route A itself begins with a choice. Ahead of you is a fork. One route, with grass between the tire tracks, goes down closer to the river. This route is more naturalistic and takes you by private gardens and small (nonthreatening) riverbank houses and shacks. The other, the regular stone-asphalt path that you're on, goes up. This route is pleasant but less intimate. At some points the two paths are so close you can move from one to the other simply by going up or down a small hill. If you take the left route, in about fifteen minutes, when you can see the yellow ACEA electric building ahead, move to your right to merge with the regular path. Regardless of the path you've chosen, when they merge, you then go past the metal bar across the path and beyond the small garbage dump (sorry about that; efforts to post this with park signs seem not to have helped), curving left along the ACEA wall to the very large and busy road below: via dei Prati Fiscali, which merges into via Salaria (another Roman consular road, named for the salt trade). Move through the *brutta* (ugly) piazza. At your left is a green needle-exchange machine for drug addicts, and you may see a prostitute or two soliciting here—we did. Take the sidewalk ahead, walking against the traffic, past the bus stop and several businesses below, curving left over the bridge.

On the Aniene path. There will be trash.

Once across the bridge, turn left immediately onto the bike path. In about five minutes, the path bears right at the yellow train viaduct and dips down into an alleylike space completely covered with graffiti, then turns left under the tracks, then right into the open, onto the path. Although this last stretch can seem a bit intimidating, it really isn't, and once onto the path, you can expect bikers and joggers (we saw a woman jogging alone). Enjoy the path. Follow it upriver—you're heading back. It will emerge in a small park.

GETTING BACK

A hundred yards ahead beyond the park you'll find the now familiar via Nomentana Nuova. Turn left toward Piazza Sempione and find Bus 90 or another to take you back.

ROUTE B

Just before your path goes under the next, smaller railroad bridge, set at an angle, take a hairpin right, then curve left, past the cement-making facility on your right, and up into a regular park. On weekends, at least, you'll find locals walking, bicycling (you can rent [*noleggio*] bikes here), and even jogging (not yet a sport with much appeal to the Roman temperament); you can explore this park as you like. Work your way to the big street ahead, via Conca d'Oro, and turn right. You'll pass the large, white-tented flea market, Mercatino Conca d'Oro (9 a.m.–1 p.m., 3–8 p.m. every day, plus Saturday and Sunday nonstop). If you need a lunch break, we recommend two reasonably priced, casual restaurants ahead on via Conca d'Oro: Trattoria dei Briganti at No. 94 and Mediterraneo at No. 76.

For Route B, take the hairpin right.

If you're completing your loop, stop at the bridge, cross the road that goes over the river (to your right), and move over the bridge, past the Agip gas station, to the stairway, on the far side of the river. (There's a small luna park here, on a road running off near the gas station, if you have children who want to try a few rides.) The stairway leads to a bike-walking path. Follow it (to the right, upriver—you're heading back). It will emerge in a small park.

GETTING BACK

A hundred yards ahead beyond the park is the now familiar via Nomentana Nuova. Turn left toward Piazza Sempione and find Bus 90 or another to take you back.

ITINERARY 11: PARCO DEL PINETO

This itinerary offers the opportunity to see two kinds of Rome parks—the one for grandmothers pushing strollers and the one that drops us into the wild ravines that once covered many of Rome's nearby hillsides. The city has made great strides in setting aside these areas, even if they are not especially well maintained. We like this one because it adds the flavor of ancient settlers; it was inhabited by forts, factories, furnaces, fancy villas, and squatters, some of whom are still around, as we will see. There are no signed paths, no directions in the middle of the park. And the basic park runs the long way (as does its valley) from south (where you enter) to north, and the short way from west (you actually enter on the southwest corner) to east. We've given you some general suggestions for getting in and around the wilder part of the park. Beyond that, it's really up to you. The area has some fine views of St. Peter's and at the same time allows one to see firsthand the encroachment of city dwellers on the wild countryside. Dropping down into Parco del Pineto's many levels, one can imagine the *campagna romana*—the Roman countryside—that so fascinated nineteenth-century romantic writers and painters. You can spend one or more hours in this park. So let's get trekking!

HOW TO GET THERE

The main entrance to the park is at the corner of via della Pineta Sacchetti and via Albergotti. It's an easy half-mile walk straight north from Metro A, stop Cornelia, on the very busy Circonvallazione Cornelia. The

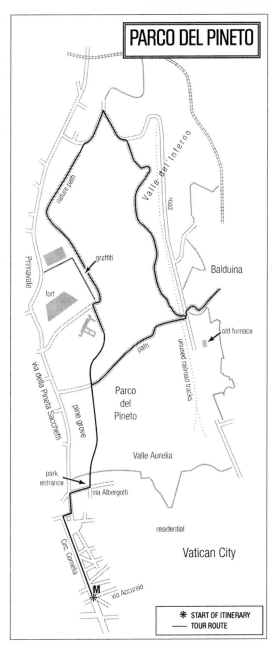

street becomes via della *Pineta Sacchetti* (the pine grove named for the family who once owned most of this land). The first small street to the right is via Albergotti. Don't let the graffiti-filled walls leading to the park entrance gates stop you; one day when we were here, there were about twenty elderly women having a picnic lunch with the graffiti as their backdrop. It's all quite colorful, the purple, blue, and black of the graffiti, the green of the *pini* (pine trees), and the yellow of the construction fences and equipment (ever present, it seems).

PARK 1: GRANDPARENTS AND BABIES

The upper park, which you enter now, is the one that looks like a traditional Roman park—grandmas with their *nipotini* (grandchildren; interestingly, the same word means nieces and nephews—a sign of the historical closeness of Italian extended families), couples lying on the grass, a few balls being kicked around. There are kiddie rides (swings, slides) that have graffiti on them too and are overgrown, but still clearly usable and used. A typical Roman park. The tall, lovely pines you see, which give Rome its distinctive skyline (the *pini*), are sometimes called umbrella trees. As you walk into this park you can see why and how the park got its name—park of the pine grove. Walk along the upper park; you'll get some of the views across the way of the dense, fairly new, middle-class and politically conservative Balduina neighborhood, with its layers of cement apartment buildings, and of St. Peter's dome. You'll also see directly east the tall towers on

Monte Mario (see Itinerary 9 above).

PARK 2: HOVELS, INFERNO, WARNINGS, FLORA, FAUNA (WHAT ELSE?)

About halfway along the upper park (you will see

Entrance to Parco del Pineto.

unrestored nineteenth-century buildings at the end of this track), take a right (east) on a worn path heading into the valley below. We don't recommend you head down to your right just as you enter the park, even if the path seems well worn. If a path looks too good, as this one did, it can lead to squatter encampments. The path we advise you not to take has dirt stairs built into it. We came, all of a sudden, onto a group of hovels pieced together of various materials and somewhat disguised by green plastic netting. There were at least twenty people, apparently not Italian, around on this Sunday afternoon, and they were friendly and showed us the path—which went right through their housing area. We did it, but we wouldn't do it again. (Less than a month after our visit, and in response to complaints from area residents, police moved into the park at dawn, demolishing twenty-five shacks and removing forty Romanian squatters—for the time being, anyway).

So stick to the path that leads off the middle of the upper park. You can follow paths directly to the opposite side of the park, under the railroad via a cement underpass, and up into a middle-class park on the other side. When you're at the bottom, you're in the *Valle dell'Inferno*—the Valley of Hell. This up and down and through is all worth the effort, the views, and the contrast. On this well-groomed park on the east side, you're in Balduina. You can see below one of the remaining furnaces, which operated here in ancient times and in modern times. There were a dozen of these furnaces in the late nineteenth century, and the last one ceased operation in the 1940s. They supplied the various factories in this area. Almost as stunning are the immense towerlike apartment buildings that block the southern end of the valley.

The trail down, city in the distance.

SAFETY WARNINGS

In this upper park on the east side, we read signs posted on signboards describing this and other parks (including Monte Mario) as "oases of illegality," sites of "illegal shantytowns inhabited by numerous immigrants," and warning of criminal activity—robberies, thefts, breaking into apartments. The signs were put up by a right-wing political party and its youth group. We can't make any guaranties, but neither do we think crime is as plentiful as these signs suggest. There is no question immigrants are living in these parks and that crime exists. It's not enough to keep us out of the parks, and Italian crime is famously not physically harmful. But we recommend walking with someone else, walking in broad daylight, and, if you choose, walking on a Saturday or Sunday when there are many more people around.

VALLE DELL'INFERNO AND UP

Once you have reentered the bottom of the park (cross back under the railroad), turn right along well-worn paths heading north and up toward the buildings you see in the distance. At the bottom, you're in the oldest part of the park, and you may see signs of an ancient spring and an old fort. When you reach the top, north end of the park, you'll also see signs of a marked path, with large information boards (these may still be in place when you take this walk). There is a nice path lined with these boards and benches (even an exercise par course that may survive another year or two). It's called "Sentiero Natura Il Costone"—or, Nature Path "Il Costone." There are boards on the fauna, showing pictures of various animals such as the gray crow, kestrel, owl, and the surmolotto (a rodentlike creature, sometimes domesticated). Another on the flora, such as cork-oak, myrtle, mastic tree (lentiscus), Turkey oak (cerris), and hazel-nut tree. Yet others on geology. One gives information on the noble Florentine family that gives the park its longer name *Parco della Pineta Sacchetti* (Park of the Sacchetti Pine Grove).

GRAFFITI, SACCHETTI, AND OUT

If you've kept on the path, you'll skirt the military installation that uses another of Rome's many nineteenth-century forts (Forte Braschi) and the amazing graffiti along the walls, painted under the noses—but out of sight—of the military. Keep in the park, rather than out on the roads, and head south. You'll come out at the buildings the Sacchetti built in the sixteenth to nineteenth centuries; unfortunately these have not been restored. Interestingly, here we found a letter posted on a park board that defended the immigrants and noted that the Italians themselves are not the best maintainers of their parks.

GETTING BACK

You're now at the north end of the tame part of the park; skip your way out and back to Metro A's Cornelia stop and home.

5

GETTING AWAY OUTSIDE ROME

THE ALLURE of the hills that dot the landscape some twenty to thirty miles to the east and south of Rome is impossible to overestimate. The Colli Albani (Alban Hills) or the *Castelli Romani* (Roman Castles), as they also are fondly called, in particular have drawn urban Romans since they began inhabiting the area, the Etruscans before them, and even prehistoric people. These seven-hundred-thousand-year-old volcanic mountains, reaching more than three thousand feet in elevation, have been witness to all the significant events of Roman history. With Tivoli in the Monti Tiburtini and other towns, the Colli Albani have participated in the mythological birth of Rome starring Romulus and Remus. They have seen Cicero's villas, Caligula's wild parties, Hannibal's invasion, medieval farms, opulent villas of sixteenth- to nineteenth-century Roman nobility, popes' retreats, poems by Goethe and Byron singing the hills' beauty, and the battles of World War II. Today, Romans by the thousands engorge the roads to Tivoli and the Castelli as they escape the city on Sundays in search of the best meals and the best wines and a cool escape from the summer heat.

The itineraries we describe in this chapter take you to the Castelli and Tivoli and beyond the crowded roads and cafés to wonderful woods, Roman ruins, Renaissance gardens, and incomparable views. You'll have to tolerate some detritus, unkempt properties, illegal overbuilding, fences in unsuitable places, military installations, and poor signage. We encourage you to get over (as we had to) an initial impression of overbuilt, overadvertised, oversold tourist destinations. We keep returning to all these hills, and to Tivoli and the Colli Albani especially, and now find we are never disappointed. They are always enchanting and refreshing. Just like the Frascati wine we initially repudiated, the Colli Albani seem to get better and better.

GENERAL ADVICE ON GETTING TO (AND FROM) THE HILLS

TRAIN: You can go into the Colli Albani and Tivoli by train or by regional bus (COTRAL). Both means of transportation depart Rome about as early as you want to go. The last runs return from the hills at 9:30 or 10 p.m. Expect fewer runs ending earlier on Sundays and holidays. The train to Tivoli (FR 2) leaves from Stazione Tiburtina (which you can get to by train from Termini, but more easily by Metro B from Termini). The train to Frascati (FR 1) leaves from Termini itself (on tracks a bit out of the way, so leave yourself time). Walking from the train stations into the towns is relatively quick, in our opinion, although uphill in both cases. Train tickets cost about €2.5 each way. Buy tickets at the stations, most easily at the station newsstands. Be sure to get return tickets as well (*andata e ritorno* [going and returning]). It's often more difficult to get tickets in smaller towns and later at night (we've made that mistake). You can buy tickets well in advance. All tickets are general second class that can be used at any time. Remember to validate the ticket by stamping it in the (usually yellow) machines near the platforms before beginning the trip (each way). The trains are fairly frequent, especially at peak times, and the rides are lovely. Rome to Tivoli takes about an hour; Rome to Frascati about thirty minutes.

BUS: To take the COTRAL bus to Tivoli, go to the next to the last Metro B stop in the Rebibbia direction, Ponte Mammolo, and catch a bus marked "Tivoli" in the large bus lot outside the Metro exit. To take the COTRAL bus to Frascati, take Metro A to its Anagnina end stop and catch a bus marked "Frascati" in the large bus lot outside the Metro exit. Bus tickets require stamping (on the first bus or Metro) as well. We recommend a BIRG ticket—that's a one-day regional bus ticket that should allow you to get on and off, back and forth, and ride everywhere, for about €6 (three zones). BIRG covers the Metro ride for the day as well. Make sure it's a BIRG, not a BIT. BITs are not valid outside Rome's metro area. Bear in mind that the Metro closes at 11:30 p.m. on most days. The last COTRAL buses depart from Frascati and Tivoli generally before 10 p.m. Be sure you're not left stranded. Winter buses are much less frequent than summer buses. Sundays and holidays will have fewer runs and end earlier. Ask about return times on your arrival, rather than on your way back.

TWO FOR ONE OVERNIGHT: Two of the itineraries, Monte Cavo (Itinerary 12) and Tuscolo, from Frascati (Itinerary 13), could be combined with an overnight stay in Frascati, because the route to the beginning of the Monte Cavo hike goes through Frascati.

ITINERARY 12: MONTE CAVO

This itinerary is less than two hours of pleasant hiking in the woods on very good paths. You'll be walking to the top of Monte Cavo at 3,113 feet (949 meters). Total elevation on the hike is about 1,150 feet (350 meters), accomplished gently with switchbacks and excellent footing. This hike has nice picnic areas, stunning views, and great significance in Roman history. Finding the start is the hardest part, but we have pinpointed the beginning quite well (having made a couple of false starts over the years). And in some ways, you can't miss it if you just slog around in the woods.

WHAT TO BRING

Sneakers will suffice. Take the kids if they're just a bit hardy. Bring a bottle of water per person and a picnic lunch or snacks. Although not required, we recommend—to reduce anxiety and have more fun—that you acquire the map *Roma e Dintorni* (Rome and Its Environs), basically a topographical and road map of the Colli Albani that includes some hiking paths. It has a red cover, costs about ten dollars, and can be found in most bookstores. The one most certain to have it is Libreria Esedra (not open midday) in Galleria Esedra, just off Piazza della Repubblica (Metro

A stop). Galleria Esedra is between via Orlando and via Torino; while you're in the Galleria, stop at Dagnino's (Dianne says) for some Sicilian food and pastries.

HOW TO GET THERE

You can take a train from Termini to Frascati fairly easily (see "General Advice on Getting to [and From] the Hills" above), and take a COTRAL bus from Frascati, but it might be easier to take a bus all the way. To do that, take Metro A to the Anagnina stop, as indicated in "General Advice on Getting to (and From) the Hills" above, and catch a bus in the large bus lot there marked "Rocca di Papa" (instead of simply "Frascati"—some will go through Frascati and Grottaferrata to Rocca di Papa). Many of the Rocca di Papa buses will take you very close to the beginning of this hike.

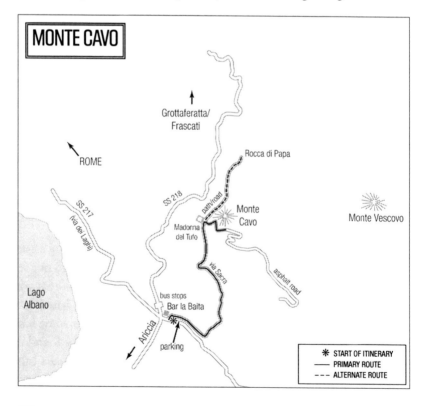

"Parking lot" for Monte Cavo.
That's Bill with his new Malaguti.

Ask for the intersection of SS 218 and *via dei Laghi* (Lake Road), SS 217. There are COTRAL stops on request (*fermata a richiesta*) each direction on the cross road, SS 218, that runs north-south from Rocca di Papa to Ariccia (you don't want to go all the way to Ariccia), a few yards north of the intersection with via dei Laghi. Once you turn left onto via dei Laghi at this busy intersection (walk carefully), you'll see Bar la Baita on your left and a sign for Ristorante La Foresta across the street (where one day we saw traffic held up as "*i big*"—Italian big shots—arrived in a multicar caravan for Sunday lunch).

Take the left at the intersection and go past Bar la Baita (a nice place to have coffee before your trek or a sit-down snack or lunch when you return; their outside counter, made of marble and very casual, is hard to resist). You are at about kilometer 11.7 on via dei Laghi. (The kilometer [KM] signs are large cement markers. Smaller white metal markers give the number 11 for the kilometer and above it in Roman numerals the tenths of kilometers; here 11 on the bottom and VII above it). If you're driving, park here. A word to the barista should take care of your parking for a few hours, especially if you have a drink or snack on your way up or down.

INTO THE WOODS

Continue about 100 feet from the bar, still on the left side. (Our estimates of minutes of walking begin here.) You'll see two large boulders marking a path. The boulders are yellow or gold colored, perhaps *tufo*. Enter the woods here and walk basically right, then straight, about 700 yards, paralleling the road (ignore the first trail left). The path then turns left toward the hill, toward Monte Cavo. You may see in the bushes just ahead of you, as you turn, the fencing for where via Sacra really begins—but you can't get to it here. Continue following the well-traveled hard-dirt path. It's also frequented by bikers and riders on horseback. Continue about 250 yards on this dirt path, bearing left at the one fork. At the intersection of paths, continue straight. After about 50 feet you'll see a sign for via Sacra. Some of this path (but not all of it) has red and white painted trail markers from CAI (*Club Alpino Italiano*—Italian Alpine Club, one of Italy's oldest hiking and trail maintenance organizations).

STOP READING, UNLESS . . .

Now you've hit pay dirt, so to speak. And if you don't want the secret revealed to you before you arrive, DON'T READ FURTHER before you get to this part of the hike.

THE SECRET ROAD

In the middle of these mostly quiet woods, seemingly far from Rome, you are now on a sacred (*sacra*) Roman road leading to the top of the also once-sacred Monte Cavo. The Roman road here is in the best condition of any of the remaining Roman roads. You have a great opportunity to look at Roman road building, the concrete underneath in places, the water runoffs. And to think this road still remains in such pristine condition two thousand years later; it's another tribute to the builders of Rome. While Pompey and others were feted with processionals in Rome (on another via Sacra), generals whose feats didn't quite measure up to Pompey's received their triumphal processions here. The road also was called via Triumphalis in Roman times and was built to reach the Temple of Jupiter Latialis (*Giove Laziale*) on Monte Cavo's peak, said to have been founded by the forty-seven cities of the (Roman) Latina Confederation, but traces of the temple to confirm this have yet to be found.

VIEWS OF . . .

Continue up this extraordinary stretch of Roman road, past picnic areas (don't stop until you get one with a view!). You'll skirt a dirt road about twenty-five minutes out, then a big curve at thirty-five minutes, with a small sanctuary on your right. The path to the left and down heads to Rocca di Papa; curve right, following the Roman road. In a few minutes you can get a view of both of the volcanic lakes of the Colli Albani, Nemi (the smaller), and Albano. If you look at the ridge to the left, you can see where the German army fortified the Colli Albani area to protect the southern entryway to Rome during World War II. The area between and just beyond the two lakes was also the scene of intense partisan activity (see "Partisans of the Colli Albani," p. 161). You can see other towns, most notably Albano and Castel Gandolfo above Lake Albano—the latter (with its round dome visible in the skyline) is the pope's summer residence. From here you also can appreciate the volcanic nature of the Castelli—you can see craters and their rims all around, large and small. Monte Cavo is the second highest peak; Maschio delle Faete at 3,136 feet (956 meters) is 23 feet higher (you can find it by its cell towers too).

IN THE STEPS OF A POPE

It is reasonable to assume that you have enjoyed the walk up Monte Cavo and taken pleasure in the view from near the top. But it is also important to understand that there was a time when hiking through the woods to experience nature or scaling a peak to get an exciting, new perspective was not seen as desirable. For the most part, the idea of nature as something to be enjoyed and appreciated is a modern one, not common until the early Renaissance; until then, nature was often associated with sin and demons. When Petrarch embarked on the ascent

A shrine on the trail.

View from below the summit of Monte Cavo.

of Mount Ventoux, near Avignon, a herdsman urged him to turn back or risk all sorts of trouble and bad fortune. He persisted, and so did Aeneas Sylvius—Pope Pius II (1405–64)—described by historian Jacob Burckhardt as the first man to "enjoy the magnificence of the Italian landscape." Indeed, he climbed Monte Cavo, just as you have, and stood in rapture before much of the same panorama that meets your eyes, though centuries later.

CELL TOWER HEAVEN OR HELL

You now meet the asphalt road. Keep on the path and enter the *Zona Militare* (Military Zone). No photos are allowed. You can walk around, through a forest not of trees but of cell phone towers and satellite dishes. We can skip Dianne's lecture on the military and what it has done to a once sacred place; you could make it up yourself (perhaps have the kids count the cell towers to compare to other "sights"). What looks like a tunnel under the military installation has been blocked. You can go up to the piazza at the top of the mountain, but we're sorry to say, this is it. No trace of Jupiter or sacred ruins; just a blizzard of cell towers and the remains of a hotel and restaurant. There are no paths down the other side. Looking through the scaffold-covered hotel you can see a couple letters on a metal arch—the . . . IS . . . OR, what remains of "Ristorante." Even walking slowly, it should have taken you less than an hour to reach this point.

GETTING BACK

From here you can return to the sanctuary and, if you're adventurous, take the dirt path into Rocca di Papa (about twenty minutes) and catch a bus

THE PARTISANS OF THE *COLLI ALBANI* (ALBAN HILLS)

The partisans (*partigiani*) were active through-out Italy during World War II, fighting against the Fascist regime and its sympathizers and especially against the Germans who occupied the country in September 1943. In the province of Lazio an estimated ten thousand partisans were active combatants, and of those, more than twelve hundred were killed in the struggle.

There was considerable partisan activity in the Colli Albani, with small but active squads in and around the towns of Albano, Ariccia, Genzano, and Lanuvio (all more or less in a row to the southwest of the lakes Albano and Nemi) as well as in Frascati (one of the itineraries), Colleferro, and Marino. Other towns, including Castel S. Pietro in the Casilina valley, Zagarolo, and Palestrina, had weak partisan groups or none at all. Most of the partisans were Italians, but a contingent of about twenty Russians, escaped prisoners who had been part of a partisan band in Monterotondo, were active—and very aggressive—in the Colli Albani.

Although the area of the *Castelli* (castles, another term for Alban Hills) was never a battlefront in the sense of Cassino to the southeast, it was heavily fortified by the Germans—the strategic ridge above Velletri, in particular—because of its defensive possibilities in the event of a breakthrough at Cassino or Anzio, the nearby port where the Allies landed on January 22, 1944.

Pino Levi Cavaglioni, who was in charge of partisan activity in the Colli Albani for a crucial six-month period, offers a glimpse of the day-to-day life of the partisans in his wartime diary *Guerriglia nei Castelli Romani,* first published in 1971 and reprinted 2006 (in Italian). Born in 1911 and raised in Genoa, Cavaglioni was arrested and jailed in 1938 for his association with the Republican army during the Spanish Civil War and released in 1943. Two months later, when the Germans occupied the peninsula, he left his Jewish parents and his brother in Genoa and took the train for Rome. By early October he had been assigned to command a partisan unit near Genzano. Following a report, which proved to be accurate, that the Jews of Rome had been rounded up and sent away, and worried about his mother and father, he wrote, "When will I be able to begin killing some of these brutes?" He didn't have to wait long. On October 26 he wrote, "Tonight I killed my first German and so I possess a magnificent P.38 revolver and a superb pair of waterproof boots. . . . I had never in my life shot at a living thing, because I don't like hunting and I imagine that it would be difficult to kill a man. But are the Germans men?" (He employed the exact phrase the Germans used to refer to Jews.)

As Cavaglioni's account reveals, the partisans were not regularly or well supplied by the Allies. Most of their weapons were taken from dead Germans; explosives came from Rome, where the CLN (*Comitato di Liberazione Nazionale* [Committee for National Liberation]) attempted to structure the activities of the Colli Albani partisans. The most common partisan act, in which all the squads (usually two to five men) engaged, was to spread quantities of four-point *chiodi* (nails) on a road, wait for German vehicles (apparently the only ones using the roads) to hit the nails and grind to a stop or crash, and then ambush the occupants. Sometimes these acts were coordinated with the British air force), which would strafe and bomb the wounded vehicles. Nails were used frequently on via Appia, via Ardeatina, via Nettunense, via Casilina, and via Tuscolana. Cavaglioni reports that the Germans became enraged by these forays. When a Lanuvio farmer was caught with one of the four-pointed nails, he was brutally tortured—his fingernails and toenails and his teeth were torn out—to find the source of the nails, and then the farmer was shot.

The most important action taken by the Colli Albani partisans was undoubtedly the December 1943 destruction of the Ponte delle Sette Luci bridge on the Rome-Formia railroad line. It was accomplished by a squad of four (including Cavaglioni) during a pouring rain that turned the paths and hillsides into mud slides, an atmosphere captured in the 1961 film *Un Giorno da Leoni* (*A Day of Lions*). A troop train crossing the bridge came down with it, killing as many as four hundred German soldiers. Afterward, Cavaglioni wrote: "No, damned Germans, this time the blow doesn't come from the sky, nor from the English aviators. It comes from us! From us who in this moment feel proud of being Italian and partisans and would not change our wet and muddy tattered clothes for any uniform. And we hate you, we hate you to death."

Although the Germans were usually the object of Cavaglioni's anger, the senseless bombing of Albano, which killed hundreds of civilians, made him and many other Italians furious at what he calls the "anglo-americans."

After the war, Cavaglioni practiced law in Genoa. In a 1971 introduction to the first published edition of his diary, he writes that the conduct of the German soldiers brought him and others to hate their adversaries to a degree that, years later, he found nearly unthinkable: "Cruelty was everywhere inside us in those years. It enveloped everything and everyone."

You can imagine the partisan activity in the itineraries in and around Frascati and Monte Cavo. For more on the partisans, see the *Casa della Memoria e della Storia* (House of Memory and History), p. 206. The via Tasso museum in the German SS torture prison on the street of the same name has information (some in English) on partisan activity. See p. 87.

back to Rome (via the town of Frascati [start of the next itinerary]) from there. Or simply retrace your steps to Bar la Baita, enjoying again the Roman road, the views, and the flora—the maple trees, broom, and wildflowers in season, for which the *Colli Albani* are known. Congratulate yourselves on your own triumphal march.

ITINERARY 13: TUSCOLO FROM FRASCATI

This itinerary begins in the charming hill town of Frascati, with its magnificent view of Rome, and winds upward in the Alban Hills past enormous villas and through the countryside to the ruins of Tuscolo (in Latin, Tusculum), at one time a major Etruscan city, about one thousand feet above the town. The ascent is gradual and can be accomplished in sneakers. For the descent, we offer two options: retracing one's steps or, for those more adventurous, a much-less-traveled route. Neither descent route requires hiking boots. If you don't spend time at Villa Aldobrandini, it will take about ninety minutes to get to Tuscolo and an hour or less to come down.

HOW TO GET THERE, WHEN TO GO, WHAT TO TAKE

It's easy and economical to take the train to Frascati. You'll have a walk up steps from the station to Piazza Marconi, where the itinerary starts. Alternatively, you can take the Metro A to the Anagnina stop, and take the bus to Frascati (Piazza Marconi stop). Both these alternatives are described more fully above in the opening sections of "General Advice on Getting to (and From) the Hills." Some of the buses to Frascati keep going through the town and up to Villa Tuscolana and close to Tuscolo. For those who don't want to walk much, these buses are an option.

We recommend this trip in pleasant weather, during daylight hours. Take a standard guidebook with information on Tuscolo and Villa Aldobrandini. You're never far from water and food, but we recommend taking a small bottle of water per person. The picnic lunch part is up to you.

For many years, Frascati was best known, to Americans, anyway, as the source of bad white wine. It may still be that, but today the area's best wines, marketed as Frascati "riserva," are as tasty and enjoyable as a good pinot grigio or sauvignon blanc.

BEGINNING WITH A SPLENDID VILLA

The tour begins on the great balcony in Piazza Marconi overlooking the Roman plain. With your back to Rome, the view is dominated by the splendid front gardens of Villa Aldobrandini. The exterior of the villa is in disrepair, but it remains an exceptional site, especially for the complex series of fountains in the rear, extending up the hill. If you think you may be interested in visiting the grounds of the villa now or later in the day (Dianne says they are not to be missed), you will (or may—sometimes you can just walk in) need tickets, which are free and available only in town, not at the villa. To obtain tickets and other tourist information, cross Piazza Marconi on its left side (as you face away from the views of the Roman plain) to the tourist office. Dianne also recommends a stop at the Scuderie, the seventeenth-century stables of Villa Aldobrandini (the stables are sometimes referred to as *Frascatino*—little Frascati), which have

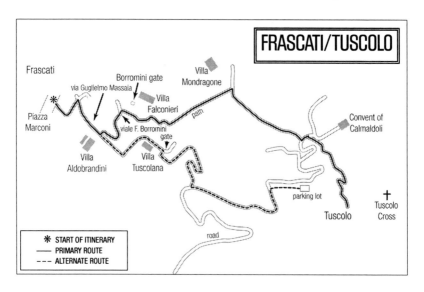

The evocative decadence of Villa Aldobrandini. Be sure to go around back.

been creatively restructured by one of Italy's renowned modern architects, Massimiliano Fuksas, into a museum with exhibition space and artifacts from the digs at Tuscolo.

Exiting the tourist office (for either Villa Aldobrandini or the hike to Tuscolo), go left up the hill and around the curve, using the steps to avoid the traffic. About two hundred yards after the curve, take via Guglielmo Massaia up to the right, following the signs for the Guardia di Finanza. Up the hill at the right at No. 18 is the entrance to Villa Aldobrandini. If you're headed to Tuscolo, go sharply left here and downhill for a few hundred yards to viale Francesco Borromini, where there are signs for a CAI path and red and white trail markers.

A GATE DEBATE

Only fifty yards ahead on the trail/road is the enormous baroque entrance to the Villa Falconieri gardens, now closed but splendid in its decadence, with a grand tree growing through it. The villa was built in the mid-1500s and enlarged in the seventeenth century by Francesco Borromini

Borromini's gate (Dianne says)
at Villa Falconieri.

(1599–1667), the great architect of Rome and Bernini rival. Farther uphill, the road ends at a second entrance, to the villa itself. One or both of these entrances is by Borromini. The *Blue Guide* says Borromini's gate has a tree growing through it. The gate to the gardens has a marble plaque with the date 1729—so either the marble plaque was done later, or Borromini's is (only) the second gate. We'll let the Borromini expert in you decide which. (Dianne thinks the first one has to be Borromini's; Bill just knows he likes that first one with the tree through it; a friend, a Borromini expert, throws up his hands.)

Follow the path uphill to the left (the green gate) as it skirts the walls of Villa Mondragone, now a Jesuit seminary, before opening onto a small piazza with a worthy arch in the romantic Gregoriana style, our way of referring to the nineteenth-century, romantic landscape of Tivoli's Villa Gregoriana (see p. 177). An earlier Gregory, Pope Gregory XIII (1572–85), had an apartment reserved for him at this villa. On the cypress-lined road leading to this villa (from another direction), Pope Gregory issued his 1582 bull reforming the calendar, giving us the "Gregorian" calendar, with its months of thirty and thirty-one days (twenty-eight or twenty-nine for February) and dating from the year of Christ's birth—the most widely used calendar in the world. These villas are not open to the public except a few times each year (we encourage you to look for those and leap at the opportunity). Getting glimpses of them as you walk along this path is satisfying in itself and gives you a sense of the great collection of sixteenth-century villas of the superrich (or superconnected to the popes or, usually, both) that once dotted these "Tuscolo hills." Several of them were damaged beyond repair during World War II, when Frascati served as Colli Albani headquarters for the German army. Others were allowed to go to ruin. Modern restorations have salvaged others.

MEDIEVAL HERMITAGE ALONG THE WAY

In a few minutes, you'll reach a crossroads of sorts, a rural piazza. One road goes left and down. Follow the signs for Tuscolo (right and up, basically) and continue on the path until it joins a larger road. Follow that road left for about fifty yards, cross the street, and take the first dirt path–road curving up at the right. In just a few minutes you'll be at a sort of intersection. The trail to Tuscolo is to the right. To the left, up the hill, is the Convent of Camaldoli, a hermitage dating from 1611 to which you may wish to make a brief side trip (no tourist visits, but they sell honey 8:30–11:30 a.m. and 3–5 p.m.—the sign says to ring the bell strongly, then wait a few minutes before ringing it again).

After about twenty minutes, as the wall appears on your left, turn back right up the dirt road. You'll emerge in a few minutes in Tuscolo, just above the ancient amphitheater. The mountain ahead with all the antennas is Monte Cavo (see Itinerary 12, p. 155), and below it, the town of Rocca di Papa. Farther to the right, above Lake Albano, is the unmistakable outline of Castel Gandolfo, the pope's summer residence.

AND FINALLY, THE ROMANS (AND OTHERS) IN TUSCOLO

Tuscolo is the ancient city of Tusculum. Legend says it was founded by a son of Ulysses and Circes. What seems to be certain is that it was inhabited by prehistoric people (as early as the end of the Bronze Age, tenth century BC), then by the Etruscans, then by Romans,

This must be the way.

then, in the Middle Ages, by the counts of Tuscolo. There are various versions of history that put Cicero's villa here and list Tuscolo as the birthplace of Cato the Censor. Archaeological remains are hard to decipher, but there are parts of an amphitheater, a forum, a cistern, and walls. Poke around up here. To your left, up the hill, is a very large cross made of steel pipes (at 670 meters, about 2,000 feet above sea level). Also here are some remains of the original citadel. To your right, not far down the hill, is a well-placed refreshment stand in the parking lot.

HEADING DOWN FROM THE MOUNT

When you're ready to go, locate the amphitheater to find the same path down and retrace your steps. For the more adventurous, we advise reading ahead to see if an alternate route is to your liking.

This alternate route is clearly not official and takes you onto property not officially open to the public. Holes in fences that were there when last we were there may not be there now. You're never really far away from civilization, and if you get lost, you always can ask for help. We've tried to streamline this and left out a few of our false starts. So if adventure appeals to you, read on.

This route down begins from the left side of the parking lot next to the refreshment stand, where you'll take the path out—a small, lovely Roman road that parallels the asphalt road. Follow this path until it ends at the regular road below. Take this road downhill until the road takes a ninety-degree curve to the left (followed, about two hundred yards farther on by another curve to the left). Just *before* the first of these left turns is a locked gate and, inside, a "road" covered with grass and weeds. To the left of the gate is an opening in the green wire. Go through, take the weedy "road" for about seventy-five yards, then go left, *downhill* (the road also goes uphill to the right), along a series of traverses through a cool, graceful forest of very large trees. You'll pass a cement waterworks on your left (explore it briefly), then, just beyond, a locked gate with a bar removed to facilitate your exit (if the gate is whole, look to the right and left for another opening; we've always found openings in fences; Italians are resourceful).

MORE SIXTEENTH-CENTURY VILLAS

(This villa and the lovely lane from it is on the alternate route, but you also can get here straight up from Villa Aldobrandini or by taking a Frascati bus up this way.) After exiting the gate, take the road, left, downhill. A few hundreds yards below is the arched entrance to the Hotel Tuscolana and the Centro Congressi. This is the beautiful sixteenth-century Villa Rufinella or Villa Tuscolana (you'll see both names on maps, the latter on the bus routes). Take the tree-lined lane up and around the corner and past the hotel on the left, where you can get a drink at the charming small fountain with objects embedded in it. The villa was damaged by World War II bombing and has been restored. It has had famous owners, including Bonaparte descendants, Victor Emmanuel II, and many others. As you move around the front of the hotel, note also the large fountain in Gregoriana-grotto-romantic style. Continue out the entrance to the hotel and down the road to Villa Aldobrandini, now on your left, where you turned off for Tuscolo earlier in the day.

RETURN TO FRASCATI

Back in Frascati, for a casual snack, we suggest the Bar dei Glicini, *a due passi* (very near) the tourist office and on the same side of the piazza, where two beers, a *tramezzino* (sandwich with the crusts cut off), and a panino (Italian sandwich) cost us €15, including a charge for table service. An alternative is to head up into the older part of Frascati to a *fraschetta,* a type of trattoria where you can drink Castelli wine, eat your own food (deli food you've purchased, especially *porchetta,* the famous Castelli roasted and seasoned pork, usually advertised as being from the Castelli town of Ariccia). Today most *fraschette* serve their own food also.

GETTING BACK

Return to Rome via train or bus, as described above in "General Advice on Getting to (and From) the Hills." Or stay overnight and try Monte Cavo tomorrow.

ITINERARY 14: WALKING AND CLIMBING AMID THE WATERS OF TIVOLI

This itinerary could have been included in chapter 1, "The Waters of Rome," for the pleasures and delights of Tivoli—Villa d'Este, Villa Gregoriana, and the spectacle of the rambunctious Aniene River—are deeply associated with water and have been for millennia. We invite you to walk through the villas and then make a stirring climb above the city to Monte Catillo and beyond, with the city of Tivoli and its river, now tamed, laid out below. Because the main attractions—the two villas and access to Monte Catillo—are not far apart, this is an efficient itinerary too. (Once you're in Tivoli, you can do everything in about three hours.) You can add more walks in and about Tivoli, a trip to Villa Adriana below Tivoli, baths at the town of Bagni di Tivoli, even closer to Rome than Villa Adriana—and make a full day or two of the trip. If you have time (or the inclination) to visit only one of the villas, we (no doubt contrary to most guides) recommend Gregoriana.

HOW TO GET THERE
Follow the routes in "General Advice on Getting to (and From) the Hills," see p. 154. If you want to stop in Villa Adriana or Bagni di Tivoli, be sure to take the bus rather than the train. The bus will drop you in the center of Tivoli (be sure to go all the way uphill to the main square). The train station is south and east of the center of town. A ten- to fifteen-minute walk will take you to the town center. Or you can go straight to Villa Gregoriana from the train station, as we describe below.

WHEN TO GO, WHAT TO TAKE
Any nice day except Monday, when both villas are closed. Note also Villa Gregoriana is closed in winter. You may want to bring a guidebook that describes the two villas, although each has informative panels in both Italian and English. Because Villa Gregoriana was reopened only in 2005, after years of decay, trashing, and then restoration (for example, the removal of five tons of garbage, including washing machines and vehicles), it does not appear in many guidebooks. (We have FAI, *Fondo per l'Ambiente*

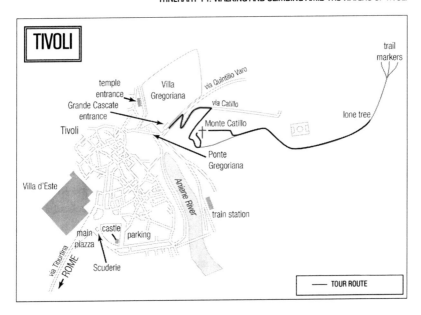

Italiano—the Fund for the Italian Environment, to thank for the restoration work.)

For the Monte Catillo excursion, you will want to take a small bottle of water per person, sunscreen, and a cap. Parts of the hike are quite rocky and a bit steep; for comfort and protection against turned ankles, we recommend some sort of boot, although there is nothing that can't be accomplished in sturdy sneakers. A map is available, but where to get it is an issue. It's published by the Provincia di Roma and may be available in Tivoli's tourist office—"Riserva Naturale Monte Catillo/Carta Escursionistica"—with a nice picture of a cow (you'll be walking through pastures) on the front.

The hours for Villa Gregoriana generally are 10 a.m. to 2:30 p.m. (March and mid-October through November) and to 6:30 p.m. (April through mid-October). It's closed from December through February. You'll need to enter at least one hour before closing time. Admission is €4. Villa d'Este is open from 8:30 a.m. until an hour before sunset all year, except nonholiday Mondays, the day after a Monday holiday, January 1,

May 1, and December 25. Admission is €9 from mid-June through mid-November.

A BRIEF DESCRIPTION OF TIVOLI, BEFORE YOU START

Tivoli, and the road that leads to it, via Tiburtina, take their names from the Tevere, or Tiber River. At first this may seem odd, because the river that flows from the mountains above and through Tivoli is not the Tiber, per se, but the Aniene. The Aniene pours into the Tevere just inside (but for most of its history, outside) Rome (see chapter 4, Itinerary 10, p. 137, which takes you on the banks of the Aniene in Rome). So the Aniene was considered a tributary of the Tiber, therefore a Tiber or Tevere river, and is so marked on some old maps. Tivoli was called Tibur in Roman times. It was home to prehistoric peoples, dates from before the Romans, saw the building of many villas of Roman greats, including Cassius and Trajan (and Hadrian, that is, Villa Adriana—about three miles below the city itself—worth a stop for sure, Dianne says), with monuments or remains of monuments to the Roman gods. You'll see more ruins and waterworks as well, especially from Ponte Gregoriano and Villa Gregoriana. Tivoli also has been famous for its healing waters, sulfur springs especially. You can try these baths at the town appropriately called *Bagni di Tivoli* (Baths of Tivoli) about five miles before Tivoli, on the road from Rome, and if you pass by on this road, you'll even smell the sulfur of the baths. Tivoli was severely damaged during World War II but shows little of that destruction now. It is home to one of the largest Romanian communities in Italy and is full of residents, rather than simply tourists, much of the time. A delightful place, Dianne says, to stop and have a snack or lunch or just wander.

VILLA D'ESTE, VILLA GREGORIANA

In Tivoli's main piazza, get a map of the city at the information kiosk or at the nearby Scuderie Estensi (seventeenth century), now a center for local tourism. If you don't have it yet, and they have a map of Monte Catillo and its environs, pick that up too—although it's not essential.

We leave you to find first Villa d'Este and then Villa Gregoriana (just across the river) on your own, using the city map or ours. You may want to change the order if you're pressed by the limited admission hours of Villa Gregoriana or if you come in on the train. From the train station, proceed straight north, keeping the river on your left, and you'll come to the Grande Cascata entrance to Villa Gregoriana after about five minutes. This is also the route to Monte Catillo, described below. Be sure to see the fountains on the right side of Villa d'Este as well as the "Rome" fountain on the upper left, and don't miss the bottom of Villa Gregoriana. There also are Web sites for the villas; for d'Este—www.villadeste-tivoli.info (be sure to use the .info—other suffixes won't get you there) in both English and Italian; on Villa Gregoriana, only in Italian (www.villagregoriana.it).

TWO VILLAS, VIEWED BRIEFLY

Villa d'Este was constructed in 1550 by a cardinal (son of the reputedly infamous Lucretia Borgia) of the d'Este family. The actual planning of the gardens and fountains was done by Pirro Ligorio, a man of enormous energy and undeniable genius, who wrote on this hillside what H. V. Morton rightly calls an "essay in perfection." Fountains were added over the years, using famous architects (even Bernini), in an effort to continually outdo the past.

Villa Gregoriana was built in part as a result of the devastating flood of 1826. The papacy asked for plans to prevent future flooding of Tivoli. More than twenty designs were considered. An innovative design by Clemente Folchi was selected by Pope Gregory XVI (1831–46) that called for building a double tunnel under Monte Catillo. When in 1832 he issued the order for the work to reroute the Aniene, the pope also called for the building of the public gardens, Villa Gregoriana; work was completed by 1835.

A TALE OF TWO VILLAS

We won't go further in competing with the panels and guidebooks here; instead we offer a few ways of thinking about and understanding these villas.

JOINING AN ITALIAN HIKING GROUP

Another way to get away outside Rome is to join a local hiking group. Several of these operate from Rome and offer hikes at different levels of difficulty. We have gone with these groups, from a day to overnight stays, including a one-day trip to (and around and up) Vesuvius, near Naples. The groups range from large (fifty people) to small (seven people), and from beginning hikers (sneakers and no muscle) to advanced ones.

Most of the groups have Web sites in Italian, and many of the hikes are listed each week in *Roma C'è*. Compared to our hiking companions in upstate New York and the northwestern Cascades, we view Roman hikers as slow, cautious, and hiking to eat (perhaps another meaning of the "slow food" movement) rather than for the views or mountaintops. That said, we've enjoyed all our treks with the groups, especially once we understood their pace and goals. And for those of you who aren't *in gamba* (in shape) but appreciate the outdoors, this is an opportunity to join a slow-paced group.

The mountains around Rome range from the hills of the Etruscan centers (Monti della Tolfa around Cerveteri) to peaks up to ten thuosand feet—the Gran Sasso, the tallest mountains in Italy outside the Alps. The Abruzzi, which straddle the border between the provinces of Lazio (Rome's province) and the Abruzzo, are rugged, stunning mountains. Often the treks include archaeological sites, like the ones near Cerveteri in the Province of Lazio, only thirty miles from Rome. Monte Gennaro is the closest real mountain (about four thousand feet high) near Rome. It's a great hike, through an enormous pasture, up to a peak with stunning views of the Roman plain. If you see it on a list, go for it, Bill says.

Don't expect to hear much English, but there are usually a few people in each group who will help you out with some English. This is an enjoyable way to meet some Italians and see some of rural and rustic Italy.

Here are a few suggestions for joining a group. Check out the *Verdenatura* (green nature) section of *Roma C'è*, under that the *Escursioni* (excursions) listings. There you'll find the basic information on five to fifteen hikes, usually on Sundays. This information includes the place, the date, the way to make a reservation (always required), the cost, and the level of difficulty. Often the level of difficulty is expressed in the net altitude (in meters) the group plans to do. For example, "disl. 400mt" means the net altitude (*dislivello*) the group plans to do is 400 meters, or about 1,300 feet. Generally below 500 meters is considered easy, 500–800 medium, and over 800 difficult.

Groups we recommend from experience are Associazione Cammina Natura (www .geocities.com/camminanatura), Altair, and Altrimonti. Cammina Natura's site has an English component. Once you click on English, click on Departures and Meeting Points; e-mail information is there too.

Altair tends to have the widest range and number of programs. Its Web site is www.associazionealtair.it. Click on *Programma* for the dates and hikes, and click on the hike for more details about it. E-mail Altair at info@associazionealtair.it.

With an Italian hiking group at Monti della Laga.

Altrimonti, while small, offers more expert-level hikes. Its Web site is www .altrimonti.it; click on *escursioni*. To e-mail Altrimonti, use altrimonti@tin.it.

If you send an e-mail to any of these groups in English, you'll get a response in English you can understand. That's the best way to get information and make your reservation.

Once you make your reservation, you'll be told the meeting time and place (many start from Piazza Bologna, which has a Metro stop—look for all the buses in front of the post office there on Sundays). Always bring your own lunch and water. Wear sturdy walking or hiking shoes. When you make your reservation, let them know you will need transportation from the meeting place to the start of the hike and back. Transportation costs will be shared. Transportation may be in a large bus (*pullman*), small van (*pulmino*), or private car. The Italian names derived from George Pullman, the American inventor of the railroad sleeping car. You will need to bring enough cash for this shared cost, for the group's annual membership (usually around €10), and for the hike itself (a range, depending on the length, place, etc., but average about €11).

As the Italians say, *buon trekking!*

The sixteenth-century formality of Villa d'Este.

Both depend on the manipulation and movement of enormous quantities of water: Villa d'Este was made possible by a two-hundred-yard tunnel, constructed in 1561, that carried water from the Aniene, and Villa Gregoriana became a park only in the 1830s, when a major diversion of water through Monte Catillo, and the controlled flow through the villa that it made possible, allowed the grotto to become a place visitors could enjoy without risking their lives. One great difference between the villas is that d'Este was a private venture by a wealthy family, who used their influence to expropriate the existing farms and gardens on which the villa was built, while Gregoriana was a public project, created—like New York's Central Park, which was designed only two decades later—to provide citizens with a park environment (see "What's in a *Villa* or *Via* [the Name]?" p. 121).

Whether private or public, the experiences offered by the villas are vastly different. Villa d'Este is all about control, order, precision, repetition, and technology; one gets the sense here of human beings making water do tricks, of water engineers engaged in modern, scientific acts of manipulation, of nature bent to human will, to the logic of science. In contrast, Villa Gregoriana is about an apparent lack of control, about the power of water to erode and carve, about singularity rather than repetition, about a ferocious nature barely restrained. Villa d'Este offers a lesson on the mind, a discourse on reason; Villa Gregoriana provides instruction on the body, on the spirit. Villa d'Este is about humanity's burgeoning self-confidence; Villa Gregoriana speaks to humanity's anxieties and fears, the nightmare of being washed away, down a dark hole. Originally designed to be entered from below, Villa d'Este brings its visitors up, always accompanied by that spectacular view of the Roman plain; Villa Gregoriana offers the eye no such respite, no relief from the downward spiral that threatens to engulf us. Villa Gregoriana confronts our fears and quiets them (one of the slogans it employs is *natura domata* or nature tamed), begs us to sit on a bench and come to terms with nature, to feel, to emote; Villa d'Este pretends that we are fearless, that emotions are to be held in abeyance. In short, Villa d'Este is the ultimate expression of the mind of the early Renaissance, reveling in the conquest of nature by the natural sciences, in the ordering of nature by engineering and mathematics, embracing nature after having exorcised its demons; Villa Gregoriana speaks to the values of nineteenth-century Romanticism, turning away from the materialism and utilitarianism of the new industrial society—and away from the order and intellectuality of Villa d'Este—while privileging instinct, spontaneity, freedom, imagination, the awesome sublime, welcoming the demons because they make us *feel* (Bill says).

The nineteenth-century Romanticism of Villa Gregoriana.

UP MONTE CATILLO

You may have entered and exited Villa Gregoriana next to the Temple of Sibyl (second century BC) (the *Sibilla* side or temple entrance-exit). If so, return or go to the farther entrance (the *Grande Cascata* or Great Cascade—that is, the waterfall—entrance, on the same side of the river as the train station). To reach this entrance, you'll cross Ponte Gregoriano (named for Pope Gregory, of course), inaugurated as part of his grand project in 1835, destroyed by the retreating Germans in World War II, and rebuilt since with some water flowing under it to form more waterfalls in Villa Gregoriana. From the Grande Cascata entrance-exit to Villa Gregoriana, turn left and proceed about 150 yards uphill on via Quintilio Varo to the arch (on your left) denoting the edge of town, turn off the main drag directly right there, up the hill on via Catillo. After about 100 feet the road turns sharply left and uphill (follow the red and yellow CAI trail markers for *sentiero* Don Nello Del Raso), the beginning of an unpleasant but short asphalt section. In five minutes the path leaves the road and goes up right onto the hill.

REACHING THE CROSS

About fifteen minutes after leaving the road and arch below, you'll see an informal trail diverge left and back, around the front of Monte Catillo. You can take that path to the top; it's rocky and has some moderately steep sections, but it is also short and manageable. You'll find a big metal cross up there, overlooking the city. You're about 380 feet above the arch here, and about 650 feet above the floor of Villa Gregoriana.

The main path offers indirect but easier access to the top. It continues around the mountain, with views of the Aniene and the city below. Here you can see and feel how much of the flow of the Aniene was diverted through the mountain, with some of the water reserved for the falls inside Villa Gregoriana. Follow the path as it goes past a large gully on your left, then up a series of switchbacks (all in about five minutes). When the main path approaches the height of the landmass to your left, strike off up the slope to the saddle between Monte Catillo (now on your left) and a green pole–athletic complex (on your right as you go up to the saddle). Once on

the saddle, work your way back left, up to the cross, if you'v
easier route to it.

WALKING THROUGH PASTURES

Descending from the cross and directly in back of it (whiche
chosen to get to it), strike out in the direction of the athletic
big green pole. About 200 feet *before* you arrive at the greer
goes off right, through a break in the bushes and around th
plex. Except for the right turn through the brush, the trail
here and in the open, mostly with large swaths of the yell
rocks in the ground. After about twenty-five minutes and
tional elevation from the cross, you'll arrive at a relatively
gins with a large isolated tree—a good place for a picnic.

In addition to the flora and fauna you'll notice, you
signs of everything from old farm and pasture structure
traces of carbon burning and limestone quarrying an
lime—all occupations in this part of the Monti Tiburtin
Catillo is a part.

If you want to go on from here, continue through
about two hundred yards to a panel, "Riserva Naturale
A trail marker and arrow show the "correct" path (amo
roads here). Continue on the marked trail as long as y
your steps (around Monte Catillo to its left, rather th
the road and back into town. If you stopped at the "pic
descent to the road should take about twenty-five min

GETTING BACK

Once you've returned to Tivoli, you can take the train
train station on the east side of the river, or you ca
town and catch a bus back.

6

AFTER SIX

Culture

THERE WAS a time, and not so long ago, when Rome went to bed early. When a fast drive up the Tevere or an illicit dip in the Trevi Fountain, à la Anita Ekberg, seemed the only late-night entertainments in town. Today, that's no longer true. Entertainment districts in San Lorenzo, Testaccio, Trastevere, and the Centro (Campo dei Fiori) bustle with activity (and irritate the residents) until the wee hours of the morning, catering mostly to the young and the restless. More important for our purposes (and yours, we think), Rome has become a cultural center, a hotspot for art, theater, dance, film, music, photography, design, and architecture, attracting talent from around the world while nurturing its own, often presenting its cultural offerings with unsurpassed flair and generosity. Although we've put many of the suggestions for eating and drinking in chapter 7 (After 8— Food and Drink), you can't go far in Rome's cultural world without finding yourself with a glass of prosecco in one hand, an hor d'oeuvres in the other, and a smile on your face. There's always plenty to do after 6 p.m. in Rome.

In this chapter, we explain how to find and get to Rome's cultural venues. We've included all kinds of events and experiences, from big, public, in-your-face to tiny, offbeat, cheap, or (best of all, Bill says) free. We group the offerings into seven areas: Contemporary Art (galleries) with Extras (openings), *Vernissage* (Gallery Opening with Extras), International Academies,

Centri Sociali (Social Centers), Bookstore Entertainment, Cinema, Jazz (with a feint to other music), and *Case* (Houses of Culture).

Let's start with a story: "Not much going on today," Bill lamented over Saturday morning coffee. "Except, maybe, this," he added, pointing to *La Repubblica*'s "Giorno e Notte" page. Translated, the brief notice read: "50 Years of Art, at Villa Iris (via Appia Antica, 107), from 3–8 p.m., opening of the show of paintings of Eugenio Sgaravatti." There was mention of an "artistic picnic to the rhythm of jazz." We arrived at 4 p.m., parked the scooter under a tree, and moments later found ourselves warmly welcomed by a handsome gray-haired man in a blue sport coat—Eugenio—who pointed the way through the woods, past his hanging watercolors (some with a Sudoku theme) and a huge serpent of metal and cloth, on which two children were playing. We were ready for ten minutes of art, a polite "grazie," and then an exit when we came over a rise to find (thank you, Bobby Darin) "a party goin' on": dozens of Italians (more arriving every minute), mounds of fava beans to open and eat with chunks of pecorino from huge rounds (the combination is a classic Roman appetizer), slices of freshly cut prosciutto, red and white wines (served in glassware), and a gelato cart. Just beyond was a large tent with more of Eugenio's art works, his collection of carved elephants, and, as promised, a jazz group (talented and sophisticated—renditions of the standards, including "Caravan"). Outside and around the artist's home, lanes, and trees, with more art to come upon, we wandered with glasses in hand, full of pleasure, astonished at Eugenio Sgaravatti's generosity in hosting this grand party—to which everyone in Rome had been invited.

CONTEMPORARY ART (WITH EXTRAS)

Gallery hopping, often complete with food and drink, is a ritual for many Romans, and we recommend you join them. The contemporary art scene has grown significantly in the last decade, with new high-end and alternative galleries opening in the city. The *New York Times* recently acknowledged Rome's emergence onto the international contemporary art scene. Below you'll find descriptions of the three major public contemporary art galleries and the concentrated areas of private galleries, accompanied by our suggestions. We explain how to find the current exhibits and specific gallery information, and, last but not least, how to hit the fun-filled openings.

PUBLIC CONTEMPORARY ART GALLERIES

MACRO. The City of Rome's most established contemporary gallery is MACRO (*Museo d'Arte Contemporanea Roma,* hence the acronym). It's two blocks outside the city walls, near Porta Pia. Not a large gallery, MACRO features one or two focused shows of well-known international artists; we've never been disappointed. MACRO is in the process of expanding, but it still won't be a huge gallery. It's also inexpensive: €1. There are infrequent openings and other events here. (One we enjoyed was on food art, where we came perilously close to eating one of the art works—a no-no.) Via Reggio Emilia, 54; www.macro.roma.museum (Web site in multiple languages, including English); 9 a.m.–7 p.m. Tuesday–Sunday; closed Mondays and January 1, May 1, and December 25.

MACRO FUTURE. MACRO expanded to a new site recently, taking over most of the former slaughterhouse, or *l'ex-mattatoio,* in Testaccio (a fascinating place—some of the cables, hooks, and pens are still in evidence).

Rubbery, touchable sculpture at MACRO.

Shows here are big, bold, and edgy, appealing to a younger crowd, as the hours and location attest. Piazza O. Giustiniani, 4; 4 p.m.–midnight Tuesday–Sunday; closed Mondays and January 1, May 1, and December 24, 25, and 31; see MACRO Web site; free.

MAXXI. See how the name ends in the Roman numeral XXI? This will be Italy's destination museum in Rome for even bigger and bolder contemporary (twenty-first-century) art and architecture. The key here is "will be." An enormous building by international architect Zaha Hadid is under construction. Shows in the old space, excellent pairings of Italian and foreign artists, were discontinued in 2008. Temporary exhibits are mounted in other spaces around the city from time to time. MAXXI expects to open in 2009, but add a couple years to that to be safe. In the meantime, the structure itself is worth a look. Via Guido Reni, 2f; www.maxxi.darc.beniculturali.it (also in English).

PRIVATE GALLERIES

One concentration of private galleries is in the "trident" area south of Piazza del Popolo, on via del Corso, via Margutta, and cross streets. Sometimes there are groups of exhibits or openings in this part of the city. Try **MARA COCCIA,** via del Vantaggio, 4 (tel. 06.322.4434); the *CASA DI GOETHE* (Goethe's House), via del Corso, 18 (tel. 06.3265.0412; www.casadigoethe .it, in English too), €4; or **AUGUSTO CONSORTI,** via Margutta 52/A (tel. 06.361.4053). We hate to be snobs, but via Margutta, once home to many impoverished artists' studios, is now pretty cheesy. Still, there are some decent galleries here, and you can see where the Gregory Peck character had his charming studio in *Roman Holiday* at via Margutta, 51.

A second area is around Piazza Navona and south of it. Try **IL PONTE CONTEMPORANEA,** via Monserrato, 23 (tel. 06.6880.1351) or **ROMBERG ART,** Piazza de' Ricci, 127 (www.romberg.it, click on the British flag), a fabulous new space.

In between these areas, **GALLERJA** (see below under "Vernissage") is cutting edge (www.gallerja.it, some sections in English). Don't miss the monumental modernist space of Larry **GAGOSIAN'S** new gallery in Rome near the bottom of the Spanish Steps at via Francesco Crispi, 16 (www.gagosian.com). We recommend also the highly rated **LORCAN O'NEILL** gallery between Trastevere and St. Peter's, at via Orti d'Alibert, 1E (www.lorcanoneill.com).

Hours of galleries vary. Your best bet is late afternoon or early evening, avoid Sunday and Monday. All these galleries have a *gallerista*—or gallery monitor—and usually have a closed door with a bell to ring. Ring it. We've never met a *gallerista* who wasn't either very nice or coolly professional. They often speak some English and have press releases in English. Try it a couple times and you'll be a natural; it's less intimidating than Soho or Chelsea, Dianne thinks.

HOW TO FIND OUT WHAT'S ON

The easiest way to check out the scene is to stop at a gallery and pick up the monthly one-sheet *Art/Guide*. It lists most of the private galleries and institutes and all the relevant information (hours, phone numbers, the exhibits), including listing by day all the openings/*vernissages*. *Art/Guide* is online at www.artguide.it. The Web site is only in Italian, but given the content— mostly times, dates, and places—it's easy to navigate (click on *Entra* to start). Ideally, print out the guide before you leave for Italy. Also, click on the *Vernissages* link for the day-by-day openings. Other art magazines for Rome are mostly advertising vehicles that you'll find in the galleries, many in English as well as Italian. Pick them up and start searching for what you like.

A second method is to parse the weekly *Roma C'è* (available at newsstands on Wednesdays, €1.5). Besides the woefully abbreviated English-language pages at the back ("This Week in Rome"), go to the *Arte* section. The first listings are the openings. At the end of the paragraph description, if you see in parentheses something like ("h.18.30")—that means there is a public opening and that it begins at the hour (h) of 6:30 p.m. on the date listed just before that. For example, "Dal 15 mag (h.18.30) al 7 giu" means the show runs from ("dal") May 15 ("15 mag"), beginning with an opening at 6:30 p.m. (h.18.30) to ("al") June 7 ("7 giu"). The ongoing (*in corso*) shows follow. All necessary information is listed (in Italian) in each exhibit description. Another weekly, *Trova Roma,* comes free with the Thursday edition of *La Repubblica*. It's a smaller and less helpful *Roma C'è* and has a two-page English-language section, "The Best in Rome," at the back.

VERNISSAGE (GALLERY OPENING WITH EXTRAS)

Here's a gallery and *vernissage* hopping that worked for us. To plan a Thursday evening, we spent an hour with *Roma C'è, La Repubblica*'s two-page entertainment section—"Giorno e Notte"—and a good map, making sure

A sumptuous *vernissage*.

we had gallery addresses and opening times, *vernissage* times, and ways of getting to, from, and between the locations. Jeans and black are the usual dress code.

We started with a show about to close, one we didn't want to miss. We had read about a new gallery in the Centro, **GALLERJA,** that had made its splash opening with a Jannis Kounellis installation featuring a mid-seventeenth-century painting. We weren't disappointed in this work by one of the world's most famous, even notorious contemporary artists (we watched several couples come and leave in short order, the men's faces revealing disinterest). Gallerja, at via della Lupa, 24, has friendly galleristas, who offered us press releases on the installation in Italian and English and had on hand a book of articles, some in English, on the artwork.

We combined Gallerja with an opening nearby in the expensive shopping area below the Spanish Steps. The setting for the show, billed as one of contemporary carpets (we were game), was the renovated *scuderie* (former stables) of a palazzo on via del Corso, Villa Ruspoli. We were a bit embarrassed at being underdressed this time, because the evening was sponsored by a high-end commercial venture, Kasthall Carpets. The carpets were stunning. The designer was on hand. Servers offered drinks of all kinds; canapés and snacks abounded. We were approached by a suave older Italian in matching gold suit and tie who overheard our English. He explained he was an architect, Piero Sartogo, who taught frequently in the United States. He also was the artist's husband and collaborator. We had an interesting talk about their work, he introduced us to a former ambassador, and the discussion came around to a building he had designed in the Piazza Bologna area, a medical office (Sede dell'Ordine dei Medici di

Roma), a building we had debated at length, from the awkward 1970s (see p. 120). We were offered a bag of posters and information (some in English) on the carpets. Then we played our window-shopping game: which carpet would you want in your dining room at home?

Having nourished ourselves physically, visually, and intellectually in style, we changed locations for our second focus of the evening—the Flaminio area north of Piazza del Popolo (some could walk the eight blocks or so; others might want to take Tram 2 or taxi—although taxis at 7 p.m. can mean being stalled in traffic).

We looked forward to the **HENDRIK CHRISTIAN ANDERSEN MUSEUM**/Villa Helene on via P. S. Mancini, 20 (www.museoandersen.beniculturali.it, in English too). A cavernous space with huge Andersen sculptures of nudes, the museum is "not to be missed by lovers of bad taste," writes Rome authority and Brit Georgina Masson, "but perhaps better avoided by the refined." The museum often has good temporary exhibitions. The installation of a Bill Viola video was sponsored by MAXXI, and many people (this time, dressed like us—all in black) were milling about inside and out. We're fans of Viola, perhaps the United States' most famous video artist, but we were disappointed in this 1975 work, more like waiting for Warhol than intriguing. MAXXI provided a nice brochure on Viola and this piece, all in Italian. And we chided ourselves for missing a chance to see (free) a photo exhibit on the second floor, because it closed minutes after we arrived. (April and May are the months to see Rome's well-publicized photo exhibitions—hundreds are put up and down over several weeks throughout the city.) Our timing could have been better.

Leaving Museo Andersen somewhat disappointed, we opted for a small gallery opening nearby. The outside looked improbable for a gallery site, but the imposing iron gates were open. So at dusk we stepped into an intimate courtyard full of people (looking like artists and their friends and relatives) and into a photo show, which we analyzed at length (was he trying to show emotion, or was he more interested in light and line?). On hand were a refreshing *frizzante* Roman white wine (from bottles without labels), an excellent cheese, and something like raw bacon (Dianne noted). Others were helping themselves, and we followed suit. We heard English spoken by some and could have struck up a conversation. We decided just to enjoy the ambience of this shaded courtyard with its celebrants. And then we headed home . . . sated with art and *vernissages,* even proud of ourselves for what does not always occur—being four for four: all four galleries were open as billed, there was art, there were artists, there was a talk with an architect whose work we knew, there was food and drink.

Hard work, but somebody's gotta do it.

INTERNATIONAL ACADEMIES

Institutes sponsored by foreign governments provide very good (usually free) entertainment. And if you speak the foreign language, so much the better. Music, art, lectures, film, photography, food, drink—all are available at various times. The best way to find offerings is through the Web sites listed below. You can locate most, but not all, of the events in *Roma C'è* under the appropriate category (music, art, culture [for lectures]) and some in *La Repubblica's* "Giorno e Notte" (under museums, shows, music, or special write-ups). You can access the Villa Borghese Web site in English (en.villaborghese.it—don't type "www" first—gets you the English Web site) and see a listing of the academies; clicking on one, you then can link to its Web site. We've listed phone numbers for the English-speaking academies.

AMERICAN ACADEMY IN ROME (www.aarome.org). On the Gianicolo, near Porta S. Pancrazio, the AAR offers lectures (ranging from Roman archaeology to contemporary authors, such as Frank McCourt), music performances, and art exhibits. All listed on the Web site are open to the public, in one of their two remarkable buildings (see chapter 1, which also has directions on p. 37). Bring your passport or other photo ID to enter. If you're in town, don't miss the end of season (usually May) Open Studios. Via Angelo Masina, 5, and also programs at the nearby Villa Aurelia, Largo di Porta di San Pancrazio, 1; tel. 06.58.461.

THE BRITISH SCHOOL AT ROME (www.bsr.ac.uk). Well situated near Rome's national modern art museum, GALLERIA NAZIONALE D'ARTE MODERNA (viale delle Belle Arti) north of Villa Borghese, the British School sponsors first-rate shows and openings. The clear Web site lists lectures too. Expect

Open Studios at the
American Academy.

a good beer at the open-
ings. Via Gramsci, 61; tel.
06.326.4939. (Trams 3
and 19 run to and from
Piazza Thorwaldsen in
front of the museum and
school; a half-mile uphill
walk from the Flaminio stop [exit to Villa Borghese] of Metro A.)

CENTRO STUDI AMERICANI (American Studies Center) (www.centros-
tudiamericani.org. The Web site is in Italian and English, but the English
portion is incomplete; you may need to go to the Italian side to see what's
really going on). Lectures are more often in Italian than English. Expect
English only from those speakers who are clearly American or British na-
tives. Great location, in the splendidly intricate Palazzo Mattei, whose
double interior courtyard is a veritable sculpture museum. Go up the
stairs to Centro Studi and get buzzed in—ask where the lecture hall is—
you'll wind through an intriguing series of Victorian rooms. You don't
need to be a member of Centro Studi to attend the lectures. Via Caetani,
32 (near Largo di Torre Argentina; Tram 8 from Trastevere and many
buses from other locations); tel. 06.6880.1613. On the other side of via
Caetani, a few steps toward Largo di Torre Argentina from Centro Studi
Americani, you will see a plaque to Aldo Moro, a popular centrist Italian
politician, twice prime minister, who in 1978 was kidnapped by the
ultra-leftist Red Brigades, held for fifty-five days, and left dead in the
trunk of a car at this spot. The failure of the Italian government to find
his kidnappers over the two months remains a mystery, the Italian equivalent of the Kennedy assassination. Often the plaque is marked with
wreaths and flowers.

HUNGARIAN ACADEMY IN ROME (www.magyarintezet.hu. Click on
Roma and then on English at the top; the site uses Forward to link to more

information). Situated in the elegant Palazzo Falconieri at the beginning of via Guilia in the Centro, this is an active academy. Some lectures and films may be only in Magyar; there are good art exhibits and musical performances for the non-Magyar-speaking. The sixteenth-century building and courtyard, modified by Borromini, are compelling. We've never experienced a charge here. Via Giulia, 1 (just behind Campo dei Fiori).

FRENCH ACADEMY AT VILLA MEDICI (www.villamedici.it. The Web site is in French and Italian; events usually have a fee). This magnificent sixteenth-century palazzo, with interventions by Michelangelo and extensive gardens, is near the top of the Spanish Steps, on the Pincio. The art exhibits are high quality and sometimes occupy unusual spaces, including the villa's sixth-century cistern, constructed to store rainwater should the barbarians cut the aqueducts (see p. 27). Musical performances range from jazz to classical. Via Trinità dei Monti, 1 (walk up the Spanish Steps, then left about three hundred feet).

ROYAL SPANISH ACADEMY (www.raer.it. The Web site is in Spanish and Italian). A great location, next to the Church of S. Pietro in Montorio (try to visit when you can go into the church too) and just below the gracious Acqua Paola Fountain (see p. 39). Frequent concerts and art exhibits are hosted here—and they throw a grand opening party with ample food and wine. Piazza San Pietro in Montorio, 3 (reached by walking uphill from via Garibaldi in Trastevere, or walking down from the American Academy or Porta S. Pancrazio [see p. 33 for directions]).

ROMANIAN ACADEMY (www.accadromania.it. The Web site is in Romanian and Italian). Like the British School, which it faces, the Romanian Academy is located in "Academy Valley," Valle

Before a concert at the French Academy, Villa Medici.

Giulia, near the GALLERIA NAZIONALE D'ARTE MODERNA, in a sumptuous palazzo. This academy has good art exhibits, often with a youthful flair, and infrequent concerts; sometimes wine is offered at openings. Piazza José de San Martin, 1 (same directions as to the British School).

GERMAN ACADEMY, Villa Massimo (www.villamassimo.de. The Web site is in German and Italian). The academy hosts a small art exhibit now and then (in our view, not worth making a special trip). It is worth visiting if you're in the Piazza Bologna area (see p. 114 generally and for directions), and not to be missed, if you're in town, are their Open Studios, usually in April. Largo di Villa Massimo, 1–2.

CENTRI SOCIALI (SOCIAL CENTERS)

If you'd like to discover what Rome's twentysomething, creative, avant-garde leftists are doing, there's no better way than to visit one of Rome's "social centers." Although they're not on the tourist beaten track, they are often listed on *La Repubblica*'s "Giorno e Notte" pages, usually in the upper right, as well as in *Roma C'è*. The entertainment can be spectacular, and the atmosphere—chic messy, lots of smoking, young people doing their thing, imaginative settings—for those so inclined, will be worth the visit.

RIALTO SANTAMBROGIO (www.rialtosantambrogio.org. The Web site is in Italian only.) A place for theater, dance, music, and exhibits. Centrally located but tricky to find. From via Portico d'Ottavia, one of the major streets in the Jewish ghetto, follow the narrow alley, via di S. Ambrogio, as it turns left into a small piazza. Rialto Santambrogio (founded 1999) is in the last building on the right, via S. Ambrogio, 4, before the street turns right. Feel free to walk in and look around. Upstairs one floor, the hallway wraps around an enchanting courtyard (poke your head out and have a look at the hanging vines), past art exhibits, bathrooms (should you need one), and an open performance space where we saw an evening of dance to die for (Bill says). Another theater on the first floor seats about fifty on padded risers. Despite the excellence of its offerings, Rialto Santambrogio is facing pressure from the city government that may force it to shut down or at least leave its current funky premises. The police have already closed the social space in the courtyard where the association served drinks and food, and a right-wing city government, elected in 2008, is likely to try to find a way to get rid of this troublesome bunch of cultural activists (as even the prior center-left government did with other *centri sociali*). A sign on the bulletin board reads "Vogliono Chiudere Il Rialto" (They Want to Close the Rialto) and urges readers to sign a petition. We say, get there before it closes.

FORTE PRENESTINO (www.forteprenestino.net. The Web site is in Italian only.) Forte Prenestino is both a social center and a fort. The complex was constructed in the 1880s for Italy's military, then given to the city government (the Comune di Roma) in 1977. Abandoned for a decade, the fort was "taken" on May 1, 1986 (May Day), by youthful anarchists who declared it an occupied and self-governing social center. The anarchists have since been replaced by modern-day hippies and other leftist activists and countercultural types. The fort remains an occupied space—another thorn in the side of the city's 2008-elected rightist government.

And what a space it is! Massive underground passageways provide access to a series of rooms and tunnels that house a cinema, a theater, exhibits, performance spaces for dance and music, a cycling shop, a recording studio, workshops, classes in Kung Fu, and places to eat and drink: a pub, an *enoteca*, and a *taverna* (the latter open for lunch 1:30–3:30 p.m. and dinner 8:30–11:00 p.m. [Monday and Saturday only for lunch]). Outside, two huge parade grounds host major concerts and the bigger parties. There's even a moat. Our first experience of Forte Prenestino was in April 2007, when we heard '60s U.S. radical John Sinclair (founder of the White Panthers, leader of the band MC5, notorious for having been sentenced to three years in jail for possession of two marijuana cigarettes) chant his beat poetry over the rumble of his blues band. A dream world, powerfully evocative, enchanting, and exuberant—a bit scary, even, but perfectly safe. Smoking everywhere, despite the nationwide prohibition. Check *La Repubblica*'s "Giorno e Notte" for notable events.

How to get to and from the fort, which is a ways from the center: Tram 5 from Termini (runs every eight to twelve minutes) will get you to (direction "Amendola") and from (direction "Gerani") via Federico Delpino.

When the tram stops at the Delpino stop (just as the tram turns onto via Parlatore), get off and walk about two hundred yards north (back) to the end of the street; the entrance to the fort is over a berm. For rides back after midnight (and before 5 a.m.), use the night Bus n12 from the same intersection (via Parlatore) where the tram stopped (runs every twenty minutes [beginning shortly after midnight] to sixty minutes [as it approaches 5 a.m.]). Via Federico Delpino, tel. 06.2180.7855.

BOOKSTORE ENTERTAINMENT

Bookstores in Rome are a source of usually free entertainment: talks and music, book signings, and even personal meetings with authors. They're well publicized in the newspapers and *Roma C'è,* under *Libri* (books), *Appuntamenti* (appointments), or *Cultura* (culture). Events usually take place in the early evening, about 6 p.m. To make sure you hear a talk in English, focus on native English speakers.

FELTRINELLI, in the Centro at Galleria Sordi, has a small downstairs space for these purposes. Get there early if you want a seat, especially for music. If you'd like an English-language book signed, you may have to bring it with you; don't expect the bookstore to carry English versions of the books of the author who is present. (The best sources for English-language books in the city are FELTRINELLI INTERNATIONAL on via Vittorio Emanuele Orlando near Piazza della Repubblica and THE LION BOOK-SHOP AND CAFÉ, via dei Greci, 33/36, between the Spanish Steps and via del Corso; www.thelionbookshop.com; tel. 06.3265.4007.) Feltrinelli has several bookstores in Rome, some of them well outside the Center. Be sure you know which one you're going to. (Web site, only in Italian, www.lafeltrinelli.it; click on *Eventi* at the top, *Roma,* etc.) A side note on this media megabusiness run by Carlo Feltrinelli: The literary enterprise was started in Milan by Carlo's father, Giangiacomo Feltrinelli, son of a powerful northern Italian timber magnate. Giangiacomo was a Marxist political activist who died in an accident while he may have been trying to plant a bomb. His son, whom we met one day at one of his bookstores, has written an intriguing biography of his partisan/communist/archivist/businessman father

Galleria Sordi, a Victorian treasure. The entrance to Feltrinelli's is at the left.

(*Feltrinelli: A Story of Riches, Revolution, and Violent Death*).

Galleria Sordi itself (named for the immensely popular Italian comic actor, Alberto Sordi), refurbished recently after languishing for years, is a beautiful late "Victorian" space (originally built in 1914) with many upscale shops. There's a piano bar–café in the atrium. The glitterati come here; Will Smith signed autographs here in 2008.

BIBLI, in Trastevere, is another bookstore with a host of activities, many of them musical performances in a large back room. The music ranges from jazz to chamber, with a focus on classical. Sometimes there's a charge, but you might get a CD in the bargain. Bibli has a small cafeteria. Via dei Fienaroli, 28. (Web site, only in Italian, www.bibli.it; click on *Bibli Musica* and *Bibli Cultura.*)

There are other bookstores and locations that feature authors and music. We recommend you be adventurous, bearing in mind that, as in much of Rome, a particular venture may not pan out. One day the musicians couldn't play; their union contract wasn't approved in time. Another time the pop singer was so mobbed we couldn't even see her. A third day the talk was by an American nut (in our personal opinion).

Erica Jong presents her latest book.

Basilica di Massenzio, site of Rome's annual literary festival.

But when it works, the bookstore experience is not to be missed. We've seen Erica Jong (*Fear of Flying*), talked with Richard Ford (*The Sportswriter*), listened to an intriguing interview with British mystery writer Ruth Rendell, heard drummer Roberto Gatto jam with young musicians, and more.

SUNSET OVER THE FORUM. Another singular literary event (Dianne says) is Rome's annual May–June Literary Festival in the Forum. The setting is magical: sunset over the Basilica di Massenzio, glimpses of the Coliseum. The number of English-language speakers has diminished over the years. But the combination of setting and music is enough for Dianne. She even recommends a pure Italian evening (but Bill doesn't). Although the events are free, you need tickets and must line up to get them. The ticket office is across from the Coliseum on via dei Fori Imperiali. It opens about 8 p.m. the day of the event. Some of the events "sell out"; we recommend you get there early to assure yourself entry and a decent seat. Even in the back you'll have a lot to enjoy; the large screens, video projections, and sound system are of rock-concert quality. The gates open shortly before the event, which is scheduled to begin at 9 p.m. Web site www.festivaldelleletterature.it gives the authors and dates clearly, no matter your language, and it has a limited English-language version; click on .ENG at the top right.

CINEMA

For English speakers who long for a good film, Rome has a number of "v.o." (*versione originale*/version original)—original-language offerings. We assume most people visiting Rome won't want to see the latest Hollywood hits, but if you do or if you need to give the kids a break, **METROPOLITAN,** on via Corso, two steps from Piazza del Popolo, offers popular films in their original languages, for example, English. You can check the newspapers (*La Repubblica*'s film listing looks a lot like any in the United States—it's near the back of the daily paper) for places, films, and times, and look for "v.o." **NUOVO OLIMPIA,** just off via Corso near Piazza Colonna, is almost an art house. It shows films we in the United States might consider to be independent, and they are not all English-language. So check the paper for details. You also can find a listing of original-language films in *Roma C'è* (see page 197) and at www.inromenow.com (see page 198).

There are several true cinephile film houses, including **CINEMA TREVI,** very near the Trevi Fountain (vicolo del Puttarello, 25), and **GRAUCO FILM RICERCA,** in the Pigneto area (via Perugia, 4), the latter harder to reach by mass transit but accessible by Tram 5 or 14 (see p. 218, Itinerary 15: An Evening in Pigneto.) Both of these sponsor film series—that is, films of a particular director, from a specific country, on specific topics. Likely the films will be subtitled in Italian only, although sometimes non-English-language films are subtitled in English. **PALAZZO DELLE ESPOSIZIONI** has reopened its theater space on its via Milano side (off via Nazionale) and has some foreign film offerings with some English subtitling; check the newspaper or *Roma C'è.* Grauco is a small operation with a theater seating about twenty in the basement of a building in upcoming Pigneto. When you open the door to the lobby-ticket area, it's like stepping into a Victorian living room that houses an extensive library of film books. Grauco requires an annual membership; that includes a film, and as they say, it is worth the price of admission, about €6. Trevi, in contrast, is a large updated auditorium, with modern equipment, couched in Roman ruins. It also is inexpensive at €4–6 per film. And you can get a gelato at San Crispino when the film lets out (via della Panetteria, 42).

The theater of Italy's most famous independent film director, Nanni Moretti (*Dear Diary* and *The Son's Room,* which won the Palme D'Or at Cannes), is **NUOVO SACHER,** in the Trastevere area. (Nuovo Sacher is a restored *dopolavoro*—"afterwork"—space from the Fascist era; Largo Ascianghi,

1; see p. 52.) And you might see Moretti himself, as we did twice. On Tuesdays, whatever film is showing is in its original language, not often English.

Rome also is host to several international film series, including shorts, animations, documentaries, Europe festivals, and our favorite, early June's *Cannes a Roma*—or Cannes in Rome, that brings about forty festival films to Rome immediately after the conclusion of the Cannes festival. Usually several of these are in English or with English subtitles. They show mainly in Trastevere's film houses. See Cannes before your friends at home!

CASA DEL CINEMA (see the *Case* section, p. 204) also has some subtitled foreign films.

LA DOLCE VITA

We recommend a good dose of *La Dolce Vita* to provide a glimpse of 1960 Rome (see p. 77). It shows, with English subtitles, every Sunday at 5 p.m. at an historic film club in Prati, AZZURRO SCIPIONI (via degli Scipioni, 82; take Metro A to Ottaviano and you're almost there).

HOW TO FIND FILMS IN *ROMA C'È*

The first section of *Roma C'è* is the *Cinema* section. Within it, go to the heading *Lingua Originale* (Original Language, the last section of film descriptions). Films are listed alphabetically by language first and then by title. Look for I—*Inglese* (English). The end of the thumbnail film description gives the theater and a number, for example, "Grauco Film Ricerca—76." Go to the numbered listings of theaters (at the end of the *Cinema* section) to No. 76 and you'll find the days, times, and films for Grauco. Note also in *La Repubblica*'s daily listings, both Trevi and Grauco are listed after the primary listings under *D'Essai* (basically second-run, quality films). Also see the information about www.inromenow.com on page 198.

JAZZ

Italy has a long history of support and enthusiasm for American jazz; among others, 1950s trumpeter Chet Baker played and recorded in the Bel Paese. Rome has been slower to take to jazz than Milan or Bologna, but in the last fifteen years, thanks especially to the construction of new performance centers that regularly program the music, the city has emerged as a world jazz center. The club scene, too, is vibrant, with long-established spaces and new ones. Although some of the best American jazz musicians perform in Rome—trumpeter Tom Harrell, for example, seems to stop here every spring, and McCoy Tyner and Joe Lovano played in Rome recently—most of the performers you'll see will be Italian. Among those you shouldn't miss are trumpeters (playing the *tromba*) Paolo Fresu and Enrico Rava; drummer (*batteria*) Roberto Gatto; saxophonist Stefano di Battista; pianists (*pianoforte*) Danilo Rea and Stefano Bollani; emerging guitarist Marco Bonini; and Antonello Salis, the manic, inventive Sardinian pianist and accordionist (*fisarmonica*), who blew us away one evening at Alexanderplatz.

FINDING OUT WHAT'S PLAYING

Check the *Musica* listings in *Roma C'è* (they are by day and by type of music) or listings at the top of the pages in "Giorno e Notte" in *La Repubblica*. We've provided Web sites below. The best English-language Web site for events in Rome is www.inromenow.com. It lists weekly the bigger exhibits, concerts, plays, and films in English. We recommend checking it both before you go and once you're in Rome. No source is foolproof, as we have learned from experience (Alexanderplatz's music was listed in several print media and on its Web site; yet when we got there, a sign on the door said that it was closed for the week).

A NOTE ON THE SEASONS

Rome's offerings are governed by the seasons. In the summer, *tutti al mare!* (everyone to the sea!); the action moves to the beach. Closing parties for Rome clubs abound in late May and early June, and the opening parties start up in September and October. What you get in recompense in the summer and in holiday periods are lavish shows with top Italian and international performers to give those Romans left in the city something to do. These shows run across all cultural types—music, theater, dance, opera—and often have evocative locations. One example is jazz at Celimontana, described below.

Renzo Piano's Parco della Musica.

PERFORMANCE CENTERS
PARCO DELLA MUSICA
(Music Park), also called
the Auditorium. Situated
about one mile north of
Piazza del Popolo in the
Flaminio neighborhood
(viale Pietro de Coubertin), Parco della Musica is an evocative complex of au-
ditoriums designed by world-famous architect Renzo Piano. It contains several
spaces, large and small, where jazz and other performances take place. Events
here are well publicized and cost from €5 to €25. (See www
.auditorium.com, a limited English site.) If you arrive early, the Parco has
an intriguing (but a bit pricey) sidewalk café (**RED**); an attractive
cafeteria-style café and bar; an excellent CD and bookstore (carrying
books only in Italian); and a small gallery with focused art exhibits (usually €2). The wine bar **ANNIBALE** is nearby (see p. 217), as are the
Flaminio-area restaurants (see p. 214). Parco della Musica is served by the
M (for Music) bus, which leaves to and from Termini every fifteen minutes from about 5 p.m. to midnight.

CASA DEL JAZZ (House of Jazz). At the opposite end of the city from Parco
della Musica, Casa del Jazz has the added attraction of being developed on a
site taken over by the city from a Mafia don and converted into a luxurious
park space. This recent addition to the city's jazz scene hosts performances in
two environments: an intimate, steeply sloped auditorium, where every seat
(of about two hundred) is a good one and the sound system is excellent; and
in warm weather, on the lawn (they have one of the few lawnmowers in town),
where the musicians hold forth from a large portable sound stage and patrons
lounge in plastic chairs or sit on the grass. Inside there's a perfunctory bar and
a good jazz CD shop. In a separate building on your left, after you pass
through the gates, is a rather desolate restaurant. Otherwise the Casa is isolated

Casa del Jazz.

from commerce. Popular artists will sell out, and the ticket office is open only for the hour before performances (generally 9 p.m.), so it can be difficult to make sure you'll get in. Admission €5–15.

The Web site, www.casajazz.it, has a wealth of information in Italian. Given most of the information is on musical groups with dates and times, you should be able to figure this out, along with opening times for the restaurant. Viale di Porta Ardeatina, 55; tel. 06.70.4731. Access by public transportation is not great, making taxi service ideal. Alternatives to taxis include taking Metro B to Piramide and walking up viale di Porta Ardeatina—a lonely walk at night. Bus 714 from Termini stops nearby at Colombo/Marco Polo, the tenth stop from Termini. Walk a few steps forward to the first cross street and take it two hundred yards or so. The bus stop back is across the exceedingly busy street (via Cristoforo Colombo) from where you got off. Bus 714 runs every fifteen minutes until midnight.

VILLA CELIMONTANA (www.villacelimontanajazz.com. The Web site is in Italian and English.) In June, most of the jazz clubs close and the action goes outdoors—at Casa del Jazz and Villa Celimontana, a park just a ten-minute walk uphill from the Coliseum, decked out for the summer season with a huge sound stage and hundreds of tables, which are served by bars and restaurants at the periphery. Once you've paid the price of admission (free to €10), you can order beer or wine and find a place to sit, either in the arranged seating near the stage or some place informal around the sides or a nonreserved table (and order from a waiter). Summer 2008's musical fare included Enrico Rava, Paolo Fresu, and Stefano Bollani (see the introduction to this section), as well as pianist and orchestra director Carla Bley,

plus midnight shows. Giampiero Rubei, who runs Alexanderplatz (see the next section) books the music. Lights, glitter, the pleasures of food, drink, and music, all in an enchanting setting. Days vary; box office opens at 7:30 p.m. on the evening of an event; doors open at 9 p.m.; performances begin at 10:15 p.m. Via della Navicella, up the Celio Hill from the Coliseum (Metro B stop; see Web site for map).

CLUBS

ALEXANDERPLATZ. The city's premier jazz club, this ratskeller space was opened in the city's Prati section by jazz entrepreneur Giampiero Rubei in the 1980s. The inviting club consists of four or five rooms running off a small central one in which the musicians perform. The walls are adorned with photos and signatures of jazz greats who have played here. Sight lines are unusual, sometimes perverse. The bar has a few stools that offer satisfying views, and the room stage right is well positioned. Avoid the loft-balcony stage left. Performances begin at 10 or 10:15 p.m. To be assured of a good seat, arrive about 9 p.m., when the club opens, and have dinner—the food is tasty. Cover €5–15 plus a €10 monthly *tessera* (membership; note *tessera* policies seem to change from year to year). Via Ostia, 9, within walking distance of the Vatican and Metro A, Ottaviano; www .alexanderplatz.it (the English site is not up-to-date); tel. 06.3974.2171.

CHARITY CAFÉ. Situated in the Monti district, between the Coliseum and via Nazionale, Charity has transcended its origins as a social club (*circolo*) and its cramped, funky quarters to become a jazz hot spot of local renown. The stars don't play here, but the up-and-comers do (along with those of lesser ability). When the mix is right, nothing beats

Charity Café

a seat in the main room (it holds about fifteen), two feet from the stage, the *sassofonista* blowing his guts out in your face. The seating in the second room, for those given more to talking than listening, consists of church pews. The crowd is mostly under thirty-five. No cover, no *tessera*. Sunday's *Aperitivo Jazz* (7 p.m.) features a help-yourself smorgasbord at the bar for the price of one drink. Beers are €5–7, cocktails €6–8, wine €5; drink prices may be somewhat higher on Sunday. Performances begin between 10 and 11 p.m. Via Panisperna, 68, a short walk from the Cavour or Colosseo stops on Metro B; www.charitycafe.it (in English too); tel. 06.4782.5881.

COTTON CLUB. A recent addition to the city's jazz scene, Cotton Club (Bill says) looks as if it were a set for a *Saturday Night Live* skit about a jazz club, its round tables set a tad too far apart, table service by the owner, not quite enough customers. Dianne's more positive. Although unusual for jazz, the elevated stage guarantees a good view. The music is excellent. One can expect ballroom dancing to live music and a garden space in early summer. Cover €10 per person includes a drink and chips. Via Bellinzona, 2, at corso Trieste, one block from Piazza Istria; www.cottonclubroma.it (no English, map on *Dove siamo* link); tel. 06.9761.5246. About five blocks southwest of Cotton Club is Quartiere Coppedè, a fascinating, architecturally distinct area, built by Gino Coppedè in the 1920s in that decade's Art Nouveau style—seductive at night.

BE BOP JAZZ BLUES LIVE CLUB. Another subterranean experience, this one with brick walls and arches. Good music. Dianne likes it ("always something going on," "I feel like I'm in a real club"); Bill doesn't (uncomfortable chairs, spotlight in his eyes, indifferent service, band's an hour late starting). You decide. *Tessera* €5 required. Performances are supposed to start at 10:30 p.m. Via Giuseppe Giulietti, 14, a three-minute walk from the Piramide stop of Metro B on the via Ostiense side; www.bebopjazzclub.it (no English; has a map, click on *Dove Siamo*); tel. 347.177.1710.

IL PENTAGRAPPOLO. More a piano bar than a jazz club, catering to young somethings who would rather chat than listen to the music, which can be pleasant if uninspired. Performances begin at 10 p.m. Two high-ceilinged rooms tastefully combine the rustic Roman and the modern. Candles on the tables. By the glass, wine is reasonable (€4–6), but if the *bruschettine* were any more "ine," Bill says, they would cease to exist. Poor value if you're hungry, but perhaps worth it if you're in the Coliseum area and want a yuppie setting—with music. Via Celimontana, 21/B (Metro B, Colosseo); www.ilpentagrappolo.com (Italian only); tel. 06.709.6301.

LA PALMA. Off the beaten track, but for many years second only to Alexanderplatz in jazz and other music offerings (blues, soul, indie, etc.). The club ranges over an indoor and expansive outdoor space in an industrial neighborhood. Good music, food and drink, reasonable charges. The downside: La Palma closed in 2007 for restoration (a good thing; one night the entire electrical system went out as we listened to a group, but the pianist played on—in the dark), and it's not clear it will reopen. Check the local media when you get to Rome. Hard to reach with public transportation at night; night Bus n2 gets you within a half mile. Via G. Mirri, 35; www.lapalmaclub.it (in Italian only; not much on it while they're closed); tel. 06.4359.9029.

OTHER MUSIC

There are many other music and dance offerings in Rome on any given evening. Some are free (*gratis*). You can find these listed in clearly marked sections (classical set apart from dance, from jazz, from rock, etc.) in the *Roma C'è* and *La Repubblica* listings, and on institute Web sites (see "International Academies," p. 188).

CASE (HOUSES OF CULTURE)

Among its burgeoning cultural institutions are Rome's *case,* or houses of culture. Penetrating these is not straightforward, but we think it's worth the effort, especially if you have an interest in one of the *casa* topics. The *case* were part of the push to expand Rome's cultural offerings by the prior mayor, liberal Walter Veltroni, a published author and advocate of culture (it's not clear if these houses will continue to thrive under Gianni Alemanno, the conservative mayor elected in 2008 on an anticulture platform). The problem with penetrating the houses is that they normally do not provide programs or information in English. To the extent they do, you likely will find the information in the other sources we've mentioned, such as *Roma C'è*, *Trova Roma*, and *La Repubblica*'s "Giorno e Notte" pages. The descriptions below give you the best chance at finding culture in the houses of culture.

The main houses of culture are:

Casa del Jazz (House of Jazz)
Casa del Cinema (House of Film)
Casa delle Letterature (House of Literature)
Casa dei Teatri (House of Theater)
Casa dell'Architettura (House of Architecture)
Casa della Memoria e della Storia (House of Memory and History)
Casa Internazionale delle Donne (International Women's House)

CASA DEL JAZZ (House of Jazz) is described in the Jazz section (see p. 199).

CASA DEL CINEMA (House of Film) is in a prominent building at the beginning of the large Villa Borghese park, just beyond the city's wall off corso d'Italia where via Veneto comes in. You can walk there from Termini (or take Metro A to Spagna and follow the via Veneto signs). Like some of the other *case*, it has a restaurant and bar, open most of the day. The €8 lunch buffet (about 1–3 p.m.; drinks extra) is a good deal. Often films are in original language (subtitles likely to be in Italian). Note "v.o." means *versione originale* or shown in original language (don't confuse this with "v.m."—*vietato ai minori*, prohibited to minors). So you should be able to find films in languages you understand. It also has a small bookstore devoted to film and a viewing room (generally opens at 4 p.m. Tuesday–Sunday) with many carrels and DVDs available. If you have the time, we recommend stopping by the ticket office and picking up the literature listing the current and upcoming films. Information at www.casadelcinema.it; Italian only. Also see Cinema, p. 195.

CASA DELLE LETTERATURE (House of Literature) occasionally has readings in English. Some of its Web site (www.casadelleletterature.it) is in English, so you should be able to determine when English-language programs are available. It often has a worthy photo or art show. Because this *casa* is in

Casa del Cinema, honoring
Sophia Loren

the Center, it's easy to stop by and check it out. Piazza dell'Orologio, 3, behind Chiesa Nuova (and part of a Borromini complex), off corso V. Emmanule II; Monday–Friday 8:30 a.m.–6:30 p.m. Bus 64 (watch your pockets—this is the tourist bus to the Vatican from Termini) gets you there and back.

CASA DEI TEATRI (House of Theater) is in Villa Corsini in the park of Villa Pamphili. This *casa* (open Tuesday–Saturday, 10 a.m.–7 p.m.; 10 a.m.–5p.m. October through March) hosts some events understandable to English speakers, including exhibitions. It's in a pretty spot, snug against a functioning aqueduct, and is worth a stop if you're in Villa Pamphili. Information in Italian at www.casadeiteatri.culturaroma.it. For bus and walking directions, follow the tour in chapter 1, Itinerary 2: The Strange Career of the Tevere, beginning on p. 42, which heads into Villa Pamphili.

CASA DELL'ARCHITETTURA (House of Architecture) inhabits an unusual late-nineteenth-century building restored to its late baroque beauty, the Acquario Romano (built to house an aquarium [*acquario*] and fish hatchery). It has excellent exhibits on architecture, often in multiple languages, a good bookstore on architecture, and a Web site with some English (www.casadellarchitettura.it, click on English version—right side). The Web site offers a history of the building in English. Open Monday–Friday, 9 a.m.–1 p.m.; also Monday and Wednesday 2:30–4:30 p.m.; gardens open each day 10 a.m.–7 p.m. (summer), 10 a.m.–5:30 p.m. (winter), 10 a.m.–1:30 p.m. on Sundays. The location, halfway between Termini Station and Piazza Vittorio, makes this *casa* a convenient stop. Take either Metro line to Termini and walk a few blocks down to Piazza M. Fanti (or, as the Web site says, almost any bus headed toward Termini should get you close enough).

CASA DELLA MEMORIA E DELLA STORIA (House of Memory and History) is on an out-of-the-way side street on the Vatican end of Trastevere, appropriately alongside the still-used prison, Regina Coeli, that housed political prisoners, including many of those murdered by the German SS in the Ardeatine Caves (see p. 92). Because the *casa's* primary mission is to recoup the oral histories of Italians, everything is in Italian. The *casa* focuses on the twentieth century and emphasizes the history of the anti-Fascist movement and the partisan resistance to the German occupation of 1943/44 by hosting talks and small photo shows. It has a library and sells just-published memoirs, among other books, all in Italian. It does not have a dedicated Web site; a general description of it on the city's cultural Web site is translated in English (www.culturaroma.it/english; click on Casa della Memoria e della Storia on the left). Look for announcements of presentations here in *Roma C'è* and *La Repubblica's* "Giorno e Notte." Hours: Monday–Saturday, 10 a.m.–6 p.m., via San Francesco di Sales, 3. Bus 64 from Termini to Chiesa Nuova (where you get off for Casa delle Letterature) takes you within a half mile of Casa della Memoria e della Storia; you cross the Mazzini bridge over the Tevere, head down the steep street or steps in front of you to your left, and jog around the prison to the left and then right on via San Francesco di Sales to No. 3. Or take Bus 64 across the Tevere to Santo Spirito hospital and walk along the Tevere until you are just past the Mazzini bridge, then follow the prior directions. The walk this second way is a bit shorter. Backtrack to head home, or go farther north into Trastevere and catch Tram 8 back to Largo di Torre Argentina.

CASA INTERNAZIONALE DELLE DONNE (International Women's House) is on the same street as Casa della Memoria e della Storia, again in Trastevere, but closer to the river. For women, this is an important resource, in part because in addition to being a meeting center and archive, it hosts a small women-only hotel, including dorm rooms. The *casa* includes a restaurant and cafeteria, a biofriendly tea and snack shop, and a courtyard overhung with ancient magnolias. The restaurant is open to men and women for lunch; women only in the evenings. It's a calm and peaceful break from the hubbub that is now Trastevere. The Web site (www.casainternazionaledelledonne.org) is in Italian, except for the hotel section, which has a clear description of rooms, offerings, and prices. The hotel is Foresteria Orsa Maggiore and can be reached through the *casa*'s Web site; click on Foresteria Orsa Maggiore, then on English. Dorm rooms with showers down the hall are €26; other rooms run €52 to €138—this last is for a four-bed room (for four people) with private bath, breakfast included. Via San Francesco di Sales, 1/a, corner via della Lungara; tel. 06.689.3753.

7

AFTER EIGHT

Food and Drink

AT THE end of this chapter, as we explore the city's rooftop bars in search of spectacular views, we come perilously close to breaking a promise made on the cover of this book: that we wouldn't take you to the Coliseum. But first things first, and that means dinner at a ristorante or trattoria or pizzeria—none of them, we hasten to add, anywhere near the Coliseum or, for that matter, in the standard tourist areas. Our suggestions include three very different neighborhoods just outside the Centro—Appio Latino, Flaminio, and Pigneto—each with a variety of authentic Roman restaurants and none yet exposed to tourists. We have outlined one itinerary, An Evening in Pigneto, that will guide you to and through one of our favorite neighborhoods and one that isn't in the guidebooks. After all, this is Rome the *second* time. Following these descriptions are a selection of wine bars and some tips on finding wine tastings. We close, as we hope your evening will, with rooftop bars with views.

APPIO LATINO RESTAURANTS

The suggestions here offer you real Roman food, and you'll be surrounded by real Romans. Don't expect tourists or English translations. What you can expect is good, basic Roman cuisine, all cooked on site (*fatta in casa*—

homemade), and economical prices. You can find all the "trendy" (that's the way the Italians say it) and expensive restaurants in the usual guidebooks. The Appio Latino neighborhood in south Rome is large, and within it are subdivisions like this one we recommend, tucked away between the busy San Giovanni and Appia Nuova areas. This part of Appio Latino is almost like a small town, or close-in suburb, of its own. It's mostly middle class and perhaps on the lower end of that. It is not glitzy or refined, but it offers a real taste of how most Romans live. It has its own shopping areas and plenty of places to eat and drink. We've selected four restaurants that would be labeled inexpensive in any English-language guidebook, a wine bar that offers dinners, and the city's top-rated *gelateria*.

SOME GUIDANCE ON COURSES

A *primo* is a first course, more than an appetizer (*antipasto*). A *secondo* is a second course (for example, a meat course), often served without sides or *contorni*. We've compromised the language a bit to use *primis* as the plural for first courses and *seconds* for second courses.

If we had to pick one, we'd go to **MITHOS—LA TAVERNA DELL'ALLEGRIA.** The name implies Greek, but the couple who own and run Mithos are Italian. Charming Mario will greet and serve you; his wife, Vittoria, does the cooking. Everything on the handwritten menu changes daily, as Vittoria chooses and experiments. If you have trouble reading Italian handwriting, and even if you don't, ask Mario for recommendations. Everything is a daily special. There's Antipasti Mithos at €10, primis run €6–8, seconds €6–9, sides (*contorni*) €3.5, and desserts (*dolci*) €4. Expect fish dishes on only Tuesdays and Fridays. A half liter of house wine is €3. The space is tiny, with a small outdoor area in warm weather. Dianne thinks it's romantic. A reservation usually is required. Via Benedetto Varchi, 3 (just off Piazza Scipione Ammirato); tel. 06.784.0034; open evenings, beginning about 8 p.m. (you might be able to get in at 7:30 p.m.); closed Wednesdays (and other days when they need a break). Mithos is a third of a mile from the Metro A stop Furio Camillo, off via Appia Nuova. Directions: From the Furio Camillo Metro stop, head southwest on via Cesare Baronio, take your first ninety-degree right on via Giuseppe La Farina. Go through Piazza Scipione Ammirato (two short blocks ahead) and out diagonally opposite the way you came in, on the narrow via Benedetto Varchi. You'll see Mithos's outdoor space on your left. Note also the lovely stork and palms bas-relief on the building opposite.

LA ZINGARELLA ("the Gypsy Girl") is a large, bustling Roman restaurant also run by a husband-and-wife team, Carlo and Marina. It features classic Roman cuisine, including an ample antipasto bar and many pastas, and lives up to the quote on their business card: "the most authentic Roman cuisine; fresh fish every day." You'll find large groups, families with small children, and romantic younger and older couples—in other words, the gamut. Service can be prompt or slow, friendly or brusque, depending on the crowd and the waiter. Marina cares about the patrons, visiting at tables to make sure everything is right, and the food, chopping tomatoes into salads only when the salad has been ordered. One night we saw her teaching her teenage son how to do this. We like the seafood pastas, but everything is good here. Wood-oven pizza is on the menu too. You'll likely get some of the sugary Sorrento liqueur, *limoncello,* free to finish your meal (a digestive, so the Italians say). Newly refurbished, but unchanged in style; check out the paintings on the walls of happy gypsy life—a far cry from Italy's current distaste for anything gypsy. At La Zingarella, for €30 you can have wine, water, two primis, and two desserts (plus the *limoncello*). Follow the directions to Mithos but stop in Piazza Scipione Ammirato; La Zingarella is practically on the piazza, kitty-corner from Mithos, via G. Capponi, 61/63; tel. 06.781.0687; closed Mondays.

TRATTORIA ADA E MARIO is another local institution run by a family. It features simple, homemade Roman food at bargain prices. The menu is

Mario, host at *Mithos*, in Appio Latino.

handwritten, and there will be specials of the day not listed; ask for recommendations. Appetizers €4.5, primis €5, seconds €8, sides and desserts €3, and a half liter of wine €1.5. It's hard to go wrong trying anything here. We recommend focusing on the primis, including ones favored by Romans like *pasta alla boscaiola* (mushrooms, ham, onions—a "woodsman's pasta"—usually a fall dish) or *norcina* (mushrooms) *e tonnarelli all'ortica* (small, square pasta with nettles!). The restaurant is made up of small spaces up, down, and outside (surrounded by walls). Sit wherever they put you and watch the family run around serving everyone. Circonvallazione Appia, 81, tel. 06.78.6615; open evenings, beginning at 8 p.m., closed Sundays. Trattoria Ada e Mario is a third of a mile from the Metro A stop Ponte Lungo, off via Appia Nuova (this is one stop closer to the center of Rome than the Furio Camillo stop). Directions: From the Ponte Lungo Metro stop, head toward the bridge, away from the Center, and turn just before the bridge, right on via Ivrea. Follow via Ivrea one long block to a street and bridge crossing the train tracks. Turn left across that bridge on via A. Baccarini and take your first right onto Circonvallazione Appia. Halfway down this block on the left, you'll see the sign for Trattoria Ada e Mario at No. 81. (If you want to go to the San Crispino Gelateria from Trattoria Ada e Mario, you're a half mile from Piazza Zama, and from there it's a snap. Take a left out of Ada e Mario and proceed to via Siria, where you take a right and go over the bridge to Piazza Zama. To get to the gelateria from there, see the directions on p. 214.)

PIZZERIA LA MADIA, unlike Mithos and Ada e Mario, is large. It's a bustling, often noisy, two-story pizzeria, with outdoor space in front and on the second floor (don't get stuck in the basement). The list of pizzas is long, and you can't go wrong. These are classic thin Roman pizzas, €4–9, average €7. La Madia is also known for its made-on-site fried appetizers, the very Roman *fritti* (average €4). We've enjoyed the primis here too (€6–10). And the menu is complete with appetizers (€4–9), bruschette (€1–2.5), meat dishes (€15), and salads and sides (€4). A half liter of wine is €3. Expect daily specials. La Madia is on busy Piazza Zama, at No. 5; tel. 06.7709.6875; open evenings, beginning 7:30 p.m., closed Tuesdays; reservations not needed. Directions: From the Termini Station, take Bus

360, which has Piazza Zama as one of its endpoints. (See directions to the gelateria on p. 214.)

For a more sophisticated and modern setting, the **TABERNA RECINA** is a small wine bar on the west, or Centro, side of busy via Britannia (the three restaurants are on the east side). The knowledgeable owners serve good wines at €3.5–4 per glass. You can order bottles as well or buy some to take home. They now serve dinners that include Antipasto della Taberna at €8.5, primis at €8, seconds at €12–14, and sides at €4–5. The Taberna is open until late at night for wine and appetizers. The organization *Slow Food* named Taberna Recina among the best *osterias* of Italy in 2006. Signs and its Web site say it's open 7:30 a.m.–11:30 p.m. (closed Sundays), but we've seen it open only in the evenings. If you plan on arriving before 7:30 p.m., we suggest you call first. Via Elvia Recina, 26; www.tabernarecina.it (in English too); tel. 06.700.0413. Directions: Using Metro A to the San Giovanni stop, exit on the via Appia Nuova (Piazzale Appio) side; take a diagonal right, straight south on via Magna Grecia, which becomes via Britannia right after Piazza Tuscolo. Via Elvia Recina is a small street heading southwest off the bottom of Piazza Tuscolo (on your right). That's a half-mile walk from the Metro stop. You also can take Bus 360 from Termini and ask to get off at the stop nearest Piazza Tuscolo (Magna Grecia/Tuscolo, nine stops from Termini). You're now in front of Piazza Tuscolo. Keep walking south (in the direction the bus was going) to the

ONE-GLASS TRATTORIA

Years ago, while traveling in Tuscany, we stopped in Montepulciano for lunch. On the main street we found a spot, once someone's basement but now handsomely decorated, cool, and inviting. The clientele was mostly local businessmen. We ordered water, white wine, and the specialty of the house, a bean soup. When the water and wine arrived, we realized we each had only one glass and stopped the waiter to ask for wine glasses. "What do you think this is," he replied, "a restaurant? This is a trattoria." To be sure, many trattorias will provide two glasses. But when there is only one, we alternate wine and water and say to each other, "one-glass trattoria."

small via Elvia Recina heading southwest (on your right) off the south end of Piazza Tuscolo. Using the bus, you're walking an eighth of a mile.

ROME'S BEST GELATO

We hope you've left room for dessert, because Rome's number-one gelateria has one of its two outlets not far from Piazzas Tuscolo (about a quarter of a mile) and Zama (about four hundred feet). GELATERIA SAN CRISPINO is at via Acaia, 56; via Acaia is the extension (farther away from S. Giovanni) of via Britannia (which is the extension of via Magna Grecia); open 11 a.m.–midnight, closed Tuesdays.

AROUND THE BLOCK IN FLAMINIO

Maybe the best way (Bill says) to find a good restaurant is to go to a neighborhood where there are lots of restaurants in close proximity. We found such a block in the Flaminio quarter. Flaminio begins just north of Piazza del Popolo and extends north of the historic center for two miles. The restaurant area is three-quarters of a mile from Piazza del Popolo and a ten-minute walk from Parco della Musica. From Piazza del Popolo, walk through the porta to Piazzale Flaminio (the name of the piazza on the other side of the wall), take Tram 2, and get off at Piazzale Ankara (the name ideally will appear on the tram's electronic board), the stop after the long, bright green gas station on your right. Walk east (left from the tram direction), over several sets of trolley tracks, to the corner of via Flaminia and via Cesare Fracassini (a newsstand sits in the middle of this divided street). The block on the right has five restaurants. For those without a reservation, we suggest a clockwise stroll around the block to have a brief look at each.

You'll first come across PERILLI AL FLAMINIO, at via Fracassini, 36. A recent write-up in *La Repubblica* described it as "an institution in the capital" dedicated to authentic Roman cooking. The décor is classic upper-middle-class Roman, the waiters seem to have been there for years, and the clientele is more "refined" and somewhat older than that in the other restaurants on this block. Despite its reputation (perhaps attributable more to its sister restaurant of the same name in Testaccio), the night we visited, the food

Charming *Bistrot*, in Flaminio.

was only ordinary: sinfully, the *osso buco* not tender and the *tagliatelle ai funghi* unexceptional. This is the most expensive of the five restaurants (by a small margin) and probably not worth the money, although you may be willing to pay for a classic subdued Roman atmosphere. Open for lunch and dinner; closed Wednesdays; tel. 06.322.7591.

Our next stop—around the corner right and then a right turn at the driveway for the Cinema Politecnico Fandango, bearing left once in the small courtyard—is the charming **BISTROT** (via Tiepolo, 13a). A fixture of the neighborhood for more than twenty years, Bistrot has two narrow stories of small, candle-lit tables and is warm, informal, and inviting. We passed up the renowned French onion soup for the seasonal *vignarola*—a soup of artichokes, fava beans, and other vegetables. (One theory of the name *vignarola* is that most of the ingredients come from produce at one time cultivated in vineyards [*vigne*], among the rows of vines.) Most of the main courses are of the casserole type, many of them unusual and complex dishes made fresh that day. We recommend the (noncasserole) *cosce alla cacciatora* (chicken thighs, hunter's style—stuffed with a mix of mushrooms and spices). Bistrot is not typically Roman by any means, but worth a visit. Actor Steve Buscemi ate here while attending the photocall for his 2007 film *Interview*; note the signed poster across from the entrance. Bistrot can seem empty, but it fills up quickly when the film or play next door lets out. Reservations recommended. Opens at 8 p.m.; closed Sundays and Mondays; tel. 06.322.4005.

Exiting the driveway onto via Tiepolo, turn right and continue to the end of the block. **TIEPOLO** (via Tiepolo, 3/5) has the feel of a French café, bustling with young people smoking at the tables outside, shades of Sartre and de Beauvoir. A cozy interior, taverna style. Soups and salads, large crostini, stuffed potatoes (a signature dish) €6–10 each. No pastas, no *secondi,* no pizza. Lots of desserts listed on the big blackboard inside. Open every day from 8 p.m. until very late at night; tel. 06.322.7449.

Around the corner from Tiepolo, about halfway down viale del Vignola toward the tram, is **PIZZERIA VIGNOLA** (viale del Vignola, 25/27), a self-described "family" restaurant serving the Flaminio community for two decades. The place is charming in that haphazard Italian way: cured hams hanging from a metal bar in the dining room, athletic trophies stacked on a shelf, fluorescent lights protruding awkwardly from wall sconces, pics of the pope and soccer players. It's always been a bit hectic when we've been here, but that can be invigorating, and the food—the standard Roman menu, with an English translation—is good. The wood-oven pizza (most at €7) was the most popular choice of those around us, but the serve-yourself antipasto bar offers a nice selection, and the pasta dishes (€7–8) we've tried were more than acceptable. Red and white house wine (*vino della casa*) is €5 for a liter. There are tables outside too. Avoid the basement. Closed Wednesdays; www.ristorantevignola.it (only in Italian, map at *Dove siamo* link); tel. 06.322.7451.

The last stop, at the end of the block, is **LA FRISERIA** (viale del Vignola 1/a), whose "Mediterranean" cuisine is a mixture of standard Roman and dishes from the southern province of Puglia. The Pugliese "macaroni" dishes are tasty and run about €8–10. We ate here twice. The first time we were pleased, and Bill considered the restaurant something of a "find" (for Dianne, just okay). The second time, with visitors from the United States, the service was atrocious—thoughtless, perhaps hostile—and the food ordinary. We should have taken heed at the sign in the window: Waiter Wanted. By the time you read this, they may have hired one. Open every day for lunch and dinner; special lunch prices.

BEFORE—OR AFTER—DINNER IN FLAMINIO

Less than a ten-minute walk from the five restaurants in the Flaminio block (and closer to Parco della Musica) is one of Rome's growing number of modern wine bars. *ANNIBALE VINI & SPIRITI* ("Hannibal Wine & Spirits," Piazza dei Carracci, 4—the first name of one of the Renaissance painter Carracci brothers, for whom the piazza is named, was Annibale; you may notice most of the streets here are named for Italian painters) is in a small piazza that intersects with via Flaminia just a bit north—away from the city center. You'll find it on the west, far side of the piazza. Opened in 2007, Annibale combines high-ceiling, white, droplight vertical modernism with wooden chairs and paper-covered tables—a leavening hint of the rustic. There's space inside for fewer than twenty, while the outside expands as the weather warms. The wines are few but well chosen (€6/glass) and served with inviting *stuzzichini* (appetizers). A nice sound system, with speakers up high, plays jazz and other music loud enough to enjoy without interfering with conversation. Live music on Tuesdays. A few of the thirty-somethings that constitute much of the clientele were eating dinner one night we were there, but the restaurant has no kitchen as such, which means everything is prepared beforehand and heated up; stick to the *stuzzichini,* Dianne says. The place closed about midnight one cool Monday we were there, but it stays open later in the heat of the summer. Chic atmosphere, friendly service. Tel. 06.322.3835.

Film enthusiasts will appreciate that the Flaminio neighborhood was the location for the final scenes of Vittorio De Sica's 1948 neorealist classic *The Bicycle Thief.* The Italian title is *Ladri di Biciclette* (bicycle *thieves*) and for good reason: there are two thefts of a bicycle in the film. The second theft was filmed on via Pietro da Cortona, a short street that runs perpendicular to via Flaminia, across from **TREE BAR,** a two-minute walk south (toward Piazza del Popolo) from the restaurant block and the Piazza Ankara tram stop. As you look up via Pietro da Cortona from via Flaminia, you'll see on the left the doorway of the apartment building (No. 1) from where the bicycle was stolen. In the film, the thief circles the apartment building's block and emerges on via Flaminia (the film reveals the trams were running in 1948, but without the fencing and concrete barriers that exist today) where, pursued by an angry crowd, he turns left, then veers right before being captured. The film ends with the father (now himself a thief) walking hand-in-hand with his confused son, up via Flaminia, toward the very old round church on their (and your) left. An additional note: we once rented the apartment above where the bicycle was stolen—identifiable in the film by the first-floor corner balcony.

ITINERARY 15: AN EVENING IN PIGNETO

Only in the last two or three years has Pigneto—a gritty, compact neighborhood on the city's northwest side—begun to attract attention as a favored entertainment destination of Rome's students and young professionals. Indeed, despite its proximity to Termini Station, Piazza di Porta Maggiore, and the larger and better-known entertainment district of San Lorenzo, the area remains somewhat difficult to access by public transport (service on Metro line C is scheduled to begin in 2013). The highways that sandwich the area—the elevated via Prenestina on one side, the busy via Casilina on the other—isolate Pigneto and have, over the years, reinforced its character as a hardscrabble, working-class neighborhood. Moreover, to strangers, the highways can seem intimidating barriers. Some will be put off by the volume of graffiti that decorates the neighborhood and by the beer bottles and other debris that litter the streets. You can feel here what Trastevere and San Lorenzo were like as they were starting to gentrify and before they became the crowded (sometimes with unpleasant drunken throngs of Americans) destinations they now are. Get to Pigneto before it gentrifies too much, Dianne says.

Recently, Pigneto's isolation has softened, with the arrival of upscale restaurants and wine bars and an active pedestrian mall. Restoration of buildings, freshly painted exteriors, and rising real estate prices all signal the coming gentrification. At the same time, Pigneto has become home to thousands of new immigrants, including many from East Asia, India, Morocco, and Senegal. Although the area historically has been accepting and tolerant of the new groups, tensions between the older Italian population and the ethnic minorities can run high. In May 2008, several small, minority-owned stores were trashed by what the authorities (at first)

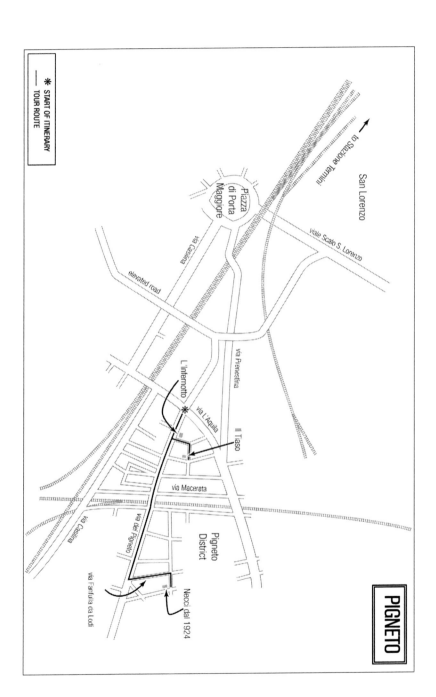

PIGNETO

★ START OF ITINERARY
— TOUR ROUTE

Piazza
di Porta
Maggiore

San Lorenzo

to Stazione Termini

viale Scalo S. Lorenzo

via Casilina

elevated road

via Prenestina

L'Infernotto

via L'Aquila

Il Tiaso

via Macerata

Pigneto
District

via del Pigneto

via Casilina

Necci dal 1924

via Fanfulla da Lodi

believed were neo-Nazis. An investigation was underway as we wrote this, and when we visited just days after the incident, the area was humming with its usual activity.

We suggest you engage Pigneto on a weeknight (but not Monday), when it will be less crowded. Arrive at 6:30 or 7:00 p.m. On the left of the pedestrian mall–via del Pigneto (walking slightly downhill), stop at the restaurant L'INFERNOTTO (via del Pigneto, 31/33; tel. 06.7030.4040, closed Mondays) and make a reservation (specifying indoor or outdoor seating) for later that evening—say, 8:00 or 8:30 p.m. Continue down via del Pigneto. As you cross via Macerata, look to your left at the small food store near the corner—one of three trashed in the attack described above, this one owned by an Indian immigrant. Cross the tracks and take the third street on the left, via Fanfulla da Lodi, where poet, novelist, and film director Pier Paolo Pasolini—a great admirer of Pigneto and its working class—shot many scenes for the film *Accattone* (1961). One block down, at No. 68, is NECCI DAL 1924, the recently restored bar and restaurant that was a favorite haunt of Pasolini. Find a table on the two-level patio, shaded by locust trees. Have a glass of wine (several choices at €4.5–6, with a complimentary generous plate of pizza pieces and fried vegetables), and enjoy the casual atmosphere. One evening we were there, one table was occupied by older men playing cards, another by a couple with an active child, a third by two women reading documents and working on a notebook computer. Imagine Pasolini

sitting here forty years ago, reveling in Pigneto's warmth and authenticity, planning the next day's shoot. Open 8 a.m.–1 a.m. every day. (Great Web site, only in Italian, www.necci1924.com, map at *Contattaci* link.)

Pigneto's *L'Infernotto.*

Retrace your steps to L'Infernotto (the name is a takeoff on *inferno* or hell). Your table should be waiting for you outside in the pedestrian mall, if the weather permits, or in the small back room, prettily restored and decorated with posters that tend toward the Left politically. There's a daily menu with interesting combinations of flavors and some of the best tasting and presented primis (€9–12) we've had anywhere. We recommend the ravioli *noci e* (walnuts and) *radicchio* and *risotto agli asparagi su crema di piselli* (risotto with asparagus and a creamed pea sauce—served in the form of a star). But you can't go wrong. Ordering wine is a minor challenge. There is no house wine. The owner only has bottles on the shelves (he also operates as a wine store), and the prices are unmarked; you can get a nice bottle of white wine for €15. The whites are all available chilled. We recommend you go into the bar area (the first room you enter) with your server and do the point-and-ask routine; it's just a quirk of the place. The main host/waiter can be a bit sullen, but don't take it personally.

There are other, more trendy spots on via del Pigneto, including the highly rated restaurant **PRIMO AL PIGNETO** (via del Pigneto, 46, closed Mondays). For an after-dinner drink, we recommend the new and nearby **IL TIASO,** a self-described *enolibreria* (book bar) that's open every day 6 p.m. to 1:30 a.m. (Exit left from L'Infernotto and take the first street, via Pesaro, left one block.) On the corner is **LO YETI,** one of those eclectic places preferred by the young and hip: computer terminals, a library, snacks and drinks, now and then live music, the action spilling into the street. Turn right at Lo Yeti onto via Perugia. At the next corner, at via Ascoli Piceno, 25, is Il Tiaso, with high ceilings, comfortable chairs, and tall bookcases (when we were last there, there was no sign outside; just check for action at the corner). The wine list is on a blackboard near the door. Order at the counter and await delivery at your table. Prices are reasonable, and pourings are generous. Afterward, if it's not too late and you have a moment, we suggest a glance into the "lobby" of the Grauco cinema (see p. 196), one of Pigneto's cultural gems, just steps down via Perugia, on the right, at No. 34.

WINE BARS

You will see the words "wine bar" (in English) everywhere in Rome. Yet wine bars as Americans know them are not authentic Italian institutions. Don't be misled; most of the establishments behind the wine bar sign are simply regular bars or restaurants, more likely not very good ones, designed to appeal to American tourists, or perhaps reflecting the Italian fascination with American culture. But there are wine bars in Rome that are real, in most cases derived from a wine store (*enoteca*) with tastings that have evolved into something like American wine bars. We describe and highly recommend four wine bars here (in addition to the two we described above, Il Tiaso in Pigneto and Taberna Recina near Appio Latino), all in very different areas, three in the Centro—one near the Coliseum and Forum, one near the ghetto (Campo dei Fiori, Piazza Navona), one near the train station (Stazione Termini), and one off Piazza Bologna. They are all reasonably priced, patronized by locals as well as tourists (one might appear occasionally in a guide), and they offer different atmospheres and wine and food selections.

BUON APERITIVO!

The last few years have seen a growth in a delectable custom: the late afternoon–evening (usually 6–8 p.m., before the restaurants open for dinner) drink with buffet. This custom, advertised with the word *aperitivo,* is spreading to more wine bars and other locales. A glass of wine and the often expansive spread of good food run about €5–12. You'll find *aperitivi* at places from Charity Café on Sundays to **RED** at **PARCO DELLA MUSICA** every day at 6 p.m.

AL VINO AL VINO is situated in the heart of "Monti," the hilly area bordered by the Coliseum, via Nazionale, and the Roman Forum. It's an ideal place to stop for a glass of wine and an appetizer. The wine list by the glass (or *mescita*—by the pouring)—both on a board and a typed menu—generally features a half dozen reds, three or four whites, and three or four sparkling wines. The price range is €3–10, with the average glass (a good portion) costing €4. Even if you don't see them in the case or on the menu, you can ask for appetizers—a cheese and meat plate or small hors d'oeuvres with homemade spreads. The shop was formerly a drugstore. Lovely wooden shelves filled with bottles of wine and a marble counter on the bar evoke that past. Graceful tiles sport grape designs that are the wine bar's symbol. *Vino al vino* is part of a saying "[dire] pane al pane, vino al vino," literally translated as "say bread to bread, wine to wine," but in Italian approximates the American expression, "call a spade a spade." You can buy bottles of wine to go as well—there are hundreds to choose from. The front room is the

Il Goccetto: the wine list is on the blackboard above the case.

nicest, but there are only four stools (we like to sit at the bar) and four tables; so you may have to share a table with others. One day we offered to share our table with a woman who turned out to be a writer for *Gourmet*. It was her first time at Al vino al vino, and she shared her appetizers with us—a good trade. The nearest Metro stop is Metro B Cavour. Al vino al vino is open every evening, starting about 5 p.m. (unless you want to wait outside, you may want to get there later) until after midnight. Some reports say they're open for lunch (except Sundays), but we haven't seen that. Via dei Serpenti, 19; tel. 06.48.5803.

IL GOCCETTO means a little drop. It's a few blocks from Campo dei Fiori and Piazza Navona (and only two blocks from the Tevere), but worlds away in terms of authenticity (rustic décor; note the wood-beamed ceiling with newer metal earthquake supports; no background music). Out front an old sign says simply *Vino/Olio* (wine, oil), and there's a much smaller sign up high with the name Il Goccetto. Sergio, the proprietor, is usually behind the bar. The list on the blackboard of wines by the glass is lengthy, thirty to forty selections ranging from €3.5 to €9, more for some champagnes. You can point and choose from a variety of appetizers in the case, or ask Sergio to bring you some that suit the wine you've selected; prices vary. The locals who frequent Il Goccetto spill out into the street and the steps, smoking, talking on their cell phones, or playing with their children and dogs. The doors are usually wide open, giving the place a neighborhood atmosphere. And that's about as close to outdoor seating as you get at Il Goccetto. The walls are lined with wooden shelves holding hundreds of bottles of wine, with prices marked. You can easily select some to buy. We found Il Goccetto by accident one day and have been coming back ever since. Via dei Banchi Vecchi, 14, 11:30 a.m.–2 p.m. and 7:30 p.m.–midnight; closed Sundays and midday Mondays; tel. 06.686.4268.

TRIMANI IL (THE) WINE BAR is a modern contrast to the prior two establishments. It was established in the early 1990s and has a low-key, blond wood, and plain warm-colored plaster décor with wood tables and chairs—designed to blend the modern with the Roman *enoteca* tradition. Don't let the simplicity fool you. The appetizers that could be meals (menus in multiple languages) and the wine selection are excellent. The menu is short, and there are daily specials. Plates start at €8 for soups and pastas and €14 for seconds. The by-the-glass wine list provides ample choice in variety and price (€3 to more than €20—yes, by the glass). There are plenty at €3.5–4.5. Open Monday–Saturday 11:30 a.m.–3:30 p.m.

TOASTING TACTICS

Toasting is a minor art form in Rome, and Romans are very superstitious. Here are a few of the basics to keep you in good form and prevent your bringing bad luck on yourself and your companions:

- Don't sneak a sip before the toast.
- Look the other person in the eye (not at his or her wine glass) as you clink your glasses.
- Don't "cross" another couple's toast; that is, clink glasses pretty much one pair at a time. It's bad luck to cross.
- Don't toast with water.
- Only after everyone has clinked, sip some wine.
- Don't set down your glass until you've completed all of the above steps.

SALUTE!

and 5:30 p.m.–12:30 a.m.; via Cernaia, 37b (corner of via Cernaia and via Goito); tel. 06.446.9630.

One reason the wines are so good and varied at Trimani Il Wine Bar is that it's an offshoot of the Trimani *enoteca* (wine store) around the corner, which traces its history to 1821 and is often listed as the best and most complete wine store in the city—no mean feat. The *enoteca* is still owned and run, as is the wine bar, by the Trimani family. You'll find English-speaking staff (they won't pressure you). Trimani (the *enoteca*) has free wine tastings with some frequency—one or two per month—even of wines not yet on the market and that are not for sale. And they have some higher-end wine tasting plus dinner events (for example, €60 per session per person). Some of this information is on the Web site (www.trimani.com, under *Incontri*) in Italian, but you should be able to ask and get a response in English through e-mail: info@trimani.com. The *enoteca* was refurbished in the early 1990s—with an arched but modern interior, graced by an enormous marble counter and the old spigots. Trimani's substantial inventory, arranged by region, includes many low-priced wines. Open Monday–Saturday, 9 a.m.–1:30 p.m. and 3:30–8:30 p.m.; via Goito, 20 (corner of via Cernaia and via Goito), tel. 06.446.9661.

The middle-class Piazza Bologna area has added a serious wine bar–bistrot, UVE E FORME, via Padova, 6/8. You can glimpse the attractive interior at www.uveeforme.it (in Italian); after dark, avoid the tables outside—too brightly lit (Bill says). Uve e forme serves lunch, dinner, and an appealing *aperitivo* (see p. 222). Glasses of wines listed on the blackboard run €4–7; *aperitivo* 6–8 p.m. daily, €6. The owners of this wine bar offer biologically correct products, a "slow food" approach, and wine appreciation classes. It's a nice break when you're on one of the Piazza Bologna itineraries (especially chapter 3's Itinerary 7: Piazza Bologna, see p. 102). Open noon–12:30 a.m. Monday–Friday, and 4:30 p.m.–12:30 a.m. Saturday; tel. 06.4423.6801.

WINE TASTINGS

In addition to occasional tastings at Trimani, wine tastings are frequently listed in *Roma C'è*. Most of these are expensive (€50 and up). Excellent

Tasting of wines from Italy's Friuli region at the International Wine Academy of Roma.

free wine tastings, sponsored by an Italian region, take place in locations ranging from the spectacular (Palazzo Rospigliosi on the Quirinale) to the interesting (Palazzo dei Congressi at EUR) to the mundane (Fiera di Roma—"fairgrounds of Rome"—now distant from the city center). Our favorite is the **INTERNATIONAL WINE ACADEMY OF ROMA** (yes, that's its name) at the north side of the Spanish Steps. At the time and day of the event, walk in, ask where to go for the *degustazione di vino* (wine tasting)—up a flight or two, get a ticket you'll exchange for a glass (hang on to it), and enjoy the indoor and outdoor spaces that nestle against the Spanish Steps. One rainy day we were in a close group of tasters under tents on the patio; about twenty-five vintners from the northern Italian region of Friuli presented a hundred wines. We talked with the vintners about their wineries and products as we were offered chunks of parmesan cheese, fatty meats on a stick, and other (to us, by now) delectables. Crowd watching comes a close second to the wines. At this and other tastings, you'll see hardcore types, complete with leather bags around their necks to spit in. Academy tastings run from free (*entrata libera*) to €20–35 per person. The schedule is on the academy's Web site (www.wineacademyroma.com; to make sure you access it in English, use www.wineacademyroma.com/uk/uk-home.asp, and click on Events). The academy is the brainchild of, and run by, the owners of the nearby luxury Hotel Hassler. International Wine Academy of Roma, tel. 06.699.0878; vicolo del Bottino, 8; entrance on the other side of the building, on via di S. Sebastianello, right (south) side, just before the Spagna Metro entrance.

ROOFTOP BARS WITH VIEWS

HOTEL RAPHAËL

Leave the hordes of tourists and hawkers behind in Piazza Navona and step into a small piazza tucked northwest behind the big one. The warm glow of Hotel Raphaël's lights beckons you into its garlanded doorway. You'll enter a lobby that is in essence a museum, with Picasso ceramics and a DeChirico-esque painting from the 1930s featuring a flapper and Nazi officer. Take the elevator (a hard left from the registration desk) to the top and climb one set of stairs to the two-level terrace, Roof Garden Bramante. The lower is for diners, the upper, with about ten tables, is for those of us who want to drink a glass of wine. Drink in the view as well, which is of rooftops—but, oh, those rooftops! You can see all the way to St. Peter's, or look down into Bramante's famed courtyard (from which the terrace gets its name) and almost touch the dome of diminutive Santa Maria della Pace. Borromini's imposing church, Sant'Agnese in Agone (St. Agnes in Agony), which faces Piazza Navona, is visible too. The €10 glass of wine, or cocktails and beer at €14 and €11, respectively, seem a good value. Largo Febo, 2; tel. 06.68.2831.

HOTEL RAPHAËL is a favorite of out-of-town Italian parliamentarians. As you leave the hotel, picture Socialist politician Bettino Craxi, the second-longest-serving postwar prime minister of Italy, as he went out from Hotel Raphaël one day in 1993. He had been finagling to get absolved of his misdeeds in office. Unexpectedly, a huge crowd confronted him, throwing coins at him and yelling, "Do you want these too?" Craxi died in Tunisia in 2000, after fleeing Italy.

GRAND HOTEL DE LA MINERVE

For a bird's eye view of the Pantheon, you can't do better than the Roof Garden bar at the Grand Hotel de la Minerve. If you've been running around sightseeing all day, this is an ideal place to relax and unwind. It's two steps behind the Pantheon and close to Piazza Navona and the Trevi Fountain. If you have remaining energy before you enter, take a moment to look at the obelisk held up by Bernini's elephant in Piazza della Minerva, in front of the hotel. This was unveiled in 1667; according to the inscription, the elephant was chosen to show that it requires a robust intelligence to uphold wisdom. (Dianne says the church here, Santa Maria sopra Minerva, is worth a stop; it has been rightly described as a museum of art treasures. In the adjoining monastery in 1633, the Inquisition tried Galileo and found him guilty of blasphemy, because he asserted the earth revolved around the sun.)

The Grand Hotel de la Minerve is a graceful 1600s palazzo, one of the first big Renaissance residences in central Rome and appropriately appointed for a five-star deluxe hotel; don't miss the glass ceiling in the main lobby. Take the elevator to the top floor and follow the Roof signs—you'll climb a flight of stairs to a large rooftop with a panoramic view of Rome's rooftops, including perhaps its most famous, the Pantheon. The waiters speak English. A menu lists drinks by the glass; don't hesitate to ask for it if the menu isn't offered (unless, Bill says, you don't care what anything costs). The terrace is adorned with white tent umbrellas to shade you, and in one section alone has twenty-five round tables with yellow tablecloths, chairs with padded seats, a tiled floor, and petunias all around (in season). The times are shortened before it's warm enough for the Romans; an 8 p.m. closing until mid-May. After that the bar will be open very late each night until it is too cool again in October. A glass of wine or beer is €10, cocktails €14–15, and a bottle of red or white wine €30 and up. Expect a few small appetizers (olives, tiny bruschette) with your drinks.

Wander around the terrace a bit to absorb the full view. You can contemplate the removal of the gilded sheets of bronze from the Pantheon dome (by Byzantine emperor Constans II in 655; replaced with lead by Pope Gregory III in the eighth century), and the engineering feat of this second-century Roman masterpiece. The Pantheon is still the largest unreinforced solid concrete dome in the world, and it was the largest dome in the world for more than sixteen centuries. Although the Roof Garden view is an urban one, mainly of roofs rather than an expansive one in terms of distance, you can see St. Peter's, which is lined up with the domes of Sant'Ivo alla Sapienza and Chiesa Nuova (not too shabby!). Piazza della Minerva, 69; tel. 06.69.5201.

View from Roof Garden Bramante, Hotel Raphaël. The dome of St. Peter's is visible on the left.

HOTEL FORTY-SEVEN

Circus Bar at **HOTEL FORTY-SEVEN** offers striking views at a reasonable price. The hotel is at via Petroselli, 47, a short block from the Tevere and a ten-minute walk south from Piazza Venezia. Your guidebook will have directions to Bocca della Verità; from there, with your back to the church, look up to your right and across the piazza, and you'll see the bar. Open to the public (6:30 p.m.–after midnight daily), it sits atop a Fascist-era building with a high-modernist interior. You can ask in the lobby for directions or follow ours: enter the hotel, access the interior courtyard (straight ahead), and take the glass elevator on the right to the sixth floor, where you'll exit on the left end of a long, wraparound lounge. There are some standard round tables, some tables set for diners, and comfortable lounge furniture—couches and the like—at both ends. We recommend the first section. Drinks are mostly reasonable: good wine (on a different list from the other drinks) is €4–6/glass; beer €7; soft drinks and juices €5; cocktails €10; all accompanied by salty crackers, mixed nuts, and chips. Dinner is costly. From left to right, the view includes the edge of the Palatine Hill, Circo Massimo, the tower of S. Maria in Cosmedin (the church that houses Bocca della Verità), and the Aventine Hill. Below, the round building is the oldest surviving marble temple in Rome; the rectangular one was constructed about 100 BC to protect the port (which was right here and

229

dates to about 1500 BC) and the sailors who labored there. Bill says the best part of the view, especially after sunset, is of the traffic on the curve in front of the Cosmedin church, where one can watch the scooters practice the perilous art of "riding the white line"—actually, the lane reserved for oncoming vehicles (see "Scooters and Cycles," p. 54). The Tevere bridge seen here is known familiarly as the "English bridge," because vehicles crossing in either direction follow the custom of driving on the left side—appropriate because the bridge is used to reverse one's direction of travel along the river. The remainder of the view from the bar is less spectacular although not uninteresting; the buildings across and down the street were constructed by the Mussolini regime in the 1930s. Visible farther down is the Theater of Marcellus and beyond it, to the right, portions of the Campidoglio, the hill (and Michelangelo-designed piazza) where the city government is headquartered.

HOTEL GLADIATORI

We promised we wouldn't take you to the Coliseum. Still, as we close this book, we can't resist offering you a spectacular view of Rome's most famous attraction from the terrace of the **HOTEL GLADIATORI** (via Labicana, 125), uphill to the east. The entrance to the hotel, on via Labicana, is small, as is the lobby. The reception desk is in a room set back to the left; you can ask there for directions to the roof, but it's easy enough to get there. Take the elevator to 3 and then the stairs around the corner one more flight. The terrace bar, which has both an inside (not for views) and outside, is named the American Bar. Except for the music (jazz, world), there's nothing American about it. There are only ten tables outside, five at the outer edge, where you'll want to sit. The décor is reserved: small marble-topped tables, cushioned chairs, a pergola with canvas for shade, candles and mini rock gardens on the tables, a terrazzo floor. The personable waiter will speak some English.

The evening we were there, a sliver of the moon hung, as if by a cord, over the seductively lit Coliseum. As Dianne said, "It almost makes me cry." The bill—€30 for two glasses of wine, paid at the reception desk off the lobby—"almost makes me cry," Bill said, but worth it, he added—

once anyway. Within sight are St. Peter's dome in the distance, the Vittoriano, stretches of the Palatine Forum hills, the Colle Oppio (where Nero built his famous golden house), and, to give the hotel its name, the ruins directly below of ancient Rome's largest school for gladiators, the *Ludus Magnus*—the main barracks for gladiators of ancient Rome, containing their lodgings and a training area.

And there, in all its ancient glory, the Coliseum. But remember: we didn't take you there . . .

ACKNOWLEDGMENTS

BOOKS HAVE many beginnings, and one of ours happened in the fall of 1993, when Massimo Vizzaccaro introduced us to the funky side of Rome with a tour of the city's all-night bakeries. We were hooked. A second occurred several years later, when Maurizio Marinelli, in a moment of temporary insanity, agreed to let us pick up his Piaggio Hexagon in Bologna and drive it to Rome over one of the country's most perilous mountain roads only months after Bill had acquired a motorcycle license in a weekend course. We survived.

Our lives and this book have been enriched in ways we can hardly express by friends—two of them American, all of them Roman—who have welcomed us into their homes and families, found us housing when we were in need, taught us about their remarkable city, treated us as if we belonged, and tolerated—at least on the surface—our hubris in writing this book. We are deeply grateful to Chiara Midolo, Donald Carroll and Dana Prescott, Luca Briasco and Alessandra Tozzi, Matteo Sanfilippo and Grazia Trabbatone, Mattia Carratello, Patrizio Nissirio and Patrizia Tariciotti, Susanna Garroni and Goffredo Galeozzi, Daniele Fiorentino and Barbara Ronchetti, Cesare Nissirio, and Marina Camboni. Among those condemned to live in something less than an "eternal" city, we express our gratitude to Nando Fasce and Carla Viale (in Genova) and to Lilia Cerone and Cesare Corbelli (in Vado, near Bologna).

To Massimo, whose talents as a linguist are exceeded only by his fondness for his native Rome, and to Matteo, a historian whose encyclopedic knowledge has led us to associate him with the phrase "ask Matteo," we offer special thanks, for they graciously accepted the task of reading the manuscript for errors, infelicities, and omissions. To our consternation (and relief), they found more than a few. Those that remain, we hasten to add, are our own. We also benefitted from the editorial talents and experience of Ed Curtis, who dealt nimbly with two opinionated authors.

One evening this spring, at our favorite Roman rooftop bar, we will pull ourselves away from the sunset and raise our glasses to all of you.

—Dianne Bennett and William Graebner

INDEX

CPSIA information can be obtained at www.ICGtesting.com
Printed in the USA
LVOW10s1204220913

353551LV00011B/281/P